Reducing Process Costs with Lean, Six Sigma, and Value Engineering Techniques

OTHER TITLES FROM AUERBACH PUBLICATIONS AND CRC PRESS

The 7 Qualities of Highly Secure Software
Mano Paul
ISBN 978-1-4398-1446-8

Communication and Networking in
Smart Grids
Edited by Yang Xiao
ISBN 978-1-4398-7873-6

Developing Essbase Applications: Advanced
Techniques for Finance and IT Professionals
Cameron Lackpour
ISBN 978-1-4665-5330-9

Drupal Web Profiles
Timi Ogunjobi
ISBN 978-1-4665-0381-6

Effective Methods for Software and
Systems Integration
Boyd L. Summers
ISBN 978-1-4398-7662-6

Electronically Stored Information:
The Complete Guide to Management,
Understanding, Acquisition, Storage,
Search, and Retrieval
David R. Matthews
ISBN 978-1-4398-7726-5

Enterprise 2.0: Social Networking Tools to
Transform Your Organization
Jessica Keyes
ISBN 978-1-4398-8043-2

Game Theory in Communication Networks:
Cooperative Resolution of Interactive
Networking Scenarios
Josephina Antoniou and Andreas Pitsillides
ISBN 978-1-4398-4808-1

Green Mobile Devices and Networks:
Energy Optimization and
ScavengingTechniques
Hrishikesh Venkataraman and
Gabriel-Miro Muntean
ISBN 978-1-4398-5989-6

Handbook of Mobile Systems
Applications and Services
Anup Kumar and Bin Xie
ISBN 978-1-4398-0152-9

The IFPUG Guide to IT and Software
Measurement
Edited by IFPUG
ISBN 978-1-4398-6930-7

Machine-to-Machine Marketing (M3)
via Anonymous Advertising Apps
Anywhere Anytime (A5)
Jesus Mena
ISBN 978-1-4398-8191-0

Media Networks: Architectures,
Applications, and Standards
Edited by Hassnaa Moustafa
and Sherali Zeadally
ISBN 978-1-4398-7728-9

Multimedia Communications and Networking
Mario Marques da Silva
ISBN 978-1-4398-7484-4

The New Triple Constraints for Sustainable
Projects, Programs, and Portfolios
Gregory T. Haugan
ISBN 978-1-4665-0518-6

Noiseless Steganography:
The Key to Covert Communications
Abdelrahman Desoky
ISBN 978-1-4398-4621-6

Open Source Data Warehousing and
Business Intelligence
Lakshman Bulusu
ISBN 978-1-4398-1640-0

Physical Principles of Wireless
Communications, Second Edition
Victor L. Granatstein
ISBN 978-1-4398-7897-2

Software Engineering Design:
Theory and Practice
Carlos E. Otero
ISBN 978-1-4398-5168-5

Strategy and Business Process Management
Techniques for Improving Execution,
Adaptability, and Consistency
Carl F. Lehmann
ISBN 978-1-4398-9023-3

Theory and Approaches of Unascertained
Group Decision-Making
Jianjun Zhu
ISBN 978-1-4200-8750-5

TV Content Analysis: Techniques
and Applications
Yiannis Kompatsiaris, Bernard Merialdo,
and Shiguo Lian
ISBN 978-1-4398-5560-7

Reducing Process Costs with Lean, Six Sigma, and Value Engineering Techniques

Kim H. Pries
Jon M. Quigley

CRC Press
Taylor & Francis Group
Boca Raton London New York

CRC Press is an imprint of the
Taylor & Francis Group, an **informa** business
AN AUERBACH BOOK

CRC Press
Taylor & Francis Group
6000 Broken Sound Parkway NW, Suite 300
Boca Raton, FL 33487-2742

First issued in paperback 2019

ISBN-13: 978-1-4398-8725-7 (hbk)
ISBN-13: 978-0-367-38051-9 (pbk)

Library of Congress Cataloging-in-Publication Data

Pries, Kim H., 1955-
    Reducing process costs with lean, six sigma, and value engineering techniques / Kim H. Pries, Jon M. Quigley.
        p. cm.
    Includes bibliographical references and index.
    ISBN 978-1-4398-8725-7 (hbk. : alk. paper)
    1. Cost control. 2. Production management--Cost control. 3. Six sigma (Quality control standard) 4. Lean manufacturing. 5. Value analysis (Cost control) I. Quigley, Jon M. II. Title.

HD47.3.P75 2013
658.15'52--dc23   2012033224

Visit the Taylor & Francis Web site at
http://www.taylorandfrancis.com

and the CRC Press Web site at
http://www.crcpress.com

Contents

Preface

We might ask, why this book? We describe several reasons.

A. Tight Economic Conditions!

It is easy to understand why a cost improvement book should be written. There are boom times and there are times when the business world is less secure and profit margins erode. One typical company response to economic downturn is to eliminate staff as if that were the only way to become a thriving company again. We wonder if these companies have some cost improvement methodology behind them that would give their management other options than removal of people. A company that has ongoing effective cost improvement activities will be more adaptable to changing economic climates.

Innovation provides value to an organization. New product or service generation is important for business growth. However, we want to maximize our return on this investment in the development of a product or a new service. In order to do that, we must frequently critique how we are meeting our customers' needs. What is our value proposition? How can we improve upon the existing proposition?

Certainly, it is not necessary to wait until we have delivered our product or service to start thinking about cost. It is sound business practice to understand the market and whether a particular course of action has an economic benefit for the undertaking organization.

This book contains multiple ways of reviewing your value proposition. Some more sophisticated than others. We provide examples of cost improvement opportunities and questions to help you think through how you can help your company improve its margins.

This book will show you a wide range of tools and techniques for improving the value proposition. These tools and techniques vary in complexity and capability. We will provide examples of these tools as well as the benefits and drawbacks for their use.

The book *Value Management Practice* by Michel Thiry identifies the types of value (page 9). He defines the variety of value propositions as:

Type of Use	Definition
Use value	The amount of current resources expended to realize a finished product that performs as it was intended
Esteem value	The amount of current resources a user is willing to expend for functions attributable to pleasing rather than performing e.G., Prestige, appearance and so on
Exchange value	The amount of current resources for which a product can be traded. It is also called worth, as the minimal equivalent value considered

Type of Use	Definition
Cost value	The amount of current resources expended to achieve a function measured in dollars
Function value	The relationship of a function worth to function cost

It is also certain that cost improvement activities only go so far. An organization cannot rely solely upon cost as a competitive feature to be a long-term strategy for success. However, it is also certain that demand and competition influence the asking price for the product or service and that, in turn, influences potential profit margins. A company that does not actively seek cost improvements leaves much on the table and is not necessarily a good steward of the organization's resources.

Cost and value improvement activities for business is as old as business itself. In the days of selling pots, our ancestors crafted the best pot they could with the materials available—which were no doubt limited. Farmers met their needs through creative means such as butter churns. My father-in-law regales my family with a story of the farm upon which he was raised. To make butter, they had to manually churn the milk. One day, they elevated the drive axle of the car, placed a belt on the tire, and a belt on the churn handle in such a way that the idling car and the subsequent tire rotation would churn butter. We could argue that the value of the car was greater than that of the purchase price for the vehicle solely for its intended operation. It is difficult to say from the story whether or not there was a suitable substitute. This event occurred during the 1930s, and they may not have had an automatic butter churn available. However, this anecdote demonstrates the principle of creative thinking to meet a need.

World War II material shortages created an atmosphere teeming with opportunities to improve the value equation with great consequences for doing so. The supply of rubber from trees, for example, was cut off by Japanese military excursions into Malaya and the East Indies. The solution: develop a synthetic rubber.

Throughout the years there has been a steady stream of talented people considering this value proposition. We start with Lawrence D. Miles regarded as the "father of value engineering." Miles was an electrical engineer at General Electric. The advent of World War II and the reallocation of material and materials shortages led to radical approaches to the development process and the materials of certain products. Miles realized that when people were confronted with an obstacle to implementation, they were forced to develop other solutions. Not all obstacles are permanent impediments; rather, some obstacles become opportunities to engage our creativity to find another solution. The overall goal of Miles's technique (value analysis/value engineering) was to produce a functional product without compromising on its quality.

Total Quality Management (TQM) is a management philosophy for improving the quality of processes and products. The participants are managers, employees, suppliers, and customers. The objective is to effectively meet customer needs and expectations, which is part of the value proposition. Important activities are as follows:

1. Cross-functional design

2. Process management

3. Supplier quality

4. Customer involvement

5. Information and feedback

6. Leadership

7. Strategic planning

8. Cross-functional training

9. Employee engagement (empowerment)

Total quality management (TQM) has had a number of advocates and proponents. Some of the more noteworthy founders and contributors were:

- W. Edwards Deming

- Kaoru Ishikawa

- Philip B. Crosby

- J.M. Juran

Six Sigma is a business management strategy that improves the value proposition. This methodology was developed by Motorola in the 1980s. The Six Sigma method improves the value proposition through the understanding and control of variation. Six Sigma was originally associated with manufacturing processes and refers to the defect. A process that is Six Sigma capable is one in which the yield from the process is 99.99966% defect free. This method employs statistical analysis to understand the variation possible in products or processes. Unwanted or unaccounted for variation is often the source of defects. These defects, even when caught during the production process, produce waste in the process.

In lean manufacturing and Six Sigma, the seven wastes are the following:

1. Overproduction

2. Defects (rework, repair, scrapped)

3. Handling (transporting parts)

4. Waiting (downtime for parts)

5. Inventory

6. Motion (excess motion)

7. Processing (overprocessing)

We use our statistical tools to uncover those wastes that affect our business. We prioritize and plan to eliminate or reduce the effects of this waste on our bottom line. Corporations that have Six Sigma programs have established infrastructure and the practices are ongoing and cyclic.

Project Management

Project management is not a cost reduction technique. It is, however, a mechanism for efficiency improvements and risk reduction. Each of these have associated costs. An inefficient project management organization leaves plenty of value on the table when it comes to the creation of a new product or service. Consider, for example, when our project overspends the budget. The business case for the project was based on some identified cost to produce and deliver against the subsequent income generated. If our project exceeds the estimated development cost, then we are putting the expected revenue stream and profit margin at risk.

The same is true for the other risks associated with the project. If we are late, and we had marketing events planned for the launch, we have affected the ability of our marketing investment to improve customer awareness. This may ultimately have an affect on the rate in which we acquire customers. Lateness to market may also mean other people beat us to market—possibly killing our value proposition altogether.

Projects that deliver an inferior product or service will threaten to make our revenue stream become a trickle. We may find that our entire revenue goes toward solving these quality problems or handling legal actions.

Experience suggests that the project management area of many companies is ready for improvement. This improvement can add to the company's bottom line.

Acknowledgment

We would like to acknowledge a number of people.

John Wyzalek, the acquisitions editor at Taylor & Francis/CRC Press, has been a great help with the development, the encouragement, and the promotion of all books we have written for them.

I (Jon) would like to thank those who have contributed to refining the content and the quality of this book: John Bate, Barry Smith, Luis Correra, and Bill Klodaski to name a few. I appreciate your help with the wire harness test fixture and wire testing tool discussions.

I would also like to thank Kim Pries; I learn much from our collaborations and I appreciate the opportunity to work with you.

Last, but not least, I would like to thank my family: my wonderful wife, Nancy, and my son, Jackson, is the best boy a daddy could have.

I would like to thank my wife, Janise Pries. She is the love of my life and the reason I work such long hours to make a change in the world.

We would also like to thank the company A2Mac1 for providing graphics for the teardowns in Chapter 10. A2Mac1 provides benchmarking services to the automotive industry and others since 1998. They are a great resource to learn about a variety of vehicle systems and other equipment. Through A2Mac1's standardized processes focused upon specific characteristics. The result is the breakdown of complete systems, including weights, dimensions, 3D scanning, material composition that you find in Chapter 4, saving you time, money, and reducing risks due to cost.

MATLAB™ is a registered trademark of The MathWorks, Inc. For product information, please contact:

The MathWorks, Inc.
3 Apple Hill Drive
Natick, MA 01760-2098 USA
Tel: 508 647 7000
Fax: 508-647-7001
E-mail: info@mathworks.com
Web: www.mathworks.com

About the Authors

Kim H. Pries has four college degrees: B.A. in history from the University of Texas at El Paso (UTEP), B.S. in metallurgical engineering from UTEP, M.S. in metallurgical engineering from UTEP, and M.S. in metallurgical engineering and materials science from Carnegie-Mellon University. In addition, he holds the following certifications:

- APICS
  - Certified Production and Inventory Manager (CPIM)
- American Society for Quality (ASQ)
  - Certified Reliability Engineer (CRE)
  - Certified Quality Engineer (CQE)
  - Certified Software Quality Engineer (CSQE)
  - Certified Six Sigma Black Belt (CSSBB)
  - Certified Manager of Quality/Operational Excellence (CMQ/OE)
  - Certified Quality Auditor (CQA)

Pries worked as a computer systems manager, a software engineer for an electrical utility, a scientific programmer under a defense contract, and for Stoneridge, Incorporated (SRI), he has worked as the following:

- Software manager
- Engineering services manager
- Reliability section manager
- Product integrity and reliability director

In addition to his other responsibilities, Pries has provided Six Sigma training for both UTEP and SRI and cost reduction initiatives for SRI. Pries is also a founding faculty member of Practical Project Management. Additionally, in concert with Jon Quigley, Pries is a cofounder and principal with Value Transformation, LLC, a training, testing, cost improvement, and product development consultancy. Pries also holds Texas teacher certification in mathematics, technological education, technological applications, and special education. Pries's first book was *Six Sigma for the Next Millennium: A CSSBB Guidebook* (Quality Press, 2005), now in a second edition as *Six Sigma for the New Millennium: A CSSBB Guidebook,* Second Edition (Quality Press, 2009).

Jon M. Quigley has three college degrees: a B.S. in electronic engineering technology from the University of North Carolina at Charlotte, a M.B.A. in marketing, and a M.S. in project management from City University of Seattle. In addition to the degrees, he holds the following certifications:

- Project Management Institute

- Project Management Professional (PMP)
- International Software Testing Qualifications Board (ISTQB)
- Certified Tester Foundation Level (CTFL)

In addition to the degrees and certifications, Quigley holds a number of patents and awards:

- U.S. Patent Award 6,253,131 Steering wheel electronic interface
- U.S. Patent Award 6,130,487 Electronic interface and method for connecting the electrical systems of truck and trailer
- U.S. Patent Award 6,828,924 Integrated vehicle communications display (also a European patent)
- U.S. Patent Award 6,718,906 Dual scale vehicle gauge
- U.S. Patent Award 7,512,477 Systems and methods for guiding operators to optimized engine operation
- U.S. Patent Award 7,629,878 Measuring instrument having location controlled display
- U.S. Published Patent Application 20090198402 Method and system for operator interface with a diesel particulate filter regeneration system
- Volvo-3P Technical Award for global IC05 Instrument cluster project 2005
- Volvo Technology Award for global IC05 Instrument cluster project April 2006

Quigley has worked within a variety of capacities within the new product development organizations including:

- Embedded product development engineer (hardware and software)
- Product engineer
- Test engineer
- Project manager
- Electrical and electronic systems manager
- Verification and test manager

Quigley is on Western Carolina University's Masters of Project Management advisory board.

In concert with Pries, Quigley is cofounder and principal with Value Transformation, LLC, training, testing, cost improvement, and product development consultancy.

Collectively, Pries and Quigley are the authors of the books *Project Management of Complex and Embedded Systems: Ensuring Product Integrity and Program Quality* (CRC Press, 2008), *Testing of Complex and Embedded Systems* (CRC Press, 2010), and *Scrum Project Management* (CRC Press, 2010). Additionally, they have authored numerous magazine articles and presentations at product development conferences about various aspects of product development and project management.

- *Embedded System Design*
- *Product Design and Development*
- *Embedded Design News* (EDN)
- *Software Test and Performance* (STP)
- *Electronics Weekly* (online)
- *DSP Design Line* (online)
- *Design Reuse* (online)
- *All Business* (online)
- *Quality Magazine* (online)
- *Automotive Design Line and Automotive Design Line Europe* (online)
- *Project Magazine* (online)
- *Tech Online India* (online)
- *Embedded Design India* (online)

E-mail Quigley at jon.quigley@valuetransform.com.

Additional information about Pries and Quigley and Value Transformation, LLC, can be found at: http://www.valuetransform.com. The site has areas to ask the authors questions and exchange ideas about product development.

List of Figures

CHAPTER 1 – Introduction

I. The Use of Rubrics

For most of our chapters, we have a rubric at the very start. The idea of the rubric is to indicate levels of competence required to perform the task outlined in that chapter. We use rubrics in our company for many situations where we have to perform some kind of evaluation.

II. Questions to Ponder

- What are the benefits to the company to have annual cost improvement activities and targets?
- What is value? How do you maximize value?
- How does my company value cost improvement successes?
- What is my company's cost improvement philosophy?
- Where are the products or services of your organization in the life cycle model?
- How do you know what stage of the life cycle you are in?
- What exercises does my company do to generate cost improvement ideas?
- What is cost avoidance? Provide three examples of cost avoidance at your company.
- What is the difference between revenue improvement and cost improvement?
- What is the role of marketing in generating revenue improvement? How quickly do we see the results of our marketing efforts?
- Is it possible to improve the cost without negative impact to quality?
- Provide an example of a cost improvement exercise you were part of that eroded the product quality.
- How does sales volume impact our costs? How does outsourcing impact our costs?
- At what point in the product (or service) life cycle are cost improvement efforts best served?

III. Cost Improvement Scenario

A. Situation

An instrument cluster recently released from production is experiencing high zero kilometer rates. Zero kilometer failures are anomalies found at the manufacturing facility. The vehicle has not traveled any distance. The failures can be found throughout the vehicle manufacturing process. The contractual obligation was to have a part per million (ppm) failure rate of less than 500 ppm. Currently, the failure rate is well above 20,000 ppm.

B. Objective

The objective is to reduce the failure rate at the installation site of the product into the vehicle.

C. Action

A cross-functional team consisting of the supplier engineering, manufacturing personnel and engineering at the customer was put together. The faults reported at the installation site (vehicle manufacturer) were recorded on a weekly basis. We could see the symptom of the failures and where these failures were in the process these failures were reported.

From this weekly report we came to see some of the problems were due the vehicle manufacturer's material handling. We scheduled a review of the vehicle manufacturer's material handling processes with the supplier. We found a number of handling issues that were easily corrected, one of which resulted in a packaging improvement, which was also a cost reduction.

D. Results

The fault frequency was reduced from 20,000 ppm down to approximately 2,500 ppm. Note that we went from approximately 3.6 sigma to 4.4 sigma—not Six Sigma yet, but a decided improvement!

E. Aftermath

At the end of the exercise, the remaining significant failure was around a Bourdon tube air gauge. The air gauge was a pneumatic/mechanical device. Each instrument cluster had at least two of these gauges, and 30% of the vehicle builds had three of these gauges. The supplier of the gauges indicated the failure rate for one gauge was 500 ppm (approximately 4.8 sigma). This meant that the target for the entire cluster of 500 ppm was not feasible since there were at least two of these air gauges in each instrument cluster.

Eventually, the customer came to realize this deficiency and moved from these mechanical gauges to a more reliable transducer and analog signal to the instrument cluster with stepper motor gauges.

IV. A Brief Overview of Value Engineering

V. Product Life Cycle

Any product or service will start with some kind of development process, which may be a matter of days or a matter of years, depending on the complexity of the product or service (see Figure 1.1). Once the product is launched, the product has a metaphorical lifetime, terminated by retirement and a kind of product or service "death." If we are especially creative, we may be able to produce another product or service that will have another discrete life cycle to continue our previous product or service. Thus starting the process all over again.

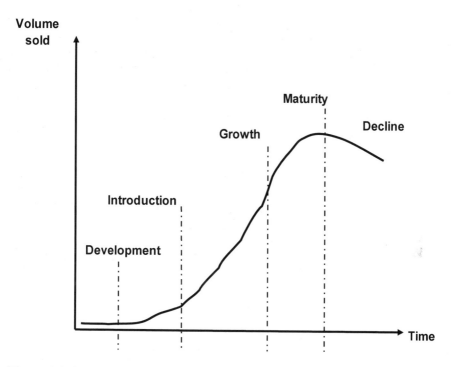

Figure 1.1 Cost opportunities are available throughout the product life cycle; however, these opportunities become more important in later stages of the life cycle.

During the growth and maturity phases of the product, our development team can revisit the product and look at it from the point of view of reducing the cost. The analysis phase of this activity is called value analysis. The design phase of this activity is called value engineering. In some ways, value engineering and value analysis may involve more creativity than the original design, simply because we are constrained by the limitations of an already existing product and the customer expectations that correspond to that product.

Use of value analysis and value engineering techniques can stave off product or service "death" for some period of time. As long as we can maintain our margins, we can still produce the product or deliver the service. If we do not have competition in the market yet, we improve our profits.

When we are in a market or delivering a product where there is some competition or if we are competing upon price to some degree, this reduction in cost can allow us to maintain our margin in the face of a decrease in product or service sale price. As we improve the value proposition we reduce any cost barrier to the customer for purchasing the product increasing the "take rate" for the product or service. The same can be true for competitive markets where the organization may have to use cost to attract or retain customers.

Value analysis and value engineering techniques need not be relegated solely to the mature phase of the product life cycle. We can couple these activities into our product or service development processes to optimize the value proposition even from the start. This does not mean we need not revisit over the remaining product life cycle. It should be clear the longer amount of time we spend optimizing the product or service margins, the better corporate stewards we are and the more probable the company will be profitable. We can also say that you can not "cost cut" your way to profitability as a long-term strategy. Generating new products and services is the other half of the equation for maintaining a profitable organization. One formula for value is as follows: Note that the formula has some intangible factors.

VI. What Is Value?

What is value? This concept has caused controversy over two centuries, from the time of Adam Smith to the time of Karl Marx to more modern economics. The point in this book is, however, what are we really doing with value engineering? We suggest in nearly every case, an improvement in value is roughly equivalent to an improvement in margin, whether it is net margin or standard gross margin. In other words, we are talking value in the sense of improving cost while holding steady on price. We can say that:

$$\text{value} = (\text{performance} + \text{capability}) / \text{cost} = \text{function} / \text{cost}$$
$$\text{Value of the time} = (\text{performance of function}) / \text{cost}$$

Improving the margin on the product or service is important to profitability, however is some instances we may be in a very competitive environment where improving the margins help us compete on price and maintain the same profit margin. Being able to adapt to the market is important. Our product or service took some amount of time, money, effort, and may have had some opportunity costs associated with the development. In those cases we want to get as much profit out of the product as possible for as long as possible. We are then maximizing the utility of the product or service. In either of these scenarios we are looking to make the most out of the company's investments.

VII. Cost Improvement Challenge

As we have indicated in our comments on value, our goal is primarily cost improvement. It is entirely possible, however, that some intelligent improvement in the design may also yield quality improvement and enhance customer satisfaction.

We use the word "challenge" in the section heading because that is exactly what we will do with our development team—the team that will perform value analysis and value engineering. In some cases, we will specify a percentage of cost reduction; in other cases, we may specify an exact dollar value. These target numbers can be generated from a critique of the product or by senior management establishing some targets for cost improvement. Sometimes these cost improvements may be contractual obligations. For the automotive industry (example of a product is shown in Figure 1.2) we can see contracts that define an annual percentage reduction in the cost of the product from the customer organization. In these instances we must constantly critique the value proposition to meet these demands.

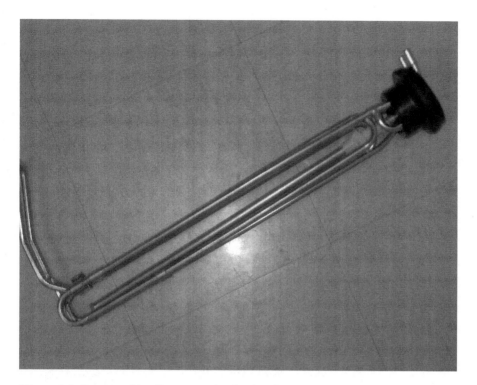

Figure 1.2 Opportunities for cost and value improvement range from the process to the product.

VIII. Cost Avoidance

Cost avoidances are tricky and will often be considered out-of-bounds by the accounting department and company controllers. The reason lies in the fact that the cost in this case is not in the expenses or capital budgets. For example, we might have an idea to spend $1 billion dollars to buy a very large iceberg. The following day, we decide not to buy the iceberg. The avoided cost is $1 billion, which is clearly deceptive.

We know of times when we legitimately avoid a cost. We may decide, for example, to revamp our manufacturing facility, improving our production capability. We may find other alternatives to improve the efficiency of the existing equipment and thereby eliminate the need for the expenditure or substituting the larger expense for a lower costing implementation. We avoid the larger expenditure by process improvement or adaptation of existing equipment.

The only way to cleanly track avoided costs is to have a third party assess the reality of the avoided cost. When the practice occurs ethically, we are then practicing good business by not spending money where we have discerned we have no need.

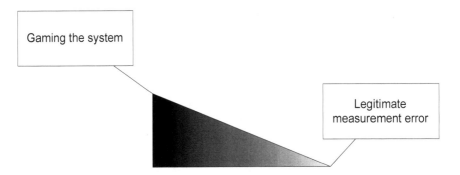

Gaming the system

Legitimate measurement error

Figure 1.3 Using the rules of the system against the system is unethical and undesirable.

IX. Cost Reduction

A true cost avoidance is always compared against the budget. This factor is the most significant difference between a cost reduction and a cost avoidance. Furthermore, cost reductions can have a significant impact on the bottom line of the enterprise. It is far easier to save money through cost reductions and improved profit at the same time, and than it is to attempt to grow profit by growing revenue. It is also true that it is easier to improve the margin through cost reduction rather than develop an entirely new product or service.

Some simple examples of cost reductions include extending the time between calibrations of laboratory equipment if we have the evidence to support this decision; we can also improve operational efficiency and reduce head count, a favorite tactic of the accounting department; many choices are available when manufacturing—when soldering electronics why not design out the selective solder process, which is effectively hiring a robot to do hand soldering? Cost reductions need not be relegated to the material costs of the product only but can encompass all of those activities and products that drive our cost.

If we are a software test facility we can automate our regression testing freeing our test staff to perform that testing which cannot be automated due to creativity and other human characteristics that cannot so easily be automated.

Cost reductions will vary from the very simple and oftentimes the most profitable to extremely complicated activities requiring Six Sigma projects and designed experimentation. Based on our experience, we know that any enterprise, be it public or private, government or nongovernment, has hundreds if not thousands of opportunities for cost reduction.

X. Profit Improvement

A profit improvement is usually a short-term situation, one of the most common of which being the sale of surplus equipment. If the equipment is truly surplus equipment, then profit improvement provides an immediate boost to the bottom line. Here are some examples of surplus equipment and other items we have sold:

- Amplifiers for EMC testing

- High altitude test equipment (had not been used in 13 years)
- Conveyor rollers for the manufacturing line
- Obsolete test equipment
- Used pallets for reuse or wood pulping
- Aluminum housing that could not be reused in product
- Solder dross

XI. Green and Corporate Stewardship Are the Same

We do not believe that there is a huge separation between green and corporate stewardship. The automobile manufacturing plant for Subaru in the United States is an example of how green approaches can be used to improve the environment (see Figure 1.4) and save money at the same time. Their facility produces no outgoing material—they reuse everything in their plant, even the food from the cafeteria is used for composting. At the fundamental level being green means we are aware of the resources and we take special care in minimizing how much we use or take and attempt to maximize the socictal (and personal) impact through the use of the resource.

In our experience, most green initiatives were created under externally imposed ISO-14001 certification. Many of the environmental activities in these cases were largely eyewash and produced little monetary value for the enterprise. But Subaru has led the way in showing that dedicated thought and persistent labor can indeed produce a zero-effluent facility, while saving money and setting a new standard.

We feel that green initiatives should be viewed as opportunities rather than a burden. Not only does it look good to the public and make for good marketing but also it provides opportunities for the reduction of waste in our facility—this philosophy is known as lean manufacturing. Company-wide recycling is essential for such an initiative to function at its very best. Obvious items that can be recycled are those such as the following:

- Paper of all kinds (keep in mind regulatory requirements for records storage)
- Food for composting (coffee grounds from corporate coffeepots)
- Grease from grease traps
- Solder
- Petroleum distillates
- Recycling of prototype wire harness
- Metal housings
- Rubber
- Plastic for regrinds

Figure 1.4 Recycling is not just a green proposition but a value and cost consideration as well.

XII. The Case for Cost Reductions

The following table analyzes the cost reduction situation:

Revenue	$50,000,000
Cost of goods sold or sales	$45,000,000
Standard Gross Margin	$5,000,000
SGM %	10.00%
Cost reduction at 3% of revenue	$1,500,000

Revenue	$50,000,000
Cost of goods sold or sales	$43,500,000
Standard Gross Margin	$6,500,000
SGM %	13.00%
Assume SGM = 10%	
Revenue	$51,500,000
Cost of goods sold or sales	$45,000,000
Standard Gross Margin	$6,500,000
SGM %	12.62%
% Increase in revenue	3.00%

Increasing revenue is a nontrivial task. In essence, we increased revenue by 3%. Note that in the other part of the table we made cost reductions of 3% of revenue, which is an utterly achievable goal. We know this from industrial experience—we can achieve 3% of revenue for three to four years before we have already saved money on the relatively easy projects.

We submit that it is generally easier to find cost reductions to 3% of revenue than it is to increase revenue by 3%. Furthermore, cost reductions involve no external marketing effort or any special sales activity.

While you cannot cost cut your way to profitability, cost improvement work can extend the useful life cycle of our product. We may be able to extend our product or service into markets that would have otherwise been off limits to us due to our customers' cost of the product or our margin needs.

XIII. Planning for and Managing a Value Improvement Project

A. Project Concept

Before we begin any kind of real project effort, we need to establish the project concept, which, in essence, defines what our project will be at a very high level. As we indicate in several chapters in this book, we can start a definition of our project by creating a document called a project charter. This document will evolve as we move through the value improvement process. Selecting the right concept goes a long way to improving the cost for the product or process. We see many times we accept the first concept and do not take time to generate a number of ideas from which to choose the best.

B. Project Information

As we continue our definition of the project in our project charter we will need to gather relevant data so that we have enough information to make a proposal to management such that they can make an informed decision. We will look at current design documents, current production documents, current procedures, the frequency of use of the part service, known issues, known exceptions, the people involved, the forms we use, and anything we know about the customer and their relation to the product.

Customer information is critical to our decision making. We want to understand the customer's point of view as well as any information we can gather about customer usage. We suggest that the team contact the customer's quality organization first—these people will most likely have the best information on challenges seen with the product.

Figure 1.5 There are abundant value improvements even in an office or administrative environment.

C. Project Business Case

Before management can really make a decision regarding our value improvement project, they will need to see the business case for the project. The business case, at a minimum, must include information about cost, schedule, and quality. Included in all of this will be the cost to perform tests on the product, the time it will take to make the improvement, and the probable change in quality. We will discuss the business case in subsequent chapters as well as what can happen when we eliminate some of the steps in our product development and delivery process.

Cost Goals

Cost goals can be derived from the project concept or they can be set arbitrarily. We also need to include as part of the cost of the project any efforts and labor, to make the value improvement occur. This collection of one-time costs will have to be amortized over the period we expect to see the cost reduction be valid. If we do not do this, we are then fooling ourselves about the benefit of the value improvement. We will be looking at total cost, incremental cost, annualized cost, and any of the compound of the cost that we can determine; for example, direct labor, factory overhead, and materials costs. Because we are more than likely improving the design, we include materials cost in our cost analysis.

Schedule Goals

As we move into our value improvement project, we need to remain aware of the impact of our activities on the project schedule. As we consume more time, we suffer from what is called opportunity cost, which can come from not benefiting from the cost savings quickly or from consuming the time of our engineers as they work on the project. If the time consumed to produce results is more hours spent than planned then the cost incurred may disrupt our business case. This can effectively eliminate our cost improvement exercise or at the very least make the payoff for the work at some yet future date.

Quality Goals

While we are working on our value improvement project, we should take whatever steps we can to eliminate degradation of the quality of the product. In the excitement of saving money, we may tend to overlook decisions that reduce product quality. If we do so, that act becomes self-defeating. Thus, just as we do with a new product, we consider the triad of cost, schedule, and quality.

Set Scope

As we complete our project charter, we define the boundaries of our activity by describing the project scope, the resources required, and the level of executive involvement we will need.

XIV. Conclusion

Cost improvement is not just a product activity. If we want our organization to survive during the down times and thrive during the boon times, it is in our best interest to know how to eliminate necessary cost from our organization. A construction organization may find cost savings in:

- Material acquisition
- Human resources including divisions of labor
- Excess material handling
- Remnant material
- Construction processes

Figure 1.6 We can select the right equipment for our company that maximizes our value proposition.

If we are an engineering business, we may likewise have a number of areas of cost improvement (see Figure 1.5).

- Prototype material procurement
- Prototype material generation
- Simulation
- Material procurement
- Tool procurement
- Process efficiency
- Product test efficiency
- Efficiency of the assorted development processes
- Project management capability
- Work instructions

If we are a manufacturing facility we have a substantial number of opportunities as well:

- Material handling
- Work instructions (see Figure 1.8)

- Tooling
- Tool capability
- Process variation
- Time!

Consider our business offices that have hundreds of people with numerous conference rooms available. This company can improve their operating costs through automatic light switches. These light switches (see Figure 1.7) detect people and movement and automatically switch the lights on when people enter the room. We can do this for our conference rooms as well as restrooms to ensure the lights are not left on for no reason. We can also install low water flow toilets and sinks that detect when hands are below and turn on and off automatically. All of these actions reduce our water consumption and can help lower our company's fixed operating costs. If our company provides coffee for the employees we can recover the coffee grounds and sell this to the local garden center or worm farm to either amend the soil or provide fodder for the worms to grow. We can do the same from our kitchen waste if we are a restaurant or have this service in our company for our employees. These ideas are examples of good stewardship and saving the company money as well. We are taking actions that lower our fixed operating costs for the building.

Figure 1.7 We can conserve energy by having conference room lights turn on and off automatically.

Consider again our office or administrative businesses. This company has a few hundred employees and the company graciously provides these employees with free coffee. The coffee is not that tasty; however, it is capable of getting the employees moving and is much better than no coffee! In the course of a day, the company produces many pots of coffee. The machines are capable of brewing what amounts to three pots of coffee consuming three bags of coffee to fill the entire pot. The spent coffee grounds are unceremoniously dumped into the trash after the pot is empty and

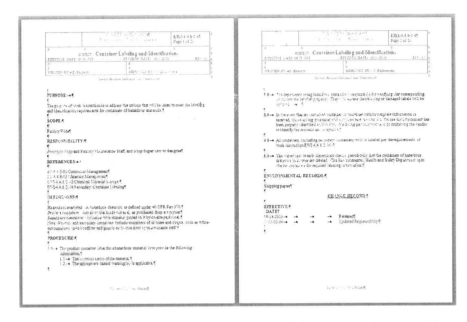

Figure 1.8 Our processes and work instructions can influence our value proposition.

an employee then restarts a new pot. Those who raise plants and worms know that coffee grounds are excellent material for compost. Exploration of the use of this waste material at farms, plant nurseries, or worm farms may tell us that money can be made from this residual material. At any rate, reuse of this material could be better for the environment than filling a plastic bag in a landfill.

If our business is a restaurant, we have opportunities for cost improvement as well. We can analyze our cost to understand the cost drivers. If our business costs were predominantly in the material costs and labor, we would look in these areas for cost improvements. Cycle times to perform the work, volume of customers over the time of day help us to optimize the restaurant's ability to maximize our value proposition.

Recycling of kitchen waste or remnant material can reduce our trash costs. If we have deep fry vats that we use to fry our customer's food, we will be periodically required to replace that vat oil. We can recover some of the cost if we find a biodiesel manufacturer that is interested in acquiring our oil for them to make fuel.

We see a local pizza restaurant using a new container when the product is a "to go" order. This new ecological container from Eco Incorporated is not just made of recycled materials, which according to some estimates saves trees by using more than 18 million pounds less paper annually, but also is a multiuse box (see Figure 1.10). The product is called the Green Box. Besides the fact that the box is recyclable, the company has understood that a "to go" order may require more handling than just the conveyance for the pizza to get home.

The design of the box is such that the top of the box becomes individual serving plates for four. There are perforated portions on the box lid that make creation of plates very simple. Customers are now able to use the box for the plates and now we have a solution that is convenient to take outside and clean up is easy. The only thing not provided in this assemblage are napkins for cleaning up face and hands. Additionally, the remaining portions of the box make it possible to save the left over pizza in the remaining half of the box. Some of you no doubt know how difficult it is to save the remaining pizza and store it in the original box. This takes up so much

Figure 1.9 Recycling can be a sustainable source of savings as well as promoting good citizenship.

room in the refrigerator. This box now is built to easily transform to meet the reduced size of pizza due to consumption complete with lid to close up the left over portions. Instead of just a transport mechanism, the box is able to handle more of the customer's demands while not increasing the same material costs, as well as recyclability. An interesting demonstration can be found at the Web address: http://www.youtube.com/watch?v=zy-pUqhB-Rg.

In keeping with the restaurant theme, suppose we have a restaurant that serves drinks. These drink conveyances consist of a straw as well as a cup and a lid. For each size cup, there could be a different lid. Contrarily, we could have a variety of cups and one lid that fit all three volumes of drinks sold. The second choice reduces our

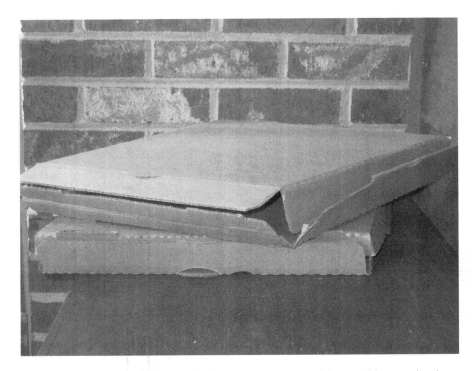

Figure 1.10 We can provide better customer value even with something as simple as a pizza box.

inventory, streamlines our ordering and reduces the risk of any one cup volume going without a lid.

If our business is in construction, we have opportunities for cost improvements as well. We can choose the equipment (see Figure 1.6 and Figure 1.11) we wish to own based upon demand from our business. Specialized equipment, we seldom use we may decide not to purchase. We can further decide if we want to keep operating expertise on staff or if we wish to subcontract that type of work from our organization altogether.

To improve the cost of the product we must know where the most promising place to look as well as the tools to use to generate ideas. We know of a company that produces heavy vehicles. This company had cost and weight activities for the various departments. One of those activities was to have the electrical group find ways to reduce the weight of the product. In this case, the electrical system on the vehicle was less than 2% of the entire weight of the vehicle. This low percentage of the total weight means looking for a large reduction in the weight due to the electrical system was not going to be very productive. While this story does not specifically discuss cost, it does illustrate that to find cost improvements, one must find a fruitful place to look. We must understand our cost generators, those things that drive the costs of our operations. This requires understanding our organization's cost drivers. What are our fixed and variable costs?

Whether we are a construction organization, an engineering firm, a service or an administrative office, we can find plenty of opportunities to improve our cost structure.

Saving the company money without degrading performance or quality is the same thing as securing new business. During tough times, we improve the probability our organization will go on in perpetuity if we are frugal. Frugal does not mean do without the necessary equipment or tools—frugality is functioning without waste. In this instance we are talking about improving the efficiency of our organization and consequently our bottom line without compromising capability or quality. In this book, we will show methods and techniques for uncovering the sources of costs for your product, organization or service. Armed with this knowledge you will be able to address the specific cost concerns in your organization.

Figure 1.11 Cost saving and value improvement are important for all businesses.

XV. EXERCISES

- What are the typical difficulties in cost improvement initiatives?

- What are the unintended consequences of rewarding employees for cost improvement achievements?

- What techniques and tools can we use to develop our cost improvement ideas?

- What tools and techniques can we use to ensure our cost improvement does not result in quality degradation?

- Describe a cost improvement process that would work at your company.

- Create a bulleted list of the cost contributions to a product in your company. What costs does your company have the most control? What costs the least control?

- Does outsourcing always mean cost improvement? How do you know when outsourcing is a cost improvement?

- What is the best way to control outsourcing, especially foreign outsourcing? What are the benefits of this kind of outsourcing?

- Why is scope demarcation so important to project completion?

- How do we know when we are exceeding our project scope?

- Who manages the project? Can we use self-directed work teams on projects for value improvement?

- Should we contract with consultants?

- Often, the best cost improvements are a little wild, mainly because nobody has thought about them before. How do we inspire breadth as well as depth of thought with regard to discovering cost reductions or profit improvements?

- We do not speak about taxation in this book, but can we not take steps to improve our tax situation as a company?

- Why not gift unused equipment and improve our tax situation? How long should the equipment have been unused?

- How do we put a value on barter? For example, we have seen a factory upgrade from simple opens/shorts testers to in-circuit testers partially through a trade.

- Make a list of 20 places where you could find a cost reduction in your enterprise.

- Make a list of 10 places where you could achieve a legitimate cost avoidance.

- Make a list of 10 potential profit improvements.

- Once you make your lists, what do you think the potential savings will be? How difficult was this exercise?

- How do we evaluate the quality of our cost reductions? Is the money the only measure?

- Recommend other metrics that would make sense in value analysis and value engineering.

CHAPTER 2 – Saving Money with Homegrown Ideas

I. Rubric for Homegrown Ideas

Criteria	Level 1 (50–59%)	Level 2 (60–69%)	Level 3 (70–79%)	Level 4 (80–100%)
Analyze concepts providing details	Analysis of concepts provides limited details	Analysis of concepts provides some details	Analysis of concepts provides considerable details	Analysis of concepts provides thorough details
Analyze given scenario	Analysis of given scenario provides limited insight	Analysis of given scenario provides some insight	Analysis of given scenario provides considerable insight	Analysis of given scenario provides thorough insight
Analyze the effect of modifications on communications systems	Analysis of the effect of modifications on communications systems demonstrates limited attentions to all factors	Analysis of the effect of modifications on communications systems demonstrates some attentions to all factors	Analysis of the effect of modifications on communications systems demonstrates considerable attentions to all factors	Analysis of the effect of modifications on communications systems demonstrates thorough attentions to all factors
Apply current production skills safely	Demonstrates limited ability to apply current production skills safely	Demonstrates some ability to apply current production skills safely	Demonstrates considerable ability to apply current production skills safely	Demonstrates a high level of ability to apply current production skills safely
Apply the design process	Applies the design process with limited effectiveness	Applies the design process with some effectiveness	Applies the design process with considerable effectiveness	Applies the design process with a high degree of effectiveness
Demonstrate effective interpersonal skills	Rarely demonstrates effective interpersonal skills	Sometimes demonstrates effective interpersonal skills	Often demonstrates effective interpersonal skills	Always or almost always demonstrates effective interpersonal skills
Demonstrate effective teamwork skills	Rarely demonstrates effective teamwork skills	Sometimes demonstrates effective teamwork skills	Often demonstrates effective teamwork skills	Always or almost always demonstrates effective teamwork skills
Demonstrate good housekeeping practices (5S)	Rarely demonstrates good housekeeping practices	Sometimes demonstrates good housekeeping practices	Often demonstrates good housekeeping practices	Routinely demonstrates good housekeeping practices
Demonstrate trouble shooting and testing skills	Demonstrates limited trouble shooting and testing skills	Demonstrates some trouble shooting and testing skills	Demonstrates considerable trouble shooting and testing skills	Demonstrates expert trouble shooting and testing skills
Describe the use of state-of-the-art technology	Description of the use of state-of-the-art technology demonstrates limited knowledge	Description of the use of state-of-the-art technology demonstrates some knowledge	Description of the use of state-of-the-art technology demonstrates considerable knowledge	Description of the use of state-of-the-art technology demonstrates thorough knowledge
Design and plan solutions to problems	Designs and plans solutions to problems with limited effectiveness	Designs and plans solutions to problems with some effectiveness	Designs and plans solutions to problems with considerable effectiveness	Designs and plans solutions to problems with a high degree of effectiveness

Criteria	Level 1 (50–59%)	Level 2 (60–69%)	Level 3 (70–79%)	Level 4 (80–100%)
Develop a production plan for a project	Develops a production plan for a project providing limited detail	Develops a production plan for a project providing some detail	Develops a production plan for a project providing considerable detail	Develops a production plan for a project providing thorough detail
Document the cost reduction process	Documents the cost reduction process providing limited detail	Documents the cost reduction process providing some detail	Documents the cost reduction process providing considerable detail	Documents the cost reduction process providing thorough detail
Follow the steps of the design process	Follows the steps of the design process with limited effectiveness	Follows the steps of the design process with some effectiveness	Follows the steps of the design process with considerable effectiveness	Follows the steps of the design process with expert effectiveness
Identify industry regulations	Identifies industry regulations with limited effectiveness	Identifies industry regulations with some effectiveness	Identifies industry regulations with considerable effectiveness	Identifies industry regulations with excellent effectiveness
Use planning tools to complete projects	Rarely uses planning tools to complete projects	Sometimes uses planning tools to complete projects	Often uses planning tools to complete projects	Always or almost always uses planning tools to complete projects
Use problem-solving skills to complete projects	Rarely uses problem-solving skills to complete projects	Sometimes uses problem-solving skills to complete projects	Often uses problem-solving skills to complete projects	Always or almost always uses problem-solving skills to complete projects

II. Questions to Ponder

- What is brainstorming?
- What is mind mapping?
- Draw a mind map of how your product is produced or service is delivered.
- What are the largest cost factors for your product or service? If you do not have a product or a service, critique another product or service.
- What is breakeven analysis?
- We can take $0.50 out of our product. To do so, we must spend $6,500.00. Assuming there are no variable costs and no other fixed costs change, how many units will we have to move to pay off the investment?
- How does your organization decide what cost improvement efforts to undertake?
- How does the market (customer) volatility impact your organization?
- How does investment payback period impact our cost improvement efforts?
- Does your organization routinely perform cost improvement exercises?
- How can TQM tools help improve our value proposition?
- What is the definition of fixed cost? What are the fixed costs of your company?

- What is variable cost? What are the variable costs of your company?
- What is the benefit of an integrated cost improvement in your organization?
- Consider where your organization's product or services are in the product life cycle.

III. Cost Improvement Scenario

A. Situation

In a cost sensitive market, the manufacturer of a vehicle electrical system identifies the need for improving the value proposition.

B. Objective

Reduce the vehicle electrical system cost without losing functionality.

C. Action

The management team of this electrical / electronic development department held a four-hour brainstorming session. The department consisted of a number of groups. The people from the groups were kept in tact, for example, the verification group worked as one of the teams in the cost rationalization providing their brainstormed ideas as contribution. It is the same for the systems engineering and component engineers. In this way, the people who routinely worked together generated ideas for improving the costs.

These ideas were put together a couple of times during the four-hour session, allowing all teams to see the other contributions. At the last hour, the walls were lined with large paper post-its with many cost improvement ideas on each of the sticky notes. The other teams then walked around adding yet more ideas to the already plenty of ideas to these sheets.

The results of the sheets were uploaded into a database where the originator of the idea and a brief description were added. The ideas were assessed in subsequent meetings by ability to implement. For example, those ideas that could be implemented within a few weeks to months were prioritized. Assignment for working these cost improvement ideas went by group that would be impacted, for example, wire harness cost "tags" were handled by the wire harness group. Ideas that required large lead time for tooling or extensive verification to implement were "back-burnered" for later work.

D. Results

In the end the target cost reduction was met without reducing the feature content.

E. Aftermath

There were so many ideas generated that for two years, there was little need to look for other cost improvement activities. Essentially, the pipeline for cost improvement of the vehicle electrical system, for the most part, was full. This meant that rather than seek additional ideas, the department spent most of its cost improvement hours toward implementation due to the previous investment of time to generate ideas.

IV. Your People Matter

Often, the truly great savings will come from the front-line level of the enterprise; after all, who knows the product better? One of the best cost reductions we have witnessed was a 27 to 1 improvement on the cost of a common screw!

Sometimes homegrown cost reductions are small; however, we follow the philosophy of "many raindrops make an ocean." Part of the goal in a cost reduction effort is to influence the corporate culture to shift in the direction of thinking about cost savings regularly. If we can persuade every employee to think about cost savings once or twice a week (at a minimum), we can expect to start seeing a flow of ideas shortly thereafter. We can establish cost improvement targets to help drive this behavior within our organization.

Experience suggests that some time creatively thinking other possible solutions can be productive. We know that a simple review of a tear down of the product or the production processes of the product can deliver success. We can do this work after the product has been in existence for some time or we can include these activities in our development effort so we make the most of the change early in the product life cycle.

V.   Laboratory Equipment

One quick way to save money in the company laboratory is to intelligently pursue the purchase of used, but well-maintained, equipment. This approach represents a cost avoidance; however, it also represents good stewardship of company monies. With the advent of the Internet, it is easy to "surf" the Web for bargains and bid on the parts. Of course, we want our technical staff to verify the equipment is in working order. In our experience, we were able to purchase amplifiers, electrostatic discharge guns, and other material for cents on the dollar. In fact, we know of one Texas laboratory that built up their capability buying equipment at auctions after other laboratories failed during an economic downturn.

Laboratory staff can also spend time building their own support equipment. Some examples of the types of equipment amenable to this approach are as follows (see Figure 2.1 and Figure 2.2):

- Transient tester (load dump)
- Antenna stands
- Equipment storage boards
- Mode stirring equipment (electromagnetic compatibility)
- Workbenches

These are just a few examples we have seen with our own eyes. Each department has hundreds of opportunities once they break away from the "I have to have the latest and greatest widget" mentality and buy what they truly need.

Laboratory staff can also design, code, and test their own test software. We have more than one laboratory use the National Instruments LabVIEW graphical programming product to run their test benches. We know of one group who became so adept, they could produce a virtual version of the product on the computer screen that had surprising verisimilitude. When a customer would not make a service tool available for the team, they produced a LabVIEW version of the service tool including a screen representation of the hardware enclosure and screen of the tool!

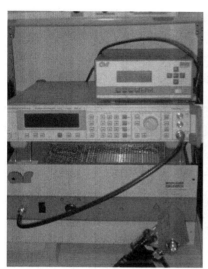

Figure 2.2 Sophisticated test equipment such as this EMC transient generation equipment improves product quality.

Figure 2.1 Laboratory equipment can be internally developed products and they can often be purchased used.

LabVIEW and National Instrument tools can help reduce the cost for testing software products. Product requirements based testing are good candidates for automation as the stimulation and the expected responses should be well documented. This automation can shorten the test cycle—saving money without compromising the test coverage.

Regression testing is another great candidate for automated testing. If we are running the test case more than one time, we should consider what it takes to automate. Regression testing, that of testing the pre-existing features, is just the sort of thing ripe for automation. You can read more about testing effectively in our book, *Testing of Complex and Embedded Systems* from Taylor & Francis (2010).

These same tools can be used to produce a hardware-in-the-loop (HIL) rig. We have seen these tools designed in such a way that the end system has similar performance to the actual vehicle in the field. We can use these tools to simulate the features interaction with the rest of the vehicle systems prior to developing the embedded hardware and software. This saves time on design iterations and prototype part costs and reduces the risk by making it possible for the customer to "virtually" test and otherwise critique the system.

For example, we can consider a heavy vehicle manufacturer. This vehicle manufacturer makes updates to the product four times in a year (see Figure 2.3). To minimize the quality risk, the organization tests each of these releases. These releases can be tested on vehicles as well as the company's hardware-in-the-loop simulator.

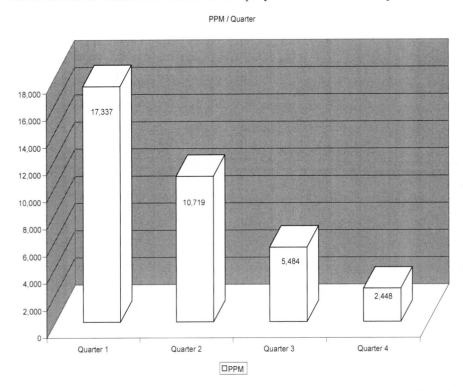

Figure 2.3 Poor quality can be very toxic to an organization and we lose profit and often customers.

The testing may well be comprehensive depending on the nature of the change and includes some level of regression testing at the system level. The company learns that development of test scripts takes roughly two times that amount of time it takes to execute the test cases. The automated test case takes only minutes to perform on the hardware in the loop rig. To perform the test manually takes hours. We cover more testing scope in less time, and more importantly, we do this without an increase in the testing human resources. The human resource can be deployed performing the exploratory test cases to uncover system performance that is not defined in the specifications. We have simultaneously reduced our cost and improved our quality.

If our testing department conducts component level testing, as well as subsystem and systems level testing, we can commonize the core operating parts using these same LabVIEW and National Instruments tools. This strategy reduces the cost for

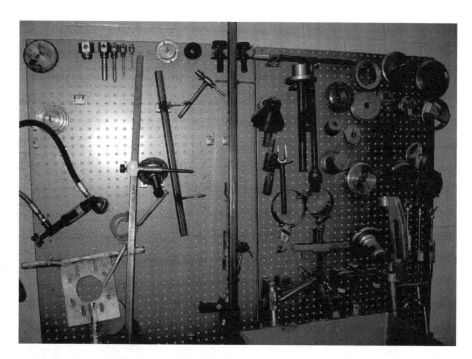

Figure 2.4 Ease of access of the tools we need for the job helps reduce waste in time.

maintaining and expanding the capabilities of the department. We can choose to focus on the testing as an alternative to maintaining a disparate set of tools that perform the testing. Recycling also reduces the time it will take one of the test team members to learn to work one of the other test fixtures.

VI. Production Equipment

Manufacturing presents hundreds if not thousands of opportunities for savings. For example, if we are an electronics firm and we use wave solder as part of our process, we can capture the solder dross and sell that to recycling firms. If our organization is going through a "lean" transformation, we can often secure some profit improvement by selling redundant equipment such as conveyor tables, storage racks, warehouse equipment, and more (see Figure 2.5). At no point should we ever take the easy path of trying to throw away this material—either recycle it, repurpose it, or sell it. Any one of these options will produce savings, either in the form of profit improvement or by way of avoided cost (again demonstrating good stewardship of enterprise monies).

Another ready source of savings occurs when we are able to analyze our processes and eliminate entire tasks out of the sequence by streamlining the operation. One of the ways for doing this is to look for points where the manufacturing operators must make a decision and work to eliminate these decision points. Firstly, a decision point will always represent the potential for an erroneous action. Secondly, decision points introduce complexity into the process.

Please be aware that recovery of floor space is not a cost reduction or a cost

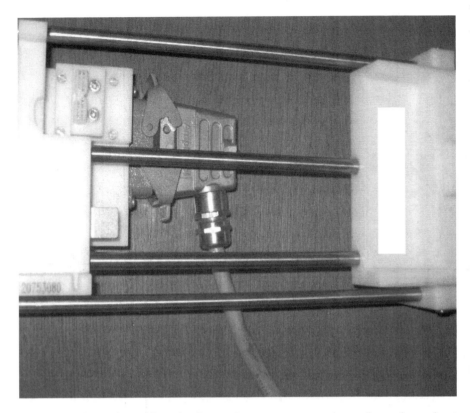

Figure 2.5 Ease of use of production equipment conserves time—the tools need not be exciting or sleek to perform the function.

avoidance unless we are able to eliminate some utilities (gas, water, electric) or we are able to rent or sell the space for a profit improvement (see Figure 2.4).

In another instance we know of an automotive company that had a diagnostics tool included within their instrument cluster. The manufacturing staff at this company used the vehicle's instrument cluster to troubleshoot the vehicle during the later portions of the vehicular production process. There came a time when the diagnostics information within the instrument cluster graphics display was deemed to be removed from the instrument cluster. However, the manufacturing team installing the instrument cluster became dependent on the instrument cluster of the vehicle as a diagnostics tool. The manufacturing people searched for a suitable tool to meet this need but this was not possible due to significant proprietary data link communication. During a brainstorming session, idea was presented to create a new product consisting of the existing graphics display and microcontroller including the software. Using an off-the-shelf enclosure, the team met this need with minimal development costs in a very short development cycle with limited risk.

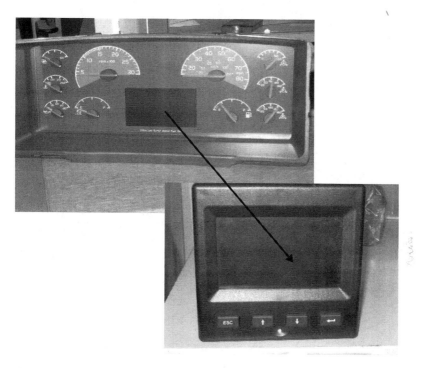

Figure 2.6 We can reuse parts of an existing design to create new products while minimizing the development and tooling costs.

VII. Production Test Equipment

Production test equipment can benefit from the same attitude used in the laboratory— the procurement of used equipment. We know of a situation where an enterprise took a collection of so-called "opens and shorts" electronic testers and traded them for much more capable, but used, in-circuit testers (ICT). The ICT equipment is capable of providing much more information than simple testers: missing parts, wrong part, open circuits, short circuits, visibility (with software) to so-called "hidden" components, and more.

Production testing can also be standardized to a software platform; for example, we can use the following tools:

- MathWorks MATLAB™

- Scilab (similar to MATLAB)

- LabVIEW

These are some obvious choices and will sometimes represent a benefit in maintainability over languages such as C++, Java, and assembly code. If we are using common equipment in different areas of the facility, it only makes sense to build modular code we can use over and over again, thus gaining the leverage of reuse of known good code. Reuse also reduces the documentation overhead because we only need to document the module once.

VIII. Logistics Material

For manufacturing facilities, much of what they receive will be on palettes or skids. The smart organization will find a way to sell the used skids to a recycling organization rather than simply disposing of these. We can say the same thing for the huge quantities of cardboard used in shipping. Paper is an easy recycle and if we can regain some money at the same time, we should pursue the option.

Returnable dunnage (the loose, protective packing material) is another solution to reducing the cost of logistics. We know many automotive companies that use this method to reduce their logistics cost and maintain the quality of the product through shipping and handling.

Returned parts constitute more potential for savings. For example, if we have metal housing, we can sell these to a recycler for meltdown if we are not allowed to reuse the parts ourselves. Aluminum parts present an excellent opportunity for recycling, as do the scarcer metals such as gold.

We have seen instances where the handling of the product was different in actuality than what was documented during the product development phase. This inappropriate handling caused problems that became product failures at the customer manufacturing facility. On review with the supplier and engineering personnel, this poor handling was identified and the handling material processes for the product was revisited including training for the people on the line. This eliminated many of the failures witnessed on the line installing the parts into the vehicle.

IX. Engineering

The primary method for saving money in the engineering function is to design out problems. The best way, of course, is to design out the problem from the start of the product development program. Sometimes, however, we do not know what problems we will have with the product and we have to design fixes later. It is at this time that we start looking for cost savings.

The engineering function can also better design the part of manufacturing. We know of one case where the operators lived with a mismatch between the screw bosses and the screw holes between a printed circuit board and housing—this situation went on for years of wasted extra effort and potential reliability and quality issues. Why? Nobody spoke up about the problem until a line engineer observed the extra effort during an audit.

If the firm is an electronics company, they can have the engineering function design out horrible and expensive manufacturing options such as selective soldering, which is really hiring an expensive robot to do hand soldering. In general, we want to see as much reflow soldering (surface mount technology or SMT) as we can, followed by wave soldering (through-hole technology). The use of a selective solder machine represents a compromise in our approach to manufacturing—even if the customer wants this approach, it is worth our while to campaign to eliminate the robots as much as possible.

While designing out defects is important, we have other opportunities to improve our costs and therefore our margins on our product. Our engineers commence by setting the cost for our product well beyond what is necessary for the quality targets. We can select development options that will affect the cost of the product beyond the quality.

We worked at an original equipment manufacturer (OEM) that had two vehicle brands that had common electrical / electronic engineering. These engineers were designing a new feature into the existing systems on the vehicle. The new feature had some elements that were mandated by the Environmental Protection Agency (EPA) and the California Air Resources Board (CARB). The systems engineering portion of the OEM, had desires to place a "smart switch" on the vehicle dash. This smart switch (see Figure 2.7) would really be a small electronic control unit (ECU) and all the attending circuitry to survive on the electrical system of a class 8 vehicle. The solution proposed by system engineer, would cost development time and money and in the end, would amount to another $40 per vehicle for the switch hardware (does not include installation at manufacturing).

This solution seemed to be contradictory to the many hours the electrical and electronic department spent trying to take cost out of the vehicle without impeding the vehicle quality. On a casual review, it was determined that the function could be easily integrated into the existing instrument cluster for development costs only (see Figure 2.8). There would be no need for material changes. One of the truck brands of this company preferred this option and the other did not. The number of vehicles

Figure 2.7 The obvious solution to meet a customer demand may not be the most cost-effective solution.

for the one brand sold per year was more than 20,000. We can see that this company saved a cost increase of $800,000 due to cost discipline and good engineering that the other vehicle brands solution was not able to overcome. In the end, the other brand in this company's product line adopted this solution also. However, at that point there was already an investment in the development of the other solution that was now

Figure 2.8 An instrument cluster can be a complex product and may present many opportunities for cost savings.

abandoned and the expenditure for more than two years, amounting to a spending of $1,600,000 that was not really necessary.

In a subsequent part of this book, we will illustrate a number of tools and techniques for achieving cost improvements. We will show methods for generating ideas for improving our costs as well as determining if the cost improvement is worthy of the investment in cost or time. Not all ideas for cost improvement are created equally. For example, we may reap great benefit, comparatively speaking, from an idea we can implement immediately with little or no cost for doing it.

X. Marketing

We might wonder how the marketing organization can contribute to value engineering. A large portion of their contribution will be in the form of avoided cost and the ephemeral concept of opportunity cost.

If the marketing department agrees to tasks that are not profitable in order to "get a foot in the door," we are committed to tasks that will not benefit the bottom line. Some examples we have seen are as follows:

- Continuing a product that had negative margin to avoid letting another supplier in the door
- Taking on a small volume product because the chief executive officer of that organization sat on the board of the supplier organization
- Bidding on a personal snow vehicle that would never yield a profit
- Participating in a personal watercraft product without understanding the ramifications
- Building some instrumentation on the word of one employee, not highly placed, of a customer and then not receiving the business

- Investing a considerable amount of time to specify a product at an original equipment manufacturer with no contract or future business case
- Participating in industry shows that have not demonstrated any return on investment
- Consuming massive engineering hours for a "one off" never to be seen again prototype part
- Ill-advised or not well-defined marketing promotion, generally performed to gather new customers, increase demand or differentiate our product. Blindly executed, we will find we are selling our product for less than we can
- Constant minor updates to the product consuming engineering resources, and not accounting for this mass-customization cost

We call some of these "opportunity costs" because we could have been working on more important, profit-making products. They are avoided costs when we choose not to do them. We can control working on products like these by setting a rigorous company-wide standard for acceptance of projects. Justifying them on the basis of some kind of accounting absorption just does not fly.

XI. Accounting/Finance

The accounting/finance function is optimally positioned to look at the flow of money through the enterprise. They also will often participate in some of the contract negotiations, which can also lead to savings. In one study we know about, we asked the accounting department to provide enough information about expenses (not capital) so that we could generate a Pareto chart of the results and look for ways to reduce the outgoing monies. Typical expenses that need oversight are the following:

- Travel
- Training/education
- Cafeteria services
- Rentals
- Maintenance

We are not suggesting these functions should not be executed; we are suggesting that accounting department oversight of these functions may lead to an increase in accountability and some reduction in cost.

Travel can be a sore spot. Some travel is necessary, often for the marketing, quality, engineering, and manufacturing functions. However, with planning, we can reduce the price of airline tickets significantly. If we are using a travel agency, appropriate timing should be part of our contractual agreement with them.

From another perspective, we have seen capital equipment identified that would improve throughput or otherwise provide a tangible benefit (in dollars). The approval and subsequent money securing through delivery process was so complicated that we consume months to acquire a modest set of tools. The effort for requesting and getting the tools delivered was nearly as costly as securing the tools.

XII. Procurement

The procurement department is often called "purchasing." They can save significant amounts of money (increasing value) just by holding the line on contractual agreements with suppliers.

We must proceed with caution in the cases where the procurement department recommends new parts as cost reductions—we have seen some of these cost reductions backfire themselves into campaigns or recalls because the substitute part was inadequate. Sometimes, even laboratory testing is insufficient to discover an issue that slowly appears across time (reliability issue).

Manufacturing procurement organizations will often conduct their own audits of suppliers. In cases where they see a sole source with their own problems, the procurement function can offer to assist by providing training, on-site auditing, and other supportive activities.

Still, procurement can be an area where we can improve our costs. We can do so not only through unilateral demands for certain percentage of reduction in the product costs as many organizations demand. We can streamline our product cost through specification of the product. If we have a firm understanding of the product use, we have the possibility of having stronger control over the product cost. We can lose some of our profits due to making the product unduly rigid for the application. For example, for a product that will mount inside a vehicle, we may need not to specify connectors that are sealed or we may not need a metal housing that will withstand corrosion, gravel bombardment and splash.

If we are a global corporation with multiple sites consuming many common parts, we can use our volumes as a way to improve our material and handling costs. Electronic and electrical parts can have significant cost improvements based on the volume of the parts ordered. The caveat is the risk to having a sole supplier for this material. While we have cost down due to this volume, if there is an event such as a tsunami or earthquake at our one supplier's location, we will most assuredly be impacted.

A. Financial Determination

Make or Buy Approach

Another tool that supports value analysis and value engineering is that of the make or buy analysis (see Figure 2.9). We use a make or buy analysis both at the strategic and operational levels. Anytime the opportunity arises to assess where we really are able to maximize the value.

Make or buy decisions are based on what our organization values or those things that our organization provides the maximum benefit. Make or buy is not necessarily restricted to equipment or hardware development. To be sure, these areas are the most prominent. However, this decision process really boils down to "can we provide maximum value" by doing the product in-house or outsourcing it. In that context, we can see even services can bear the scrutiny of a make or buy analysis.

From the material perspective, what we need to know are the following:

1. How many will be produced (per unit time)?
2. How does the volume of parts produced grow over time?
3. What are the fixed costs (and the total fixed costs)?
4. What are our direct costs for making the product (cost linked directly with the product per unit)?
5. What would be our total cost for purchasing the product (Example: including shipping)?

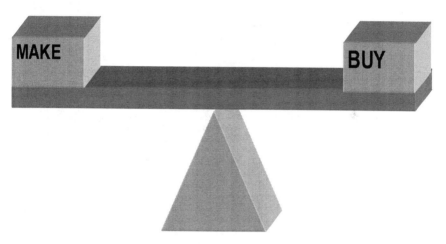

Figure 2.9 In most cases, buying is better than making.

We can see a number of reasons for making the product, the principal one of which would be that our organization can provide value to our customers. However, that is not the only reason for deciding to make the product rather than purchase. Some of these we list below:

- Volatility of the purchase price of the product
- Degree of quality control needed for our customer (dollars lost due to poor quality)
- Supplier delivery risks
- Shipping and material handling costs
- We can do it better than anybody else (intellectual property)
- Low volume price penalty

There are many reasons for purchasing the product rather than making the product. Obviously, the main reason would be that we are unable to add value for our customers by internally developing and manufacturing the product. We may have other issues, such as the following:

- We lack the requisite expertise (intellectual property of supplier)

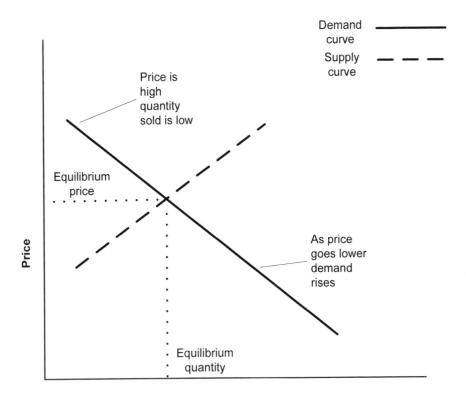

Figure 2.10 As we lower the price of the product to our customer, the demanded volume may increase.

- We lack the capacity to take on the effort (product or service)
- Cost

As stated earlier, we will use a number of techniques similar or identical to those we could use for value analysis or value engineering. For example, part of the effort to decide whether we should make or buy, must include a determination of how we could make the product and what that would cost to do so. The information we gather makes it possible to determine which equation is valid:

- Cost to make < cost to buy
- Cost to make > cost to buy
- Cost to make = cost to buy

Supply and Demand Curves

Cost improvement also has implications on the volume of the product ordered from the customer. In economics we see a generic demand curve that shows as the price comes down for a product, the customers will tend to purchase or consume more of that product (see Figure 2.10). This curve has a negative slope, which illustrates the amount of expected purchases per a level of price. As cost goes down, volume can go up if the determinants of demand constraints are met. The determinants of demand are:

1. Customer or business income

2. Customer or potential customer volume

3. Price of suitable substitutions and complimentary goods and services

4. Customer preference

It is possible to reduce our costs to deliver the product or service. Reducing the costs makes it possible for us to reduce the price at which we sell the product. We can reduce the price and still make our expected or original profit margins on the product. Reducing the price can increase the demand. Moving more products with the same profit margin makes our company more profitable. We can even keep the sale price the same, and increase our company's individual profit and therefore our company's total profit.

Breakeven Analysis

We may employ breakeven analysis to understand our costs to make the product and compare that value to the revenue generated. The breakeven analysis will tell us how much of the product we would need to make to not lose money on the endeavor (see Figure 2.11). To understand the concept of breaking even, we need to understand fixed and variable costs.

Fixed costs are the costs associated with an organization's long-term operation. Fixed costs do not fluctuate with volume of product or service the company delivers. By this definition, you can see that an improvement in the fixed costs of a company can have cost improvement implication across the entire product line or services offered. However, since fixed costs are the costs associated with the long term we can expect making fixed cost improvements to take time. Examples of fixed costs are:

• Building/rent

• Equipment

• Administration

• Marketing efforts

• Utility bills

Variable costs are costs associated with production of the product or delivery of a service. These are costs that increase and decrease with the volume of our company's production.

Examples of variable costs are:

• Raw material

• Labor for additional shifts

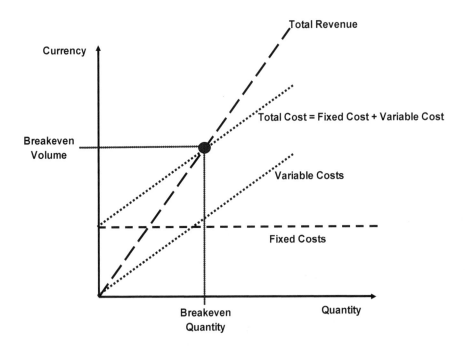

Figure 2.11 Breakeven occurs when we have no profit or loss for the investment.

To calculate breakeven cost for a particular product or service, we will likely be required to make some assumptions. Some of those assumptions are:

- Constant fixed cost
- Constant average variable cost
- Constant price

We will likely have to make some assumptions when we employ this technique. For example, we may have no historical record from which to determine our fixed costs, and it is possible our fixed costs are not always constant, though this may be the more stable or accurate of the assumptions. Fixed costs are those costs incurred by the organization that are not volume-dependent over a short term. An example of this would be the rent for a building.

Next we make the assumption that we have constant average variable costs. Variable costs are costs that increase or decrease with the volume of the organization's output. Since we are looking at change in the cost associated with volume, the assumption of a constant average variable cost has some volatility. Making this an average variable cost may reduce this volatility; however, if the range of product volumes under consideration has a large variation the average will have some impact on this assumption and therefore the real breakeven point.

Finally, we make assumptions that the sale price of the product is constant. This may not be valid as well. If the product has some variation in what our customer perceives in the value then the cost will therefore have variation.

In spite of these possible disparities, this provides a reasonable approach to understanding the cost structure for the product and a point for us to determine where to put our efforts.

We may use brainstorming techniques (discussed later) to generate a number of possible solutions. We may employ expert opinion to determine how to approach the make or buy decision. We can use tools to help decide the best approach to take through the analysis of the pros and cons of each potential design solution in support of the make or buy decision. We can use tools such as a Pugh matrix to offer a comparative perspective of the possible solutions to determine the most economically judicious approach to the decision. Ultimately we will produce a decision to either make or buy that will be based on the generated estimates of the time and material needed to make the product. Thus we will know what it costs to make and we compare that value to the cost to purchase.

If we are discussing a service, this same approach applies. If our organization provides a service to an outside customer or an internal customer, either way we can take a similar approach to determine if we really should be performing the work as part of our organization. The basic approach still applies. We really want to determine the benefits to the organization compared to the costs to supply internal and an external solution. We still go through the evaluation similarly though. We will present possible solutions, analyze those solutions and then compare that to the make solution to the buy solution.

Return on Investment (ROI)

Return on Investment is one way of evaluating the profits that are generated from an investment. Other variations on this them are listed below.

- Return on Assets
- Return on Capital
- Return on Invested Capital

Net Present Value

The net present value of an investment is the present value of its net cash inflows minus the present value of its cost outlays. An investment project is acceptable if its NPV is greater than or equal to zero.

Internal Rate of Return (IRR)

Internal Rate of Return or IRR is the net annual percentage yield of a project, obtained by solving for the discount rate that will cause the net present value of the project to be equal to zero.

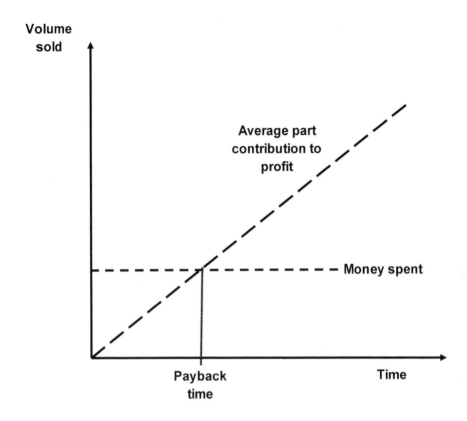

Figure 2.12 The payback period is a simple way of calculating when a project becomes profitable.

Payback Period

When we are talking about payback, we are talking about the time to recover the money we invested to produce the product (see Figure 2.12). In this instance, we know we have to spend some money to make the desired change. We use expert opinion or historical data to arrive at this cost estimate to do the work. Next, we make projections on how this change improves our cost structure, for example, we know that the product change will remove another $1.00 from the product material cost. We now have a scale of the cost for the change as compared to the revenue improvement. Knowing this makes it possible to determine how long it will take to recoup the invested money. For example, if we spend $20,000 and we improve our margin by a dollar per unit, we can expect to see the profit improvement after we have sold 20,000 units.

We may also be sensitive to how long it takes to recoup the investment and really obtain the benefit from the investment. We may decide the cost improvement comes too late for us to invest in this idea. Our needs for the cost improvement may be too imminent for the length of time it takes to see the benefit. There may be risks to the product present purchase rate from the customer. For example, we may see more competitors going into the market that could take some of our customers away reducing our volume. There may be a new generation of the product coming out from our own company or another competitor that would mean the life of the present product is too short to be worthy of investment. We may see legal regulation that could disrupt our present product sales. All of these are areas for risk that should be considered.

XIII. Brainstorming

The brainstorming technique is attributed to Alex Faickney Osborne as explained in his 1953 book, *Applied Imagination*. The technique arose from frustration with the inability of employees to develop creative solutions for problems. Personal experience suggests this is a valuable tool when deployed appropriately and the guidelines are followed. If we populate the team with diverse backgrounds we can see ideas build on other ideas very rapidly.

To really find the areas for cost improvement we must let go of our mental impediments to uncovering these opportunities. It is very probable that there are plenty of cost improvement possibilities. However, in our daily work execution we may not find the time to free our minds to consider these possibilities. A brainstorming exercise can go far to fuel the imagination, to open a "space" to think laterally at what may be possible. We have successfully employed this technique to:

- Reduce costs

- Generate intellectual property

- Reduce weight for the vehicle

- Solve product design constraints

It is not even necessary to have a team with you to accomplish this lateral thinking, creative thinking, or thinking outside the box. Whatever you call it, the objective is to alter the perspective or view of the problem in order to perceive alternative possibilities. We can do this as a solo activity or we can use a group of individuals. If we are doing this as a group exercise we must make certain the event hygiene is managed. Of course, we are not talking about cleanliness of the team but the ability of the team to work together to produce some ideas that may solve the issue (cost) at hand.

A. Product, Process or Service Preparation for Critique

We need to make sure we are well prepared for the brainstorming event. This means selecting a cross-functional team with the wherewithal to achieve the objective of the exercise. They must have example material to review or peruse before the event. It is often helpful to have the material available during the exercise as well.

Problem Statement

To be effective, we must set the objective of the brainstorming activity. This in effect is the problem statement that we wish to solve. For example:

- Reduce the product material costs by 10%

- Reduce manufacturing costs by 6%

- Reduce shipping costs by 3%

We direct the team's attention (or even our own if we are the only person involved) toward this specific objective. This is necessary lest we end up with an array of ideas of which few or any meet our objective.

Review Material

If we have a product or service that we are trying to improve the cost, we can have the product available as a teardown sample for our team to review. We can have the tools available to take the product apart during the exercise. This dissection of the product helps the team learn about the product and provides grounds for idea generation. We have had good experiences with a teaming exercise between the supplier and the customer, with each organization supplying a group of engineers from various disciplines from product design going through the product. For example, we may have mechanical and electronic engineers from both organizations generating ideas for cost and quality improvements.

We can also have drawings of the product available for our team's review. We may choose to do this prior to the brainstorming event getting our team the understanding of the product, process or service prior to the event to maximize the idea generating time available.

We need not constrain our work to drawings of products. We can use this same approach to evaluate any process or processes we have within our organization that we wish to consider for improvement. In these cases we will need the process documentation and any process performance documentation that may be available. We should have a good idea of the performance of that process the same as we would with the performance of the product.

Numbers Count

The objective of a brainstorming exercise is to put as many ideas as possible for later consideration. The operative word is *later*. At this point in the process, we are trying to educe many ideas that we will consider at a later time. At some future date we will assess these ideas.

At the start of a brainstorming exercise, we will generally see the easy ideas emerge first—those ideas that have been discussed previously in the back rooms of the organization. We may not see any unique or fresh set of perspectives until we have exhausted these recycled ideas. That is not to say that these first ideas will not be appropriate, only that the new perspective will usually appear after we have already emitted those initial clusters of ideas—those at the forefront of our minds.

The generation of a mass of ideas provides fodder for cost improvement exercises without having to start the brainstorming session again. If we generate enough ideas, we can investigate and prioritize each, thus filling the pipeline for actions the organization can take to improve the cost, all based on this one event. Consider an investment of five people during two hours that produces 40 ideas that could work, which is better than that same number of hours that produced 10 ideas that are workable. We now have a backlog of ideas for our cost improvement efforts from which we can execute.

B. Suspend Judgment

We do not want to stall progress on the idea generation by going through a premature critique of the ideas. If we are consuming time to assess the quality of the idea, we will have a reduced number of ideas for the time invested. The focus is on the problem statement and the range of possible solutions to address the demand articulated in the problem statement.

Besides the diffusion of the available time from generating ideas, if we critique what is being provided from the participants prematurely, we run the risk of shutting their contribution down. If we alienate a team member by assailing their idea, we may run the risk of reducing their contribution. We need a multitude of ideas and a safe nonjudgmental place to generate them.

Lastly, there are plenty of instances where radical or contrary ideas have produced exceptional results. Think of the Wright brothers, and Albert Einstein.

C. Build on Ideas

If we have a group of people generating the ideas, we may see a combination or building of larger ideas from a core idea or central theme. We may see a number of variations from that theme giving us a number of iterations or permutations of possible solutions. This is encouraged as well. We are looking for large volumes of ideas from which we can explore for validity at a later date. This poses the most challenging part of this process and that being the focus of the ideas. Our goal is to produce a number of solutions that could possibly meet the objective. The team may sway from the objective in the rush of ideas being proposed for consideration. While we suspend judgment, the caveat is not to diffuse the focus on the problem statement.

XIV. Mind Mapping

Mind mapping is not a new methodology. In the book *How to Think Like Leonardo da Vinci: Seven Steps to Genius Every Day* by Michael J. Gelb[2], we see that Leonardo da Vinci used this technique to build associations and ideas. We see that the technique of graphically associating or linking ideas is not new. This technique was further refined (and marketed) in the 1970s by Tony Buzan[1].

Mind mapping is a diagramming technique used to generate associations between tasks or ideas and some central theme. The technique makes it possible for the person generating to group ideas that are associated with a central theme and generate additional ideas for each of those subthemes. In the end, we have a hierarchical view of based on the central theme. Often these maps make extensive use of pictures or other graphical representation, not just text or even predominantly text[3].

If the radiant thinking ability of the brain can be applied to the left cortical skill of words, can the same power be applied to the right cortical skill of imagination and images? In 1970, *Scientific American* magazine published Ralph Haber's research showing that individuals have a recognition accuracy of images between 85% and 95%[6]. We associate and remember images because they make use of a massive range of our cortical skills, especially imagination. Images can be more evocative than words, more precise and potent in triggering a wide range of associations, thereby enhancing creative thinking and memory. These findings support the argument that the mind map is a uniquely appropriate tool. It not only uses images, it is an image.

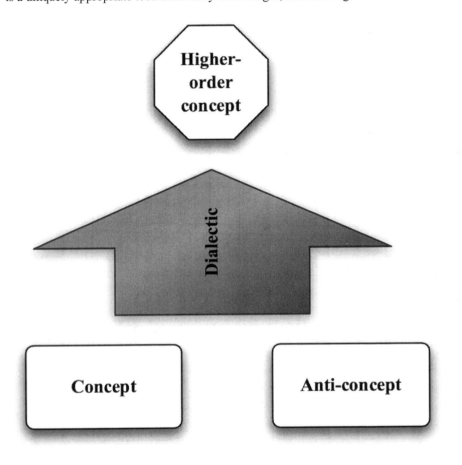

Figure 2.13 We can use conflicting ideas and concepts to produce an even better solution.

XV. Selection Method

A. Weighted Matrix Such as a Pugh Matrix

We use the tools previously discussed to generate a number of cost reduction ideas or possible solutions to improving our cost structure. We understand the financial questions we may have to ask to determine the viability of the ideas generated. We will also need to know how to assess those ideas to determine the best solution for the problem under consideration.

The Pugh matrix (shown in Figure 2.14) is a decision-making tool that allows us to compare a solution to our criteria or a number of possible solutions against the criteria we hold dear. We then evaluate each of the ideas we have generated against these attributes we value, for example:

- Compare single design
- Compare new design to existing solutions
- Compare multiple new solutions

Let us consider an individual solution under consideration. In the left most column, we will have the list of attributes we wish to assess the idea against. If we are concerned with cost, this left-hand column may have things such as:

- Cost of development

Function name: New transmission shifter

Pugh Matrix											2005-08-22
Evaluation criterion			Shifter A		Shifter B		Knob shifter Dash		T-handle on dash		Shifter on Column
	Priority - 5 is high	Rating	Weighted	Rating	Weighted	Rating	Weighted	Rating	Weighted	Rating	Weighted
Product Cost	5	1	5	3	15	2	10	2	10	1	5
Tooling Cost	2	5	10	4	8	2	4	3	6	1	2
Development time	3	4	12	2	6	1	3	1	3	1	3
Ease of entrance into sleeper compartment	5	1	5	1	5	3	15	3	15	3	15
Sight location of shifter during driving	2	0	0	1	2	3	6	2	4	3	6
Issues with extremely large people	4	1	4	1	4	4	16	4	16	1	4
Conventional acceptance	5	3	15	4	20	2	10	3	15	1	5
Instrument Panel space	3	4	12	4	12	1	3	1	3	4	12
New steering wheel with up/down & man/auto buttons	1	2	2	2	2	1	1	2	2	2	2
Reach for manual shifting	3	2	6	3	9	4	12	1	3	2	6
Clinic rating	5	3	15	3	15	3	15	3	15	1	5
Ease of diagnostics	3	2	6	2	6	1	3	1	3	1	3
Number of new parts	1	2	2	2	2	1	1	1	1	1	1
Total Score			94		106		99		96		69
Selected/Rejected/Maintained alternative											

Responsible for Pugh	
Leader:	TL
Engineering:	BT
Engineering:	JY
Advanced Engineering:	Jar
Aftermarket:	Jep
Product Planning:	BH
Product Planning:	MM
Marketing:	JF
Eng. PM:	RK

Figure 2.14 Decision-making tools, such as the Pugh matrix, help us to determine the best solution from a range of options we generate.

- Cost of material
- Cost to manufacture
- Time to manufacture
- Specialty equipment needs

We will then weigh these individual items essentially prioritizing or ranking these areas of importance. The higher we value the particular element with regard to the product or feature we are developing, the more heavily weighted that particular attribute.

B. Majority Decision

Majority decision is just that. We have a voting process to decide which of the solutions or approaches to our cost reduction effort we will pursue. If we are really interested in majority rule, we must free the voting process from undue influences between those voting. For example, we may choose to have a paper vote where each person cannot see nor do they know how the other people voted.

C. Voting Decision

The voting decision is like the majority rule, only we typically have ballots. These votes are usually such that it is not apparent how people voted.

D. Consensus

Consensus is not the same as majority voting. Consensus is a group decision-making methodology. We are seeking an agreement that meets all of the needs of the people impacted by the proposed change. We will take the time to uncover how to meet all of those demands. We may have to go through a number of iterations, ultimately we wish to address all party concerns as best possible working to find the win-win compromise. This method holds the team cohesion and team member consideration in high regard. The drawback is that decision making can be a long struggle to the final solution.

E. Rating

For rating, we are critically reviewing the ideas we have previously generated for viability. We will pick the idea that we believe the most promising based on some simple ranking or by evaluation of the advantages and disadvantages for taking the proposed cost improvement activity. If we have a number of ideas, we may compare each against the other to define which idea has what merit. This works similarly to the Pugh matrix but is typically more spontaneous and less rigorous.

F. Delphi Method

Delphi method name has origins in the "Oracle of Delphi" but has very little to do with mysticism. With this technique, we gather information from experts. We do this in a way where each of the participants will not know anything about the other members of the team. In this way, any dominant personalities will not be able to assert themselves and affect the ideation of the other contributors. These other contributors, for example, may not push their ideas as hard or vehemently in the face of strong resistance as can sometimes happen in uncontrolled exchanges.

To make this method effective, we need a facilitator to distribute the information (surveys, questionnaires, etc.) for the problem at hand. The facilitator collects the responses from these experts and compiles them, noting areas of agreement and disagreement. The results are then sent back to these experts for another round until there is some consensus with the result.

When using this technique, we find it advisable to publish the mean, the median, and the standard deviation of the results. These statistics allow a wise reader to assess the centrality and variation in the opinions of the experts.

G. Nominal Group Technique

Nominal group technique is a method that we use to include all the participants available while streamlining the process. Again, we have a facilitator for the activities and they start by explaining the purpose of the meeting and explain the mechanics of the activity. After this definition, the facilitator will get ideas generated that can meet the objective from the participants. The facilitator usually does this by a piece of paper listing the ideas possible to meet the stated objective. The participants do not discuss or share their ideas; the entire idea generation activity occurs with anonymity.

Once the team has slowed down in their idea generation phase, we stop the idea generation and start with the idea-sharing phase. Typically this happens by going around the room (what looks like laps) and getting one idea from each of the participants. The facilitator writes these ideas up on a larger flip chart.

Now we have a large sheet of paper in front of the entire team with the list of ideas. We then hold a group discussion regarding these ideas. We can question the ideas from the other members and clarify our own answers and perspectives. The same criteria apply that we used in our brainstorming method—treat all with respect and no perspective should call an undue criticism or harsh judgment of the idea or the individual.

Finally, we have the list of possible ideas and we rank the most probable to solve our problem. We will then initiate some actions to let the team know the direction taken and the next steps in securing the solution.

H. Group Passing Technique

Group passing technique is like a combination of brainstorming and nominal group technique. We have a similar explanation of the objective by the facilitator. We then hand each participant a piece of paper. Each person writes an idea on their paper and passes their paper to the next person in the chain. It does not really matter whether the direction of the passing is clockwise or counterclockwise, only that all pass in the same direction. The next person in the chain will elaborate on the idea presented in the paper as it passes them. This continues as the various papers started with each individual make it round the room to the original starting location. So now, we have an idea on each paper, with elaboration from the rest of the team on that idea. At the end, each idea will have some level of elaboration that was individually arrived at from the entire team.

I. De Bono and His Thinking Hats

Color	Area	Description
White	Information	What are the facts
Red	Emotions	Instinctive gut reaction or statements of emotional feeling
Black	Bad points judgement	Logic applied to identifying flaws or barriers

Color	Area	Description
Yellow	Good points judgement	Logic applied to identifying benefits, seeking harmony
Green	Creativity	Statements of provocation and investigation, seeing where a thought goes
Blue	Thinking	Thinking about thinking

De Bono's approach has the benefit of simplicity[5].

J. Advocacy and Inquiry

Advocacy and inquiry is usually a management function, although it can be practiced at any level. This approach is less about taking positions and defending beliefs and more about trying to understand the point of view of the other individual. Standing on one's beliefs is a simple way to produce cessation of true dialogue. Some simple steps to getting to this level are the following:

- State your position or assumptions, and then describe the information that led to them
- Clarify and manifest your position or assumptions
- Make your rationale more obvious and overt
- Reveal the frame of reference of your point of view
- Provide examples of your proposition and remember that communication is what *they* hear, not what *you* say
- Ask others to probe your model (base and superstructure), your assumptions and your data (or information if it is stronger), while avoiding defensive and counterproductive behaviors
- Acknowledge the points where you are the most opaque in your thinking
- While advocating, you should listen, remain open, and embolden others to provide alternate viewpoints

Each time we gather together to dialogue, we have four situations:

- High advocacy and high inquiry = I state, I inquire to you, I encourage you to inquire to me (the ideal)
- Low advocacy and low inquiry = stonewalling
- Low advocacy and high inquiry = speaker conceals position (21 questions)
- High advocacy and low inquiry = my way or the highway!

We are discussing true dialogue, where the attitude is more one of sharing and negotiation than it is of win at all costs. Clearly, hidden agendas, logical fallacies, and spin are going to be detrimental to a long-range partnership.

K. Strategic Assumption Surfacing and Testing (SAST)

Strategic assumptions surfacing and testing (SAST) is a method for approaching messy or poorly structured problems. It can be applied as a dialectical approach to policy and planning; a dialectic approach is one that looks for inherent contradictions from a "systems thinking" point of view. A poorly structured problem may also be called a "wicked" problem and we have also seen it associated with the term "messy data."

A poorly structured problem is one for which various strategies for providing a potential solution rest on assumptions in collision The purposes for an SAST method are:

- To help surface the underlying assumptions—for explicit examination—that analysts often unconsciously bring with them to a problem situation;

- To compare and to evaluate systematically the assumptions of different analysts;

- To examine the relationship between underlying assumptions and the resulting policies which are derived and dependent on them; and

- To attempt to formulate new, novel, and originally unforeseen policies based on previously unforeseen assumptions.

Four stages in the method include:

- Assumption specification

- Dialectic phase

- Assumption integration phase

- Composite strategy creation

We can also suggest that SAST has some fundamental principles:

- It is integrative as we pursue synthesis through the upheaval/reconciliation of the dialectical approach

- It is participative because we endeavor to involve different groups and levels in our hierarchy, since no one knows everything we need to solve problem

- It supports assumption surfacing to the managerial mentality

- It is adversarial because opposing points of view are a key part of the process

Almost by definition, a dialectical approach will be holistic. A key component of any technique that uses the word "dialectic" is that the internal contradictions present in any situation should be considered. If we want to pursue this farther, we would analyze the situation for the interpenetration of opposites, the shift from quantity to quality and back again, and the negation of the negation (hysteresis). We can use the tools of dialectical materialism without committing to a political philosophy we may not wish to support.

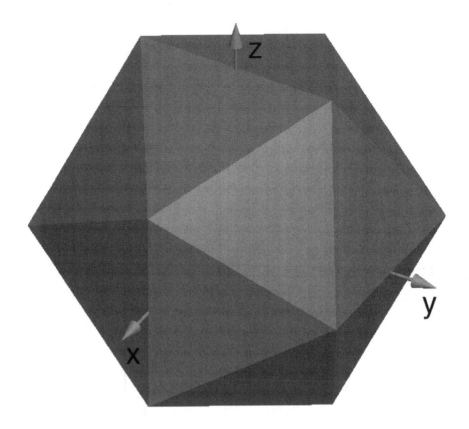

Figure 2.15 The icosahedron is a regular polyhedron having 20 faces of equilateral triangles that we can use as a communications model.

L. Team Syntegrity

Team syntegrity is a registered trademark approach to team activities based on a structural model for communication. It is a conflation of the thoughts of Stafford Beer and R. Buckminster Fuller. From Beer's point of view, effective communication is inherent in the structure on which we ground our communications. If the syntegration structure is implemented properly, the process becomes automatic. The participants in a syntegration exercise anything they think needs to be discussed. The structure provides a geometric model for who discusses what with whom, when, for how long and in what defined role.

Beer suggested that the ideal structure for this kind of communication is the icosahedron, easily the most complex of the five platonic bodies (regular polyhedra). The icosahedron is a regular polyhedron that has 20 faces, 12 vertices, and 30 edges. In turn, Buckminster Fuller showed that the equilateral triangle is the most efficient and robust structure that can be used to construct a variety of structures. Beer used the structural concept to place the topics for discussion at the 12 vertices of the icosahedron[4] and the people at its 30 edges; hence, 30 people with 12 topics.

Using this model, 30 brains network together so that they function as a single emergent brain that is more capable than any single component brain. A group with an optimal size of five people manages each of the 12 topics. The topics are then networked through the members, because each person has involvement in a defined quantity of topics. As well as a role as a team member for two topics, each person also functions in two other roles: he or she is a "critic" for two other topics and an "observer" for four others. This means that each topic is not only discussed by five members but it is also added to by five critics and observed by up to 10 observers.

We can summarize this approach with the following comments:

- We can manage 12 subtopics of one general topic in a networked and self-organizing way.

- We network the participants together to the maximum degree possible.

- The information "distance" between the topics is minimized.

- All the 12 topics are networked not only by members but also by critics and observers.

- The division of the roles into three (member, critic, and observer) makes possible a clear division of tasks and a clear focus of concentration for the participants.

The drawback to the team syntegrity approach lies in the complexity of setting up the structure as well as ensuring that all participants understand what they are supposed to do as members of the structure. The idea certainly has the attractiveness of symmetry and form. We have not personally seen one of these implemented and we suspect it would take substantial facilitation to make it occur properly; on the other hand, what is the cost of poor communications and inadequate dialogue?

M. Facilitation

The primary purpose of a facilitator is to keep a meeting "on track." What that means is that the facilitator will see to it we follow the agenda for the meeting and that we produce minutes for the meeting.

In addition, the facilitator will most likely use a technique like "Parking Lot," where side topics are collected on a flip-chart easel or white board for potential follow-up subsequent to the agenda items. The parking lot items may be considered to be new business in the parliamentary sense.

Facilitators may have certification credentials; for example, the International Institute for Facilitation (INIFAC) or the International Association of Facilitators (IAF) or a union facilitation denomination.

We can improve our group activity by laying down ground rules:

- As with SAST, we want to surface assumptions

- Also surface covert inferences

- Have an open book on information and data

- Ensure the meanings of words are discussed any time friction occurs
- Explain one's own position; that is, provide a rationale
- Focus on interests, rather than positions (sort of like "would I rather be happy or would I rather be right?")
- Use advocacy and inquiry
- Consider the use of nonviolent communication techniques
- Always discuss the next actions together
- Think the unthinkable, discuss the undiscussable, air things out
- Use decision-making rules such as a quorum or a consensus
- Try to find ways to assure a level of commitment to the driving question
- Use reframing (showing in another perspective) when it makes sense
- Make content suggestions but beware of influencing group activity directly
- Use models for solution activities
  - Eight disciplines
  - Five whys
  - Ishikawa diagram
  - Time lines
  - Value stream mapping
  - Solution matrices
  - Responsibility models
  - Affinity diagrams
  - Brainstorming
  - Force field diagrams, especially to investigate areas of resistance to proposals
  - Pugh concept selection technique

The facilitator should only be intervening when the meeting begins to move in negative directions. Otherwise, we generally expect the facilitator to stand back.

XVI. EXERCISES

- What are the benefits and limitations to reducing the fixed costs?
- What are the benefits and limitations of reducing the variable costs?
- How do variable costs figure into our profitability?
- What happens if our product or service only covers the fixed costs?
- How does a change in perspective help uncover cost improvement possibilities?

- Do we have processes for our organization? How do our processes affect our cost?

- What can we infer about our organization's process if the process is not followed? Can we tell the true cost of a process that is not followed?

- Describe a make or buy decision.

- What is IRR?

- What is NPV?

ENDNOTES

1. Buzan, Tony, and Barry Buzan. *The Mind Map Book*. New York City, NY: Plume/Penguin, 1993.

2. Gelb, Michael. *How to Think like Leonardo Da Vinci: Seven Steps to Genius Every Day*. New York City, NY: Delacorte Press, 1998.

3. http://www.mindmapping.com/Theory_Behind_Mind_Maps.htm

4. http://www.ebi.ac.uk/pdbe/docs/3dem/std_oo/icosahedron/3DEM_icosahedral.html. Retrieved June 20, 2012.

5. http://www.debonogroup.com/?gclid=CKnA66XA564CFcqe7Qodrl4RiA

6. http://www.lifetools.com/newsletters/bookblst2.html Retrieved September 20, 2012.

CHAPTER 3 – Arbitrary Cost Down Approach

I. Rubric for Costing Down

Criteria	Level 1 (50–59%)	Level 2 (60–69%)	Level 3 (70–79%)	Level 4 (80–100%)
Assess methods of accounting for capital assets if involved in costing down project	Assessment of methods of accounting for capital assets demonstrates limited understanding	Assessment of methods of accounting for capital assets demonstrates some understanding	Assessment of methods of accounting for capital assets demonstrates considerable understanding	Assessment of methods of accounting for capital assets demonstrates thorough understanding
Calculate necessary ratios	Calculates necessary ratios with limited success	Calculates necessary ratios with some success	Calculates necessary ratios with considerable success	Calculates necessary ratios with a high degree of success
Compare given components for validity	Comparison of given components demonstrates limited understanding of validity	Comparison of given components demonstrates some understanding of validity	Comparison of given components demonstrates considerable understanding of validity	Comparison of given components demonstrates thorough understanding of validity
Demonstrate skills required to analyze job costs and profitability	Demonstrates limited skills required to analyze job costs and profitability	Demonstrates some skills required to analyze job costs and profitability	Demonstrates considerable skills required to analyze job costs and profitability	Demonstrates a high degree of skills required to analyze job costs and profitability
Demonstrate skills required to interpret financial information	Demonstrates limited skills required to interpret financial information	Demonstrates some skills required to interpret financial information	Demonstrates considerable skills required to interpret financial information	Demonstrates a high degree of skills required to interpret financial information
Demonstrate understanding of cost recovery	Demonstrates limited understanding of cost recovery	Demonstrates some understanding of cost recovery	Demonstrates considerable understanding of cost recovery	Demonstrates thorough understanding of cost recovery
Demonstrate understanding of costs that are beyond the control of the business	Demonstrates limited understanding of costs that are beyond the control of the business	Demonstrates some understanding of costs that are beyond the control of the business	Demonstrates considerable understanding of costs that are beyond the control of the business	Demonstrates a thorough understanding of costs that are beyond the control of the business
Demonstrate understanding of the regulatory and ethical framework	Demonstrates limited understanding of the regulatory and ethical framework	Demonstrates some understanding of the regulatory and ethical framework	Demonstrates considerable understanding of the regulatory and ethical framework	Demonstrates a thorough understanding of the regulatory and ethical framework
Describe costing procedures for intangible assets	Description of costing procedures for intangible assets demonstrates limited knowledge	Description of costing procedures for intangible assets demonstrates some knowledge	Description of costing procedures for intangible assets demonstrates considerable knowledge	Description of costing procedures for intangible assets demonstrates thorough knowledge

Criteria	Level 1 (50–59%)	Level 2 (60–69%)	Level 3 (70–79%)	Level 4 (80–100%)
Describe costing procedures for natural resources	Description of costing procedures for natural resources demonstrates limited knowledge	Description of costing procedures for natural resources demonstrates some knowledge	Description of costing procedures for natural resources demonstrates considerable knowledge	Description of costing procedures for natural resources demonstrates thorough knowledge
Describe costing procedures for plant and equipment	Description of costing procedures for plant and equipment demonstrates limited knowledge	Description of costing procedures for plant and equipment demonstrates some knowledge	Description of costing procedures for plant and equipment demonstrates considerable knowledge	Description of costing procedures for plant and equipment demonstrates thorough knowledge
Describe the advantages and disadvantages of different types of component savings	Briefly described the advantages and disadvantages of different types of component savings	Adequately described the advantages and disadvantages of different types of component savings	Competently described the advantages and disadvantages of different types of component savings	Thoroughly described the advantages and disadvantages of different types of component savings
Distinguish between capital expenditures and revenue expenditures	Distinguishes between capital expenditures and revenue expenditures with limited clarity	Distinguishes between capital expenditures and revenue expenditures with some clarity	Distinguishes between capital expenditures and revenue expenditures with considerable clarity	Distinguishes between capital expenditures and revenue expenditures with a high degree of clarity
Evaluate costing down exercise to reach conclusions	Evaluates costing down exercise to reach conclusions with limited supporting detail	Evaluates costing down exercise to reach conclusions with some supporting detail	Evaluates costing down exercise to reach conclusions with considerable supporting detail	Evaluates costing down exercise to reach conclusions with thorough supporting detail
Evaluate information to support assumptions made	Evaluation of information provides limited support of assumptions made	Evaluation of information provides some support of assumptions made	Evaluation of information provides considerable support of assumptions made	Evaluation of information provides thorough support of assumptions made
Evaluate information using criteria	Evaluates information with limited use of criteria	Evaluates information with some use of criteria	Evaluates information with considerable use of criteria	Evaluates information with thorough use of criteria
Explain factors that influence component prices	Explains factors that influence component prices using limited critical thinking	Explains factors that influence component prices using some critical thinking	Explains factors that influence component prices using good critical thinking	Explains factors that influence component prices using excellent critical thinking
Summarize information gathered	Summarizes information gathered using limited organization	Summarizes information gathered using some organization	Summarizes information gathered using considerable organization	Summarizes information gathered using thorough organization
Use criteria to analyze information	Rarely uses criteria to analyze information	Sometimes uses criteria to analyze information	Often uses criteria to analyze information	Routinely uses criteria to analyze information
Use criteria to evaluate information	Makes limited use of criteria to evaluate information	Makes some use of criteria to evaluate information	Makes considerable use of criteria to evaluate information	Makes thorough use of criteria to evaluate information

Criteria	Level 1 (50–59%)	Level 2 (60–69%)	Level 3 (70–79%)	Level 4 (80–100%)
Use criteria to make a comparison between as-is and to-be concepts	Rarely uses criteria to make a comparison between as-is and to-be concepts	Sometimes uses criteria to make a comparison between as-is and to-be concepts	Often uses criteria to make a comparison between as-is and to-be concepts	Routinely uses criteria to make a comparison between as-is and to-be concepts

II. Questions to Ponder

- What are the benefits of arbitrary cost down approach? What are the risks or down sides to this approach?

- What happens to the team when pushed to a goal that they believe cannot be met?

- What impact does compensation based on cost improvement have on the quality of the ideas and employee engagement?

- How does small lot size and proprietary parts impact our cost control efforts?

- How does your organization manage how the suppliers charge?

- How does our purchasing and procurement efforts impact our cost?

- What are the benefits of a long-term relationship with our suppliers?

- When should we consider material handling and shipping in our cost improvement efforts?

- Where does the responsibility reside for establishing a corporate philosophy about cost?

- What is required to establish a long-term relationship with suppliers?

- How does your company's logistics impact the product costs?

- What are cost drivers for your company?

- How do we keep our people focused on cost during their work activities?

III. Cost Improvement Scenario

A. Situation

The company has requested a 6% cost reduction from the supplier for the past five years and was able to get these reductions through constant improvement of the supply chain and the manufacturing processes. Now, it is not obvious where the cost improvement opportunities are.

B. Objective

We want to improve at least 6% of the cost of the electronic control module without compromising quality or any deadlines.

C. Action

A cross-functional team from the supplier as well as the engineering discipline from the customer was created. The customer engineer went to the supplier location where a teardown of the product happened.

This teardown had the list of the constituent parts from the most costly to the least. The group dissected the product in a conference room to view how the pieces went together. The supplier provided the costs for the most significant parts of the product. The team used brainstorming of these parts for substitutes of alternative methods for achieving the objective.

Frequently, the team members went to the manufacturing floor to see the assembly process and how that affected product cost and the rationalization ideas. Assembly tools (see Figure 3.2) and processes were reviewed as well in the course of the three-day event.

Alternatively, less costly materials were considered; for example, the backlighting color for the graphics display of the product. This was not a viable alternative since this change would require re-tooling of the light guide for the new wavelength and cost considerable to get the cost improvement.

D. Results

The team managed to find a number of cost improvement ideas during the teardown exercise. In total, they found more ideas than necessary to meet the cost improvement target of 6%.

E. Aftermath

The list of the brainstorm ideas was used for the targets for the next year as well. Keeping these ideas at our beck-and-call allows us to respond to this need to reduce our internal organizational cost quickly. Quick responses to the market changes means your company is more likely to capitalize on an opportunity or, equally importantly, adapt to avoid a threat. Brainstorming cost improvement ideas often produces more ideas than we can implement in the immediate future.

IV. Why the Arbitrary Cost Down Approach

With this method of proposing a cost reduction, we set an arbitrary value for the cost reduction; for example, 25% or 50% (see Figure 3.1). We must have some sensitivity towards the people we are asking to accept this challenge—we do not want them to consider the goal unattainable and give up or balk at the idea of working with this concept.

Often, when we are developing a product or a service, we will choose a "vanilla" approach for the first release in order to reduce the risk. That means some components of the product or service may not represent optimal cost, but they do represent lower risk. Basically, we are trying to successfully release a product that will then stimulate some customer feedback, which in turn, will encourage changes that can also lead to substantial cost reductions.

V. Cost Down Process

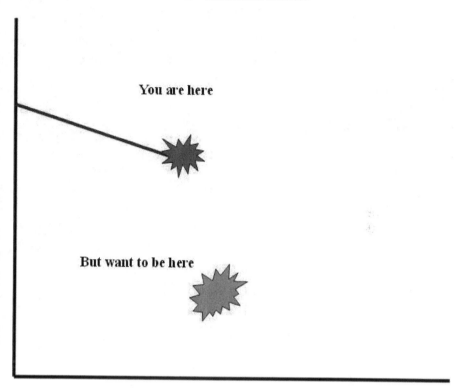

Figure 3.1 We must constantly consider how to improve, which often requires stretching goals and objectives.

As we begin this process, we must first pick a product or service on which we wish to work. How do we pick this product? We can look at several factors and see which ones make sense:

- With any product including electronics, we may wish to see if the material cost percentage is above average (other components would be factory overhead and direct labor)
- We can ascertain the age of the product or service and the location of the product within the life cycle; if we are early in the life cycle, but we have made no improvements, then we are ripe for redesign
- We can look at returns and warranty
- We can build a Pareto chart based on count of components in the product or steps in the service and see what can be removed
- We can look at the number of process steps to build the product and look for candidates for elimination
- We can look for complex processes in product or service
- We can perform a market survey to ascertain the prices our competitors are offering and whether we can beat these prices

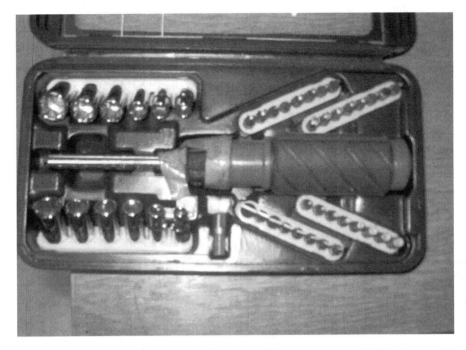

Figure 3.2 Sometimes we cost ourselves more when we remove tools that came with the larger product.

- Look at standard gross margin to see if we can find low-profit products that could benefit from a profitability boost (if they are not too far along in the product or service life cycle)—note that this step is different than simply looking at material cost

Before we begin our cost-saving, value-engineering activity, we need to clarify the rules of engagement:

- We can set some preconditions or requirements to meet to design and build products

- We can set some postconditions, which are also requirements, but we related them to postrelease behaviors

- The team will need to know the limitations; that is, restrictive conditions placed on product development and its scope of tasks

If we can control our rules ably, we may be able to bend the rules of the game. We want to be in a position to make potentially radical changes. We should also note that the word "radical" comes from the Latin root "radix" which, in fact, means "root." Our value engineering process is endeavoring to arrive at the root or essence of the product.

We have already indicated some effort to analyze cost structures for both product/

component costs and also process costs. We can look at the numbers, including:
- Types/quantities of parts and products (see Figure 3.3)
- Types/quantities of processes vis-a-vis the production system
- Types/quantities of processes vis-a-vis a service

Alternatively, we can visualize our products and processes and services as arrays of structures:
- Production site structures
    - We may be using conveyors, usually considered redundant in lean factories
    - We may be using complex and expensive manufacturing devices because our design is suboptimal (e.g., selective solder machines)
    - Excessive part routing (we used to joke that some parts traveled so much they should get frequent flyer miles!)

PART NO."	INCLUDED PART NO:s	NAME	QTY	REMARK
1078735	3944616	TACHOGRAPH, 7-DAY STD	I	
	1624632	COLOR DECAL / TACHOMETER, DI2	I	
	1624634	FRAME/COLOR DECAL	I	
	1078780	COMBI.INSTR., 24V, STD	I	
	956046	CROSS REC. SCREW M3XI	4	TACHOGRAPH – CLUSTER
1078736	3944616	TACHOGRAPH, 7-DAY STD	I	
	1624633	COLOR DECAL / TACHOMETER, DI6	I	
	1624634	FRAME/COLOR DECAL	I	
	1078780	COMBI.INSTR., 24V, STD	I	
	956046	CROSS REC. SCREW M3XI	4	TACHOGRAPH – CLUSTER
1078737	3944616	TACHOGRAPH, 7-DAY STD	I	
	1624632	COLOR DECAL / TACHOMETER, DI2	I	
	1624634	FRAME/COLOR DECAL	I	
	1078790	COMBI.INSTR., 24V, DIS. TRB	I	
	3963611	DRIVER INFO SYST., / LEAF S	I	
	956046	CROSS REC. SCREW M3XI	7	4X TACHOGRAPH – CLSTR. 3X DIS – CLUSTER
1078738	3944616	TACHOGRAPH, 7-DAY STD	I	
	1624633	COLOR DECAL / TACHOMETER, DI6	I	
	1624634	FRAME/COLOR DECAL	I	
	1078790	COMBI.INSTR., 24V, DIS. TRB	I	
	3963611	DRIVER INFO SYST., / LEAF S	I	
	956046	CROSS REC. SCREW M3XI	7	4X TACHOGRAPH – CLSTR. 3X DIS – CLUSTER

Figure 3.3 Look for entire clusters of components, which can be replaced or removed.

- In-house/outside manufacturing structures
  - Examine in-sources for factory overhead, direct labor, and device cost
  - Examine out-sources for factory overhead, direct labor, transport, and device cost
  - Investigate stockroom overhead and complexity
  - Examine out-source suppliers for lower than our internal cost pricing

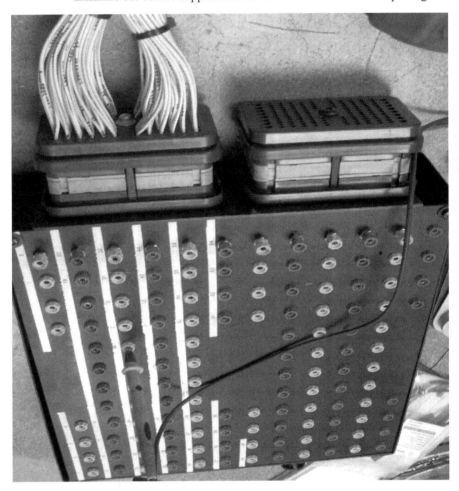

Figure 3.4 Proprietary connectors can be costly.

We should consider our procurement/purchasing assumptions (thought models or structures) for validity. "We always did it this way" (see Figure 3.4) is not good enough when we are increasing profit through value engineering. For example:

- Improve the alternate product acceptance process
- Streamline new component testing

- Set aggressive contract expectations
- Set standard cost based on most-recent, lowest price/cost to us, not on some abstraction or a value that make purchase price variance look good

Procurement can become a driving force for sharing received cost by reviewing purchased goods using the following factors (an orthogonal array in a sense and potentially possible to optimize using designed experiments in procurement):

- Small lot, low price
- Small lot, high price
- Large lot, high price
- Large lot, low price

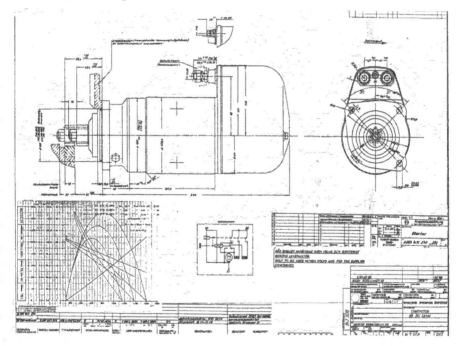

Figure 3.5 Sometimes the drawing will give us clues for cost savings.

Procurement should have a systematic review of suppliers. The function can perform this task quarterly and also set up a system where they choose a handful of suppliers at random for review (keep them on their feet!). We usually see the following orthogonal relationships when dealing with suppliers (these, too, might benefit from the use of a designed experiment):

- Small supplier, small orders
- Small supplier, large orders (tremendous leverage as long as we do not overwhelm them)

- Large supplier, large orders
- Large supplier, small orders (in this case, we have little leverage—we have seen scenarios where the supplier was a larger enterprise than the customer!)

In no case are we suggesting that the lowest cost supplier be selected as part of a value proposition. Low cost to purchase or develop parts or product does not always translate to an acceptable value proposition (see Figure 3.5), sometimes due to technical inadequacies or lack of manufacturing capacity. We have seen procurement do the development staff no favor by purchasing the product from the lowest cost (and sometimes unskilled) supplier. For example, selecting a supplier to provide us with embedded products without the prerequisite skills in software development and handling. A good and constant review of the supply base will help reduce these maladies that have the appearance of low cost, but in fact have higher costs in other places such as quality or risk.

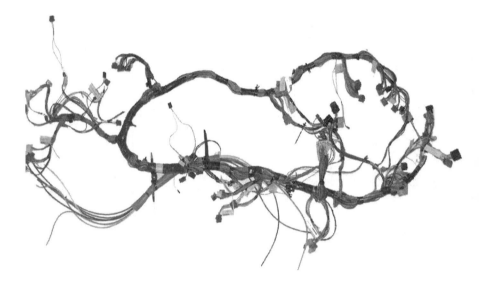

Figure 3.6 Wire harnesses can be complicated, especially in heavy vehicles, and there can be considerable weight added to the vehicle.

Changing cost-generating sources and locations is another option that may lead to cost reductions. For example, we can investigate whether a closer supplier in Mexico is actually less expensive than a supplier in China. The Chinese supplier may look less expensive on the surface, but we have to pay more in shipping and/or waiting longer to receive our supplies. Consider the logistics behind a wire harness in Figure 3.6.

We can devise a radical scenario or vision of the target cost. We want to set a challenge that inspires some creativity and we know the response is never greater than the "call." We want to avoid silly challenges; on the other hand, we do not want to create a weak cost reduction because we did not think aggressively enough.

We can also change our approaches:

- Establish cost-cutting policies enterprise-wide and make it clear cost reductions and value engineering have top management support (this applies to just about any cost or quality initiative)
- Clarify specifications and search specifications for lower cost solutions (once we have successfully launched a vanilla product or service, we can explore more exotic options); we may find areas where we can make recommendations to the customer that meet their needs but also permit significant cost relief
- Check for meaningful alternatives to any existing design we target (for example, we can examine power supplies on printed circuit boards—can we put this function externally like a laptop computer?)
- When we find alternatives, designers should then provide alternate designs, including more than one suggestion, thus opening up even more options for increased savings

We can also modify our processes. Sometimes this kind of change can become difficult because people have lost the ability to see what is lacking:

- Any time we can process products or services in parallel without adding undue complication, we should do so in order to gain the time reduction benefits as well as reducing opportunity cost
- We can assess the sources from which we get our components and services and attempt to discern the "why" of the original choice
- In the case where we have handoffs from different groups, we should ensure that coordination of effort occurs in order to eliminate waste (avoided cost) or empower fewer employees to do more
- If we have processes where more than half of the direct labor occurs before the midpoint of the process, we should investigate why this is so because we want to front load the process so we do not have to deal with the bulk of the work in the later portion of our process, which is the portion most affected by deadline/overdue pressures

We can also make changes in our activities. We can reward anticipation, execution, and follow through. We can also:

- Deal with optimization of tasks elsewhere
- Ensure that our plans and policies are clear—part of this can come from improved document design and a better understanding of how humans read instructions

Action	Actor	Information
Acquire samples for testing	Lab technician	Meet documented sample size requirements
Prepare thermal chamber	Lab technician	1350 F., stabilize for thirty minutes
Conduct test	Lab technician	Four hours
Inspect test setup during test	Lab manager	Two hours into the test

Action	Actor	Information
Finish test	Lab technician	Turn off chamber
Analyze sample parts	Lab technician/manager and design engineer	Make notes
Produce lab report	Lab manager	Use standard template

or we can use this format, which some find a little easier to follow:

Action	Lab Mgr.	Lab Tech.	Design Eng.	Information
Acquire samples for testing		x		Meet documented sample size requirements
Prepare thermal chamber		x		1350 °F, stabilize for thirty minutes
Conduct test		x		four hours
Inspect test setup during test	x			two hours into the test
Finish test		x		Turn off chamber
Analyze sample parts	x	x	x	Make notes
Produce lab report	x			Use standard template

We prefer whichever approach is the easiest for our staff to understand and follow. Note also how the "information" field allows us to use only action language (verb in the imperative mood) in the instructional column. The separation of information from action is an often-overlooked simplification of procedures. This simple step alone can result in cost savings caused by performing the process correctly rather than winging it. To continue:

- We can eliminate
  - Duplicated tasks
  - Rework (we have time to fix mistakes but no time to do it correctly the first time!)
  - Entire processes if we can prove they do not really add any value (this might include some product testing and inspection, especially if we have a better way to certify quality)
- Standardization in situations where standardization makes sense (for example, packaging, modular components)
- Knowledge management and coordination should make our enterprise more of an open book environment to both management and line employees

VI. Cost Management Cycle

The cost management cycle is linked to the product life cycle. We will see various needs and opportunities to improve the cost over the life cycle of the product. If our product or service is a monopoly, we may be less concerned with some of the later life cycle issues. For example, if there are not competitors, there is no reason for having competitive pricing; after all, we are a single source since we are a monopoly. However, there are few monopolies, and if you are a monopoly now—unless there are barriers to entry for the competition—you will probably not remain a monopoly for long. Those organizations that are close to your product will find a way to make something comparable if you are profitable. In general the lifestyle looks like:

- Idea

- Sole provider

- Multiple providers (competition)

- Mass production

- Mass production with mass customization

- Decline of product

- Extinction

We can see as we progress through the life cycle the amount of effort we wish to spend on improving the cost will increase. If we are the sole provider, we are less concerned with competitive costs while in mass production and declines we may be more willing to invest in cost improvements. This approach is counterproductive—there is never a bad time to improve your margins on a product as this adds to your organization's bottom line.

VII. When to Use

We suggest that an aggressive cost down approach be used only after a successful product or service launch. Exotic solutions introduce significant amounts of risk—we have seen cases where a poorly chosen and new technological component strained customer-supplier relationships and affected the ability of the marketing department to sell the product for years thereafter.

However, as a caveat, we council that usually the best time to make the cost improvement is during the development phase. In that case, you are able to maximize the profits from the product—from day one of the product availability for sale. It always struck us as unusual, that we would have costs to take out of the product immediately after the design has gone to production. When we see this happen, it begs the question, "How much review did we have on the cost effectiveness of the design solutions?" While it is important not to put the product launch at risk with some untried or untested technology, it is always important to start the product life cycle with the best possible value proposition possible for our customers—which translates to the best margins possible for your organization, unless we are dealing with a ruthless customer.

VIII. The Greedy Approach

We are looking for any possibility for cost savings, especially through clever design changes. If we can make low-risk design changes (e.g., different screws), the situation is even better. We may not have to invest much money in terms of development or verification dollars in order to commence alterations.

At some point, we will have to consider, as suppliers, how much we are willing to reveal to our customers. Often customers are beating on their suppliers to drop the price; hence, suppliers will do what they need to do in order to drop cost to themselves so they can still make some money. In the automotive/commercial vehicle business, customer price downs can become particularly brutal.

What is the moral position here? It is likely to be quite different depending on whether you are customer or supplier. Our recommendation is that the supplier and customer establish an honest and trusting relationship so "open book" practices can prevail; that is, we make our costs available to the customer and the customer, in turn, ensures that we as a supplier can make some reasonable amount of profit. We have seen open book work well when customer and supplier had a healthy, trusting relationship. If the relationship is frequently contentious, perhaps we need to visit that situation and see what the undercurrents are that drive the argumentation.

IX. Cost Generators

Often, in a specific industry, we will have components of our products that are known cost generators. One example of this lies with connectors in the electronics industry, especially automotive electronics. Connectors are a cost issue because only a few suppliers hold the patents (see Figure 3.4). They know if and end customer specifies their connector, then the intermediate supplier will have no choice but to use this connector. The engineering and marketing portions of our enterprise can make it part of the product strategy to find a way to bypass the use of these connectors. Sometimes we have no choice, particularly when the mating connector already exists and we must connect to it. Then, we must involve the procurement part of our organization and let them work on a more beneficial contract with the supplier. These negotiations can get really interesting if we are also a supplier to our supplier of some products; that is, one of their divisions supplies us and we supply one of their other divisions.

Though we mention connectors, it is really any proprietary product that we use that can become a source for our investigation. We know of some automotive manufacturers that develop proprietary parts for that very reason. Those customers must come back to the dealership to replace those parts. Proprietary parts are profitable but not necessarily for those using the parts.

Overspecifying the product also adds undue cost. For example, mounting a component inside the cab of a vehicle means (generally speaking) that component is in a dry location and is not affected by any of the external hazards to which the vehicle is subjected. When we have no gravel bombardment and the suspension meets the vibration profile we have a less than dynamic component. If we harden this unit to meet the external vehicle demands, the cost will go up dramatically. If we mount a hardened unit inside the vehicle we are paying for a level of performance that would not be required inside the vehicle—a poor value proposition indeed.

Another example of cost generators in motor vehicles is the copper, connectors, and coatings that are part of wire harnesses. When the price of copper escalates, we begin to look for less costly design solutions. One of these solutions is to use the idea of multiplexing, where we can use one wire for several purposes by splitting the messages into packages. This approach allows us to reduce the copper content of the harness and save cost. In some cases, multiplexing may produce improved reliability since we are normally applying a digital protocol with error management and handshaking. Also, if we take at a look at the formula for serial failure modes in reliability engineering, we will see that the fewer the components, the higher the reliability; hence, we have a theoretical motivation for reducing content whenever possible unless we have a special reason for redundancy.

X. Cost Generators and Cost Cutting

It is very seductive when we think about eliminating a major cost generator. Unfortunately, system integration requirements may lead to us being unable to effect the kind of cost reduction we have in mind. However, our cost down challenge does not have to stop with the major cost generators. For example, we might look at an ostensibly low-cost component that is used in many places, effectively making it a significant cost generator. This approach suggests that simply listing the price of the component and creating a Pareto chart from this information is an inadequate method for assessing the impact of the part; in short, we want to look at our parts from several directions: most expensive to least expensive, most content to least content, most expensive (based on price x number of parts) to least expensive (same calculation), and quality and reliability.

Another source of cost generation that is frequently overlooked is the cost of packaging. Custom-made packaging is generally more expensive than standardized packaging. If we are looking at the packaging and making adjustments for different sizes of products by using the dunnage, then we must also look at the cost of the dunnage (internal packaging). Additional cost may come from the use of glue or tape, staples, wood fitting pieces, cardboard fitting pieces, foam, and other constituents of dunnage and the outside package. We know of one company that found they could make some money by selling used pallets (sometimes called skids). Other companies have found ways to create cardboard pallets.

We know of at least one company that attempts to use as many of the developed parts in their electrical/electronics systems throughout the world. This company develops a number of electronic control units for their vehicles, and in doing this, the use of common material is a core guiding principle. We see this approach taken for the electrical systems of all of their vehicles. The primary drawback to such an approach is that products can sometimes lose their character; for example, consider how General Motors used the Cavalier platform for Chevrolet, Pontiac, and Cadillac. Why buy the Cadillac when you can get virtually the same vehicle for the cost of the Chevrolet?

Mergers and acquisitions can produce a host of problems also. Boeing merged with McDonnell-Douglas, eliminating a competitor, but ending up with a plethora of models to maintain, not to mention different philosophies of part numbers, inventory, and all the other impedimenta of running a business. A similar situation occurred when

Hewlett-Packard acquired Compaq Corporation, which in turn, had acquired Digital Equipment Corporation (DEC). Much of the cost reductions we would see in these situations would involve the aggressive cost down approach with substantial pruning of underperforming product lines. The DEC product line still exists, at least as an operating system. The Compaq line has effectively faded away.

In subsequent chapters we will review techniques for understanding these cost generators. When we are working with existing product, our parts list or bill of materials can help us determine the composition of our product cost. We must look at both the costed bill from the design engineer's point of view and also from the manufacturing bill of materials aspect, where we line up our parts in the order in which we use them in the assembly of the product. We may find savings in the design or in the process side of the house. The bill of materials should never be overlooked as a list of potential opportunities for product and process savings.

Our main point in this chapter is that aggressive cost down behaviors are unlikely to hurt us unless we use inferior material. We want to grow a culture of individuals who design for cost and who continue to look for cost savings after the product is launched. In some cases, changes in technology will allow us to improve margins years after the product is launched; for example, LCD prices have diminished over the years and our understanding of the technology has improved. They are generally much more visible in sunlight than they were and they have more or less eclipsed the much more expensive electroluminescent displays. We can also look for opportunities for greater integration electronically.

XI. EXERCISES

- What are the moral and ethical considerations involved with our relationship with the customer?

- What kind of cost reduction-oriented relationship do we want with our customer? Is it not to our benefit to show them how we are saving *them* money also?

- If we work a cost reduction with a customer, how much effort should the customer be putting in? Are they acceptable members of the cost reduction team?

- Should we make cost reduction projects a contest? What are the benefits and drawbacks of such an approach?

- How should we reward our employees for cost reductions?

- Do we not reward an employee if their cost reduction is small?

- Will rewards corrupt the cost reduction initiative?

- If we do not have rewards, then how do we inspire our employees to contribute? Saying something like "You are lucky to have a job" is not going to get us there.

- What is the value of a patent to a company? What if the patent is also a cost reducing idea? How, then, do we reward these employees or do we reward them?

- If we change packaging to save money, can we really expect our supplier to be highly motivated as their materials diminish?

- How can multiplexing of any kind (office, service, hardware product, software product) save us money? Does it?
- Can high-intensity project management (scrum) save us money?
- Do we turn down small cost reductions? Will that kill the goose that lays the golden eggs?
- How do we manage truly large cost reductions?
- How do we coordinate with the configuration management system?
- How do we manage coordinated changes (more than one change that must happen simultaneously)?
- What are the limitations of arbitrary cost down approach?
- What are the cost generators for your product line? How can these be controlled or eliminated?
- Describe the cost management process.
- Describe the cost down approach to cost reduction. What are the benefits to this approach?
- What is the greedy approach to cost reduction?
- What happens when we push cost reduction too aggressively?

CHAPTER 4 – The Isuzu Approach to Teardowns

I. Rubric for Teardowns

Criteria	Level 1 (50–59%)	Level 2 (60–69%)	Level 3 (70–79%)	Level 4 (80–100%)
Analyze a variety of system modifications and their effect on other vehicle systems	Analysis of a variety of system modifications and their effect on other vehicle systems demonstrates limited understanding	Analysis of a variety of system modifications and their effect on other vehicle systems demonstrates some understanding	Analysis of a variety of system modifications and their effect on other vehicle systems demonstrates considerable understanding	Analysis a variety of system modifications and their effect on other vehicle systems demonstrates thorough understanding
Analyze and describe the interrelationships of vehicle systems	Analyzes and describes the interrelationships of vehicle systems with limited understanding	Analyzes and describes the interrelationships of vehicle systems with some understanding	Analyzes and describes the interrelationships of vehicle systems with considerable understanding	Analyzes and describes the interrelationships of vehicle systems with thorough understanding
Analyze the power requirements of different vehicle systems	Analysis of the power requirements of different vehicle systems demonstrates limited knowledge	Analysis of the power requirements of different vehicle systems demonstrates some knowledge	Analysis of the power requirements of different vehicle systems demonstrates considerable knowledge	Analysis of the power requirements of different vehicle systems demonstrates thorough knowledge
Based on industry standards identify wear on vehicle system components	Applies few of the skills involved in the diagnostic process when inspecting vehicle system components	Applies some of the skills involved in the diagnostic process when inspecting vehicle system components	Applies most of the skills involved in the diagnostic process when inspecting vehicle system components	Applies all or almost all of the skills involved in the diagnostic process when inspecting vehicle system components
Carry out an accurate risk analysis	Demonstrates limited ability to carry out an accurate risk analysis	Demonstrates some ability to carry out an accurate risk analysis	Demonstrates considerable ability to carry out an accurate risk analysis	Demonstrates a high level of ability to carry out an accurate risk analysis
Communicate project ideas using drawings and sketches	Communicates project ideas using drawings and sketches with limited clarity	Communicates project ideas using drawings and sketches with some clarity	Communicates project ideas using drawings and sketches with considerable clarity	Communicates project ideas using drawings and sketches with thorough clarity
Demonstrate proper disposal of vehicle system components	Infrequently demonstrates proper disposal of vehicle system components	Often demonstrates proper disposal of vehicle system components	Usually demonstrates proper disposal of vehicle system components	Routinely demonstrates proper disposal of vehicle system components
Describe and evaluate the legislation pertinent to vehicles and work practices	Describes and evaluates the legislation pertinent to vehicles and work practices using limited critical thinking	Describes and evaluates the legislation pertinent to vehicles and work practices using adequate critical thinking	Describes and evaluates the legislation pertinent to vehicles and work practices using good critical thinking	Describes and evaluates the legislation pertinent to vehicles and work practices using excellent critical thinking

Criteria	Level 1 (50–59%)	Level 2 (60–69%)	Level 3 (70–79%)	Level 4 (80–100%)
Describe methods to improve the efficiency of energy consumption in vehicles	Demonstrates limited knowledge of facts related to improving the efficiency of energy consumption in vehicles	Demonstrates some knowledge of facts related to improving the efficiency of energy consumption in vehicles	Demonstrates considerable knowledge of facts related to improving the efficiency of energy consumption in vehicles	Demonstrates thorough knowledge of facts related to improving the efficiency of energy consumption in vehicles
Determine cost, quality of service and capacity considerations in existing systems	Determines cost, quality of service and capacity considerations in existing systems providing limited information	Determines cost, quality of service and capacity considerations in existing systems providing some information	Determines cost, quality of service and capacity considerations in existing systems providing considerable information	Determines cost, quality of service and capacity considerations in existing systems providing thorough information
Develop an accurate bill of materials	Develops an accurate bill of materials with limited success	Develops an accurate bill of materials with some success	Develops an accurate bill of materials with good success	Develops an accurate bill of materials with excellent success
Explain how human needs and wants can be met through a new product	Explanation of how human needs and wants can be met through a new product makes limited reference to transportation technology	Explanation of how human needs and wants can be met through a new product makes some reference to transportation technology	Explanation of how human needs and wants can be met through a new product makes considerable reference to transportation technology	Explanation of how human needs and wants can be met through a new product makes thorough reference to transportation technology
Explain the effects of modification to any of a vehicle`s components on other system	Explanation of the effects of modification to any of a vehicle's components on other systems demonstrates limited ability to make connections	Explanation of the effects of modification to any of a vehicle's components on other systems demonstrates some ability to make connections	Explanation of the effects of modification to any of a vehicle's components on other systems demonstrates considerable ability to make connections	Explanation of the effects of modification to any of a vehicle's components on other systems demonstrates thorough ability to make connections
Explain the environmental impact of materials and procedures	Explains the environmental impact of materials and procedures with limited comprehension	Explains the environmental impact of materials and procedures with some comprehension	Explains the environmental impact of materials and procedures with considerable comprehension	Explains the environmental impact of materials and procedures with thorough comprehension
Explain the function of parts of a vehicle	Explains the function of parts of a vehicle with limited understanding	Explains the function of parts of a vehicle with some understanding	Explains the function of parts of a vehicle with considerable understanding	Explains the function of parts of a vehicle with thorough understanding
Identify the legislation that applies to the transportation sector	Identifies the legislation that applies to the transportation sector with limited success	Identifies the legislation that applies to the transportation sector with some success	Identifies the legislation that applies to the transportation sector with considerable success	Identifies the legislation that applies to the transportation sector with excellent success
Suggest environmentally friendly alternatives	Suggests environmentally friendly alternatives that are based on limited knowledge	Suggests environmentally friendly alternatives that are based on some knowledge	Suggests environmentally friendly alternatives that are based on considerable knowledge	Suggests environmentally friendly alternatives that are based on thorough knowledge

Criteria	Level 1 (50–59%)	Level 2 (60–69%)	Level 3 (70–79%)	Level 4 (80–100%)
Test materials and products to determine best solution	Rarely tests materials and products to determine best solution	Sometimes tests materials and products to determine best solution	Often tests materials and products to determine best solution	Always or almost always tests materials and products to determine best solution
Use brainstorming techniques to help determine the best solution	Rarely uses brainstorming techniques to help determine the best solution	Sometimes uses brainstorming techniques to help determine the best solution	Often uses brainstorming techniques to help determine the best solution	Always or almost always uses brainstorming techniques to help determine the best solution
Work effectively with team members to do a variety of tasks	Demonstrates limited ability to work effectively with team members to do a variety of tasks	Demonstrates some ability to work effectively with team members to do a variety of tasks	Demonstrates considerable ability to work effectively with team members to do a variety of tasks	Demonstrates a high level of ability to work effectively with team members to do a variety of tasks

II. Questions to Ponder

- What are some of the obstacles to performing effective teardowns?

- How do we use teardowns to learn about our competition?

- How would you go about tearing down a service?

- In your company, what areas should be explored for cost improvement?

- How do requirements impact our product cost?

- What processes provide the least value analysis in your organization? How would you know?

- What benefit to the organization can be obtained through membership in any of the number of value engineering organization's value analysis?

- What (if any) are the ethical implications of a company that provides teardown analysis for an entire industry?

III. Cost Improvement Scenario

A. Situation

A biodiesel company wishes to increase their throughput without dramatically increasing their operating costs. The incoming material temperature has considerable variation. In the summer, the temperature of the incoming raw material can be in the range of 70°–80°F. In the winter, fall, and spring the temperature is considerably lower. This lower temperature has an impact on the viscosity of raw oil that will be converted into the biodiesel. The colder and thicker this raw material, the slower it moves though the pipes to the catalyst chamber. Also, the longer the time required for the reagent to act with the incoming oil to convert it to a biodiesel product.

Presently, the reaction is heated with electrical devices where the reagent and catalyst are mixed. To get the best performance (shortest time for the reaction) the temperature of the raw material has to be 170°F. In this experiment are mounted nine nine-kilowatt electric heaters. This consumes considerable amounts of energy. In fact, the energy presently consumed is close to the limit of the transformer that brings the power into the facility.

The owner of the building does not want to invest any money or material into the building infrastructure.

B. Objective

Improve the control over the temperature of the incoming material to improve the flow rate, and preheat the raw material so the reaction takes the least amount of time.

C. Action

Exploration of the use of increasing the amount of the electrical consumption for the facility was not viable. Solar did not seem to be an option for three reasons. The first issue was the cost of the solar panel itself. This was an expensive piece of equipment for a young company.

The second issue, the money to secure the engineering study to ascertain if and where the solar panels could be mounted on the roof. Additionally, the building owner did not want to have these panels mounted to the roof of the building.

The last concern, to install the product would have taken the company's electrician and distracted him from the main job of keeping the other systems up and running as well as improving the details of the processing.

On reflection, it was observed from the value analysis that it contained considerable amounts of residual heat postproduction. This heat went to waste as the biodiesel end product cooled prior to the truck pickup and shipping. Reuse of the heat that was applied to the value analyst during the reaction process could be recovered and applied to the raw material inlet flow.

D. Results

Heat exchangers were put in place to remove the heat after the material was moved from the reaction value analyst to the holding tank. In the holding tank, the temperature of the product is not as critical. These heat exchangers were placed in the system in such a way that the incoming material was heated (see Figure 4.1) prior to getting into the value analyst.

Additionally, the investigation uncovering what could be done to heat the incoming material uncovered an experimental blend method using a cavitation pump, which would allow the reaction tank to operate at a lower temperature. This then would reduce the electrical loads associated with maintaining the heat in the reaction. It is then possible to heat the inlet with electricity and the residual heat from the reaction and still consume less electricity and therefore money, than the heating alone.

E. Aftermath

While the project is still under way, it is possible to state that the amount of heat introduced via electricity is less than what was originally part of the production process. A constant critique and modest investments allow this company to continuously improve their throughput without increasing more cost to produce.

Figure 4.1 Rather than waste the reaction chamber heat, we use the residual heat from the main tank to heat the input pipes for a biodiesel manufacturer.

IV. What Is the Isuzu Approach?

The Isuzu approach traces its origins to Mr. Yoshihiko Sato's work experience at Isuzu in the early 1970s. Isuzu had an alliance with General Motors during this period. Mr. Sato came across the teardown method at GM, which he further developed, making it an even more effective method. The method became a part of Isuzu's operating culture and helped increase its global competitiveness. The success of the teardown method led other Japanese companies to adopt it.

The teardown method was not a concept developed from scratch by Mr. Sato. U.S. automakers were already using a form of product analysis and dissection before Sato developed his method. The method of dissecting a product to find out why it clicked in the market was not something new. Manufacturers were already incorporating some of the teardown approaches in their operations. However, Mr. Sato succeeded in making this a systematic and structured way to excel in operations. He is of the opinion that teardown methods which came from the U.S. are basically an "overall examination" type approach while the Isuzu approach was a comparative analysis, which had to be applied to competitor's products.

In his book, Mr. Sato has defined the value analysis teardown method as "a method of comparative analysis in which disassembled products, systems, components and data are visually compared; and their functions determined, analyzed and evaluated to improve the value by adding characteristics of the project under study."[2]

The Isuzu approach to teardowns is comprised of six phases and represents perhaps the most complete teardown methodology available. Common among them are material, cost, dynamic and static teardown. Process and static are the other two tear. Process and matrix teardown elements are more suited for firms that are already incorporating some of the teardown methods. In essence, we as an enterprise can acquire the product of another enterprise and analyze this product with several modalities to see what we can learn from our competition.

The definition, although seemingly simple, incorporates observable analysis, deduction and a wide range of value analysis techniques. The value analysis teardown method provides a way to understand problems and spot improvement opportunities in a systematic and analytical manner. Most engineers had initially thought teardown was a simple disassembling and inspection process. However, this process also helped in

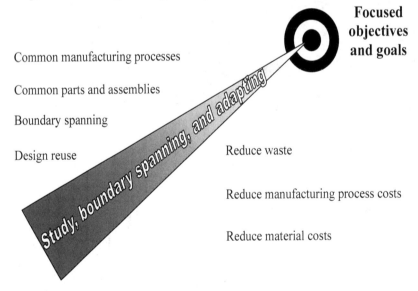

Figure 4.2 Illustration of a teardown structure.

new product development, product modifications, reverse engineering, and competitor analysis studies.

It is somewhat more difficult to do this approach with services, but we can observe or buy a service and see how they do it. We may even be able to determine their basic procedures. Teardowns are not immoral or amoral. We are simply taking a look at how they solved the problem and, in many cases, we may find that we are already doing a better job than they are; in which case, we have an opportunity to point this out in our marketing.

A. Dynamic Teardown

Dynamic teardown studies the assembly process (see Figure 4.2) of the product and then compares it to the competitor's products. The comparisons look at the time and effort taken to assemble and disassemble the product. Standard teardown focuses on the product design without spending much time on the competitor's assembly. A better understanding of the assembly helps the engineers understand the impact of their product design in the assembly process. Dynamic teardown starts by studying the product before disassembling the product. The product is disassembled one component at a time to understand how it can be assembled again. Time studies are conducted and are compared between products to understand the differences.

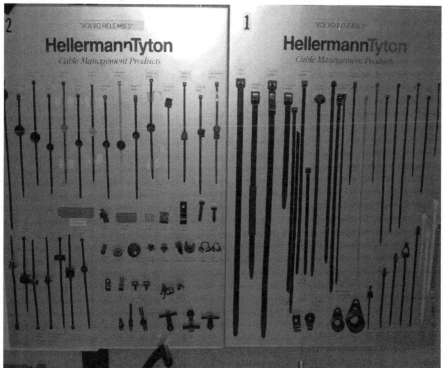

Figure 4.3 Standardizing parts can help improve throughput and reduce inventory.

Reduce Labor/Capital Expense to Assemble Product

We are looking for ideas that simplify the assembly of the product or service (see Figure 4.3). One example might be progressing from using screws to hold the product together to using snaps. We need to remain aware that sometimes snaps are not the best approach, particularly when we are dealing with a reparable product.

Another example of innovative value analysis approaches to assembly we have seen is the use of a flexible printed circuit board. A flexible PCB allows for unusual shapes in the finished product. Unfortunately, this approach almost certainly requires a modicum of hand assembly, eliminating the possibility of using a simple robot to assemble the PCB to the housing. Yet another alternative is to build programming stations (see Figure 4.4) out of common materials and components, yet keep each with differently set up as a Poke Yoke contrivance.

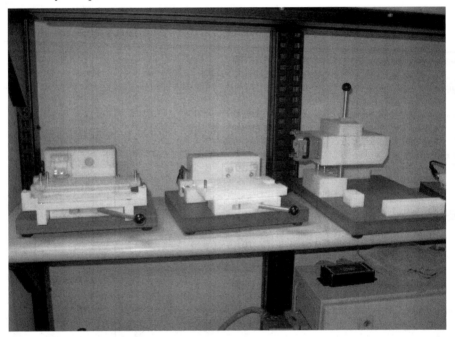

Figure 4.4 Programing a variety of controllers becomes easier with tools specifically set up using similar parts.

Reduce Assembly Time

We can reduce assembly time by automating assembly (usually) or by eliminating steps in the process. We can eliminate the assembly of a lens to a housing by having the supplier design his plastics such that we can use some kind of double shot injection molding, where the lens and the housing become one. We need to be aware that such a step may raise the piece part price enough that more assembly steps will be less costly. Sometimes we will have a discussion about whether we use screws or snap, because snaps are quicker to assemble and easier to break, screws are difficult to assemble but have good reliability.

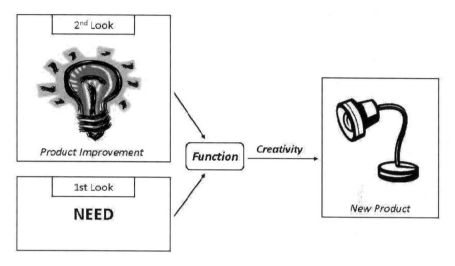

Figure 4.5 Ultimately, the value proposition is decided by the customer.

We know of companies that have established assembly time improvement targets with each new release of the parts going on the vehicle. A reduction in the assembly time becomes a target and is part of the cost improvement activities. We have seen that these ease-of-assembly activities have an added benefit when it comes to servicing the product in the field. For example, one heavy vehicle original equipment manufacturer could remove an instrument cluster from the vehicle in less than a minute. The most difficult part of the job was disconnecting the air lines to the instrument cluster.

Determine Competitive Advantage

We want to determine if our competition is doing a *worse* job than we are with the product. If we discover that is the case, then we can use this information subtly in our marketing and confidentially when speaking with customers to showcase our improved technology (see Figure 4.5).

Improve Fit and Finish Quality

We might look at fit and finish improvement if our competition has some serious advantage in this area. Alternatively, we may wish to give ourselves the advantage and outdo their product, thereby allowing our marketing department to tout the product as a higher-quality implementation than that of our competitor; remember, the Greek concept of beauty being associated with the good which still has a hold over our society.

On the other hand, we may interview our customer and arrive at the conclusion that the level of finish for our product is beyond what is needed. Maybe the customer does not desire such a high level of finish and we can improve the value analysis proposition by revising the finish down instead of improving the finish with its attending cost.

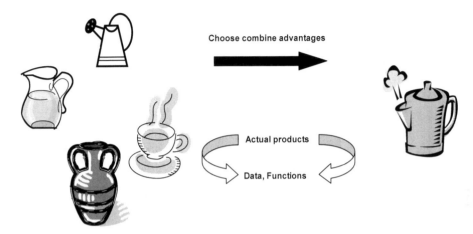

Figure 4.6 Any product is open to improvement and we can often stimulate ideas simply by comparing different versions of the same product.

Plan the Disassembly (Systematic)

We disassemble according to a systematic plan, partly because we do not want to destroy any of the evidence.

B. Cost Teardown

Cost teardown aims to study in detail the material cost of each part in our product and competitors' products. The differences in the components are noted and cost estimate for the difference is ascertained (see Figure 4.6). By making use of a comparative chart the product baseline is noted and competing product's component delta cost is calculated. The part difference ("delta") is ascertained by finding out the cost difference between our product and the competitor's product. The total of all deltas will provide the estimated cost difference of competitor's assembly. This type of teardown assumes that competitor has the same supply sources and the comparison is focused on the differences in design and not on the strategies in procurement.

We perform a cost teardown to assess and enumerate the components that comprise another product. In essence, we are trying to reverse produce the product, tearing it apart in some rational sequence instead of putting it together.

Compare Probable Competitors' Costs to Our Costs

Our goal during a cost teardown is largely to build a bill of materials and then analyze the components on the bill for cost, producing a costed bill of materials. In some cases, this costing may be difficult, particularly for the following reasons:

- Our competition may actually hide the nature of the component by covering it with epoxy or some other resin

- We may not have the procurement leverage that our competition has

- The part may actually be a one-time closeout purchase and effectively tell us very little about the overall cost of the product

Plan Disassembly

We want to plan our disassembly based on what we know about the order of production in our own facilities; for example, for electronics we would look at the following flow:

- Top-side surface mount electronics

- Bottom-side surface mount electronics

- Wave solder through-hole components

- Selective solder more difficult through-hole components such as connectors

- Assemble printed circuit board to housing

- Add mechanical parts

- Add visual parts

The above bulleted list is a very simple approach to assessing an electronic product.

Organize Parts Similar to Our Products

As we follow our disassembly process, we put like with like, so we have categories of parts; hence, we are neither creating an engineering bill of materials nor are we creating a manufacturing bill of materials.

Price the Parts

Once we have all parts categorized, by both type and, if possible, manufacturer, we can submit our bill of materials for costing analysis by the procurement agency of our enterprise (see Figure 4.7). We recommend trying to receive multiple bids for as many components as possible so that we can assess mean, median, and standard deviation for the entire assembly. This approach will provide us with low, medium, and high costing. If the results are rather "tight," then we know we may be close to the actual costed bill for the competitor.

C. Material Teardown

Material teardown focuses on the material used for similar components. The teardown looks at the choice of materials, surface treatment of materials and chemical properties. The study is normally done in a laboratory and study is done in more detail

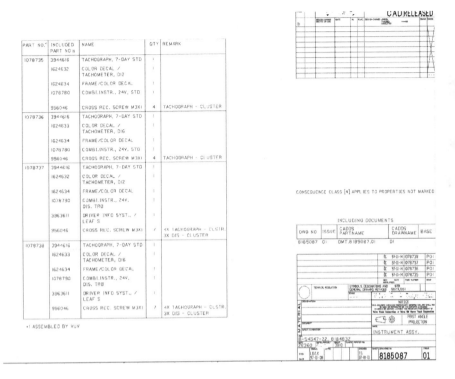

Figure 4.7 A parts list can help us find substitution parts to improve the value proposition.

than a cost teardown. Material teardown can be linked during a cost teardown to get a better comparative study.

With a material teardown, we will "deep dive" into the component structure of the competitive product. Again, we do not consider this approach to be unethical since we are unlikely to ever directly copy somebody else's solution. We can learn something about the competition and our place in the market, however.

We have been part of a complete teardown of competitor vehicles. In one instance, the complete vehicle was torn down in a very controlled way not to destroy the parts. Additionally, the associated or connecting parts were placed in close proximity enabling the employees that reviewed the systems to see how the parts went together.

If you are not part of the teardown it can be difficult to envision how some parts go together. Motor vehicles can be comprised of a number of complex systems. The less we learn from the teardown exercise the less we will profit from the exercise. The act of tearing down itself is a learning opportunity. The employees of this organization then went to the large warehouse in which the parts were laid out for review. We could readily see every subassembly on the competitor's vehicle.

Evaluate Materials and Surface Treatments

When we evaluate materials, we are talking about all of the constituent materials of the product. For example, within electronics product, we would look at the chips used on the printed circuit board, the printed circuit board itself, the solder, and the plastics used in the connectors. For the same product, we would examine the surface to see if our competitor was using conformal coat to protect the product from moisture. Furthermore, we would also investigate the conformal coat itself to see what material was used in the coating, since materials can vary from relatively soft acrylics to extremely hard epoxies.

Plan Disassembly

Before we begin to look at actual parts, we want to ensure that our disassembly occurs in an orderly manner. Consequently, we will put together a plan that allows us to expeditiously disassemble the product and organize the relevant materials to enable efficient analysis.

Comparison

Once we have the components laid out, usually on a workbench, we can compare our components with their components. We do not expect to see a one-for-one catalog of components. In most cases, we would expect to see some familial resemblance between or among the products.

Materials

When we look at the materials we use in our products, we need to look at all materials used in the product, even if we are talking about paper or cardboard or some other common material—they are all part of the product. We may be looking at obvious materials like plastic and metal. We may be looking at more subtle comparisons such as the carrier material for integrated circuits.

Surface Treatment

We mentioned conformal coating earlier in our discussion. That kind of coating applies primarily to electronic or electrical products. However, we have other kinds of surface treatment; for example, we can have tempered glass or we might have case hardened steel. Both of these are surface treatments and affect the behavior of the product.

Sometimes surface treatments can be part of the decor of the product. For example, the Apple iPod has a very Spartan exterior. This approach, while marketing based, is nonetheless a surface treatment.

Heat Treatment

We have already mentioned tempered glass. Commonly, tempered glass is a by-product of the heat treatment of the surface of the glass product although the manufacturer may use a composite system of layers with plastic support. One example of reinforced glass is the windshield of automobiles. We also find that metals are heat treated to relieve stress or to harden the surface.

Analysis of Material Scrap Rate

The analysis of the material scrap rate will be an estimate based on the knowledge of our own product. It is highly unlikely that we will ever know the actual material scrap rate for the products of our competitors. Even so, every iota of knowledge adds to our marketplace arsenal. We never know where we will find the edge that makes our product more successful than their products.

D. Matrix Teardown

Matrix teardown would benefit firms that have already made an effort to make parts common. It also helps in reducing the number of parts by making use of common parts in different products. During matrix teardown, the baseline product chosen meets most of the customer needs and is also efficiently produced. Later the value variations are compared against the baseline product with the aim of minimizing the number of parts and also adding functions to the baseline product. Matrix teardown is a good tool for standardization.

Compare Our Products with Each Other

We can look at our own solutions as we perform teardowns. If we have a large enterprise, one plant may have found solutions to problems that have not been disseminated to the other facilities.

Alternatively, we generally learn something about developing and building products over the years. We may find that solutions we are using today can be applied to legacy products for significant cost reductions. Of course, the decision will depend on where the legacy product is in the product life cycle.

Plan Disassembly

As always, we plan disassembly in a logical order just as we do with competitive products. Our goal is to improve our understanding of the differences between the products as well as to spark innovation.

Increase Number of Shared Parts, Thereby Reducing Number of Unique Parts

Often, the increasing of shared parts will lead to a reduction in raw material part numbers and concomitant savings (especially opportunity cost) in maintaining and stocking those part numbers. By so doing, we reduce the number of unique part numbers and, if we are really strategic about it, we may even increase our leverage with the suppliers as we buy larger quantities of certain part numbers.

Even though carrying cost in inventory sometimes seems like a fantasy number, it represents a real cost to the enterprise. Reducing parts is analogous to reducing steps in a manufacturing process; as always, simplicity is never easy. We can think about it this way: why do we have all the different kinds of air cleaners, spark plugs, and other filters for automobiles? Would not some continuum from tiny to huge at logical increments make a whole lot more sense? The urge to have proprietary parts can make life extremely complicated and it bars us from making truly elegant value engineering solutions.

E. Process Teardown

Process teardown is similar to matrix teardown but it focuses on process value variations. After commonization of parts, process is the next element that must be standardized. The process of baseline product and similar other products are compared to the best in class. This helps the engineers identify the best way to perform a process. Adopting the best practices help in reducing the tooling and capital investments, thereby achieving lower manufacturing costs. The reduction in process time also helps in lowering the time product takes to reach the market.

Producing a model of a competitor's manufacturing process can be somewhat like working out a puzzle. We do not really know what their process actually is, but we do know what a rational set of dependencies would look like.

Analyze the Process That *Must* Have Been Used to Build the Part

Let's look at the example of an electronic product. If we detect surface mount technology in the manufacture of this product, then we know that our competitor will be using automatic placement of components and reflow furnaces. On the other hand, if we detect through-hole components, then we know that wave solder technology is most likely part of the process. If we see both kinds of parts, we know reflow will occur on both top and bottom of the printed circuit board before they go to the wave solder device. Selective solder devices will often solder connectors and oddly-formed parts, which is hand soldering using a robot.

Record Necessary Disassembly Steps

As we disassemble the product, we will find in some cases we only have one way of taking the product apart. This feature suggests that there is only one way to put the product together as well. We would call this a necessary disassembly step and, of course, the assembly step will be necessary also.

Look for Like Processes

To improve our own processes, we want to look at the competitor's product with an eye for the case where they have solved similar problems to our own problems. Again, we are not after direct copying but, rather, we are looking for inspiration to help improve our own products and processes.

Look for Simplified Processes

Occasionally, we will see a situation where the competitor's product will provide sufficient inspiration that we can innovate within our own processes and eliminate steps. Subprocess elimination is a wonderful way to achieve a cost reduction as well as, typically, to improve the throughput on the manufacturing line.

Often, we build external test equipment in our factories, what the Department of Defense calls "peculiar support equipment," because it is often custom-made. One cost-saving innovation is to deliberately value engineer our products to have a self-test capability if they have microprocessors or microcontrollers on board. One of the most powerful approaches in electronics is the use of boundary scan (IEEE 1149.1). In essence, we briefly repurpose the integrated circuit to function as a testing device, which will then "probe" the area around the IC without external test probes. The other benefit is that this approach is normally extremely quick—often in the hundreds of milliseconds range. Additionally, boundary scan is helpful when we have a high pin density on the chip.

F. Static Teardown

Static teardown was the original teardown presented to Sato by General Motors. However, he improved this method to suit Isuzu's operational requirements. In a static teardown the focus is on visual inspection and use of display boards for baseline products and competitor's product. This helps people touch, see and smell the differences between these products. This is especially useful for people who had not taken part in the working session.

Conduct Dynamic Teardown

We will follow the usual steps of organized disassembly as we prepare to more profoundly understand these other products.

Formulate Product Strategies after Analysis of Competition

Just knowing how our competitors make their product can be enough for us to mount an informed marketing strategy. We can always look for the Achilles heel of the product. In moving towards an informed strategy, we are most likely saving money by not taking shots in the dark.

Can Be Used as a Static Display Showing Ours versus Theirs

If we have done a systematic teardown, we can take our product and their product or products and mount them on the display to show our product versus theirs. We are not likely to do this in a public display but we might use this display as a marketing tool with our customers[2].

V. Why Use This Technique

As we have acknowledged, this approach might seem a bit unethical and it would be if we copied someone else's solution immediately. The goal is to inspire us to innovative solutions! Simply duplicating some other company's solution causes regression to the mean; in short, we would all trend toward mediocrity as each company copies their competitors.

We speak about benchmarking in this book. We like to think of teardowns as a way of physically benchmarking our product against someone else's product. At a minimum, we will determine our position in the marketplace in terms of engineering and manufacturing technology.

Note that, like the benchmarking approach, we can also review techniques and ideas from noncompetitive organizations. One of us has worked with high school students, performing some teardowns of the typical electronics used by teenagers. One of the first things we noticed was the clear edge in sophistication of Apple, Inc. Their products had a high percentage (over 90%) of surface mount technology, which meant they relied on machines to provide accurate part placement and automatic soldering rather than the value variance typical of hand assembly. It would not hurt the motor vehicle industry to examine this icon of trendy, minimalistic elegance.

Process-based teardowns are most likely to occur as we describe them in the benchmarking section of this book. We doubt that our competitors will allow us into their plants to see all the "secrets" of how they build their products! However, we can always petition stellar performers in other industries to allow us to view their processes while under an ironclad nondisclosure agreement.

VI. Teardown Example

There are two approaches used for a comparative analysis process. In the first one, we look at the products, compare them and make a selection. In the above example the handles were each designed to suit a particular purpose. We would select the design that suits our purpose using imitation-type thinking.

In the second teardown approach, we let the visual of the containers in the example turn into language signals that would help us select and organize information and ideas from memory. This type of research thinking is stimulated by imitation. This resulted in a new handle, which is different from the ones being analyzed. Language signals prompt multiple ideas that include materials, production process and surface treatment.

However, there is a limitation to the creativity of a single person as they may not be able to trigger memories of something that has not been experienced. Thus is the reason for using multifunctional teams since "Two heads are better than one."

A. Design for Assembly

"Dynamic teardown is supported by commercially available computer software designed for Design for Assembly (DFA) criteria in that it can assess product designs in the same way"[1].

There are a number of guidelines that are to be noted while using DFA:

- Minimize component count by designing in multiple functions into single parts (e.g., resistor banks)

- Make multiple parts modular by moving them into subassemblies

- Ensure that proper orientation of the part is easy to discern (e.g., it is difficult to see the polarity on some small capacitors and diodes)
- Design in self-aligning parts (with electronics, ball grid arrays are self-aligning on their solder points)
- Standardizing will reduce part variety
- Optimize symmetry
- Use color coding or labeling whenever it is feasible
- Stacking is better than nesting of components
- Implement orientation for asymmetrical components
- Design any mating components or features for facile insertion
- Implement features that provide for alignment (poka-yoke)
- Design the part so that we insert new components from above
- Eradicate fasteners (especially screws) whenever feasible
- Locate any fasteners away from interference through good design
- Deep channels must be wide enough to allow the use of tools—eliminating these channels through the use of sound engineering design principles is even better
- Make sure tools can reach any fasteners
- Opt for easily manipulated parts

Use Simple Design and Lower the Number of Parts

This goal should be kept in mind, as reduction in parts would also reduce the chances for a defective part and an assembly error. The probability of a perfect product goes down exponentially as the number of parts increases. As the number of parts goes up, the total cost of fabricating and assembling the product goes up. Automation becomes more difficult and more expensive when more parts are handled and processed. Costs related to purchasing, stocking, and servicing also go down as the number of parts are reduced. Inventory and work-in-process levels will go down with fewer parts. As the product structure and required operations are simplified, fewer fabrication and assembly steps are required, manufacturing processes can be integrated and lead-times further reduced. The designer should go through the assembly part by part and evaluate whether the part can be eliminated, combined with another part, or the function can be performed in another way. To estimate the minimum number of parts we should ask the following questions

- Does the part move relative to all other moving parts?
- Must the part absolutely be of a different material from the other parts?
- Must the part be different to allow possible disassembly?

Design for parts orientation and handling to minimize nonvalue-added manual effort and ambiguity in orienting and merging parts. Product design must avoid parts which can become tangled, wedged or disoriented. Avoid holes and tabs and designed "closed" parts. This type of design will allow the use of automation in parts handling and assembly such as vibratory bowls, tubes, and magazines. Part design should incorporate symmetry around both axes of insertion wherever possible. Where parts cannot be symmetrical, the asymmetry should be emphasized to assure correct insertion or easily identifiable feature should be provided.

Parts should be designed with surfaces so that they can be easily grasped, placed, and fixtured:

- Minimize thin, flat parts or very small parts that are more difficult to pick up as this will increase handling and orientation time.

- Avoid parts with sharp edges, burrs or points. They can injure workers or customers, they require careful handling and can damage product finishes.

- Avoid parts that can be easily damaged or broken.

- Avoid parts that are sticky or slippery.

- Avoid heavy parts that increase worker fatigue, increase risk of injury, and delay the assembly process.

- Design the workstation area to minimize the distance to access and move a part.

- When purchasing components, consider acquiring materials already oriented in magazines, bands, tape, or strips.

B. Value Analysis Contribution to the Teardown Process

Value analysis was formally created in 1945 by Lawrence D. Miles at General Electric and was introduced into Japan in 1955. It has been widely used in the United States and other countries including Japan as a method for cost reduction and product improvement through function analysis.

In the mid 1950s, Japan's consumer products manufacturers made dramatic progress gaining market share from their global competitors in some targeted fields. Major credit for this success is attributed to Japan's dedicated use of these product and process control techniques. In Japan, these three initially different techniques have merged with Japan's work ethics and grown into a comprehensive technology that has enabled Japan to effectively compete and win market share over U.S. and European companies in many markets offering functionally responsive, cost effective, quality products and services to an informed market.

Many initiatives have branched out of Miles' original value analysis concepts. Among these initiatives are quality function deployment (QFD), fault tree analysis (FTA), and failure mode and effect analysis (FMEA). Value analysis and value engineering are now among the most widely used methods in Japan for controlling and directing technology. The primary emphasis of value engineering is on understanding, identifying, and classifying product related functions. Once defined, the creative value engineering steps encourage a broad search for ideas to implement those functions and produce innovative products.

In today's market, it is essential that our products have some differences in the way functions are implemented, including the cost to produce, to separate us from our competitors and attract the attention of potential customers. While it is taken for granted that our products have functions that our customers are willing to pay for, the proliferation of product offerings and model options have made determining what functions and features the customer wants a difficult marketing search. What functions in products, systems, or processes would raise the value adding perception of our customers, including aftermarket systems and services? In short, how can we improve function and reduce cost in the value equation?

Increasing functions to improve value implies that the market is willing to pay for those function improvements, or additions. Value can also be improved by reducing cost and functions, but the value analysis teardown study team must be assured that those functions being reduced or eliminated are not "customer sensitive." If not careful, the team could remove those functions that made the product successful.

C. Value Analysis Teardown and Improvement/Innovation

We are always improving existing things—products, processes, systems, and creating new things. A company dies when these activities stop. Companies must continuously improve and innovate to maintain market position. How are these two concepts different? Improvement means modifying existing things to achieve incremental enhancements. Small, but continuous improvements, piled one on top of another, are essential to the business success of any corporation. Innovation means making major change in concept and configuration. Value analysis teardown produces both improvements and innovations.

Improvement and innovation cause different degrees of change. With this distinction, value engineering is innovation focused, while value analysis is more intended for improvement. Taking the best parts of both processes, the value analysis teardown method integrates value analysis and the principles of value engineering with the creative stimuli it produces. The synergistic effect is the emergence of a powerful technique for product and process improvement and innovation.

In this technology accelerating, competition-oriented society, improvement alone cannot provide the strategic advantage to win over competitors. Some level of innovation is also needed to gain strategic advantage. The investment in capital and time in value analysis teardown activities is significantly less than traditional applied research and development activities addressing the same business improvement objectives.

D. Value Analysis Teardown Method and Its Components

Conventional teardown comparative methods were limited to displaying what is to be evaluated and letting the viewer's imagination and experience find differences (see Figure 4.8, Figure 4.9, and Figure 4.11). Lacking a systematic, structured approach, ideas were randomly produced without a focused objective or an organized way of processing them. Today's procedures, developed from past experiences and the incorporation of the value analysis/value engineering discipline, comprise a systematic way of comparison and analysis.

Any product includes a variety of factors measured in terms of cost or time. Some of those factors are: materials (see Figure 4.10 and Figure 4.12), construction, assembly, test methods, and those investment expenses classified as fixed and capital cost. The value analysis teardown process focuses on each of those factors, comparing and analyzing them in search of problems or opportunities. Then the process sets about improving each item that has surfaced in the course of the analysis.

The value analysis teardown process makes it possible to concentrate on a particular area and objective called a "theme," or an issue of concern. Since a great number of ideas develop in the course of analysis, the analysis process can be directed to meet specific objectives, or themes, such as: cost reduction, process reduction, commonality, introducing new functions, and improving existing functions. Suggestions for proposed solutions can also be collected and directed to a specific theme.

Figure 4.8 Products are often much more complicated than we think when we are sitting in them. (Image courtesy of A2Mac1 Benchmarking.)

Value Analysis Teardown Applied to Product Manufacturing

The purpose of the value analysis teardown process is to analyze and understand the competitive advantages of our, and competing products. The process also allows the products being dissected and analyzed to be benchmarked and to create product

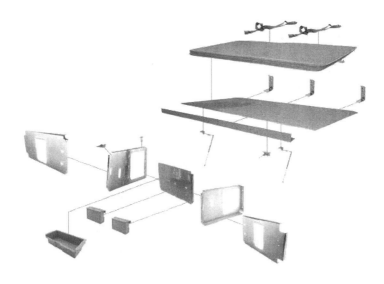

Figure 4.9 A teardown for the bunk sleeper of a class 8 vehicle. (Image courtesy of A2Mac1 Benchmarking.)

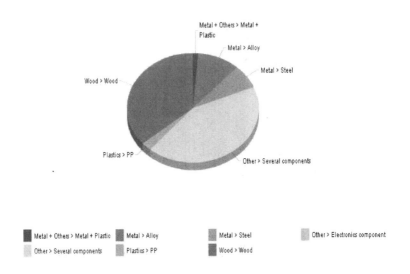

Figure 4.10 Material breakdown of the bunk sleeper can help us see specifically where the product cost resides. We can then look for alternative materials. (Image courtesy of A2Mac1 Benchmarking.)

Figure 4.11 Teardowns of systems provide material for critique of value proposition. (Image courtesy of A2Mac1 Benchmarking.)

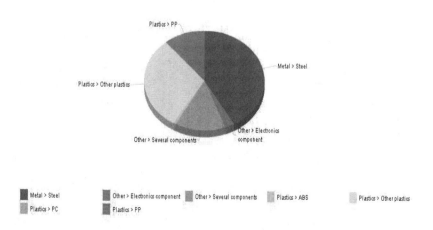

Figure 4.12 With the teardown of the system we can readily see the constituent parts contribution. (Image courtesy of A2Mac1 Benchmarking.)

improvement goals. As a creative stimulus, the process encourages developing new ideas that will improve functions, features, and attributes of products in direct competition to a targeted competitor. The products are then displayed (static) and used for information sharing and networking with everyone concerned, including top management, joint ventures, and major systems suppliers. Using the static displays to reinforce the business case with presentations adds credibility and interest to the request for new or major product improvement investments.

The following discusses the effect of value analysis teardown on manufacturing, specifically for producing component parts, assembly, and test of consumer products.

Analysis

Validating and implementing the ideas collected through the value analysis teardown process on existing products can produce some immediate, direct improvements such as, lower material and direct labor cost, or improved functions. Product improvement ideas that cannot be immediately implemented are recorded and set aside for future use. Such ideas are stored in a "Product Improvement Library" or a product development idea bank. This database, properly used, can reduce product development lead-time and capital investments, as well as the unit cost. The ideas are also used to build business cases and justify the need for acquiring new capital equipment and advanced manufacturing technology.

Setting Targets

The value analysis teardown process can be used to focus on which parts need to be improved, and to what extent and in what sequence to achieve a competitive edge. This information is used to establish cost and performance function targets for product improvement.

It is not necessary to target every component in a product. Using Pareto's maldistribution rule, approximately 80% of a product's cost resides in 20% of its components. Identifying and addressing the 20% of the components makes the target cost program more manageable to plan necessary actions and establish priorities for such actions. Setting product improvement targets on the basis of an understanding of customer needs and wants, competitive pressures, and business objectives is more credible, and generates more enthusiasm than those targets established through some abstract financial business planning processes.

Display

By presenting the results of a value analysis in an easy-to-understand physical display, concerned team members can use all of their senses to easily recognize the competitive features or disadvantage as well as scope the problems that are inherent in their products. Thus, everyone participating in the value analysis teardown activities can share their information about their individual concerns, ideas, and constraints and agree to a corrective course of action. Such actions will affect everyone involved including design, development, production and business management.

E. Recognizing Parts Suppliers' Competitive Capability

Few companies today design, produce, and assemble all of their product systems and components. It is a common practice that assemblers and parts suppliers cooperate to make a final product. As the Japanese yen appreciated and Asian manufacturers caught up with Japanese counterparts in product quality and functions, it became no longer necessary to restrict parts sourcing to a limited number of qualified domestic suppliers. Limiting supply sources could significantly detract from competitive cost and price advantage.

Determining the competitive capability of a finished product, function and quality advantages can be easily determined, but analyzing a competitor's manufacturing costs are much more difficult. Knowing the competitor's price does not give a clue to his product cost, unless his price strategy, discount policies, internal accounting structure, and level of manufacturing technology are known.

The value analysis teardown display makes it easier to determine what the competitor's product "should cost" by applying reverse engineering techniques to the dissected model. Such analysis will uncover information about the competitor's processes, assembly, materials, labor hours, capital equipment, and many other manufacturing details. Value analysis teardown is also used to evaluate parts supplier candidates. Through the value analysis teardown process a supplier's development and technological capabilities and their competitive advantage contributions can be evaluated. Based on this evaluation, supplier selection as well as potential future partners can be decided. Information retrieved in support of such decisions includes current supplier capabilities, shortfalls, and investments needed to make those suppliers better partners.

F. Collecting New Suggestions for Improvement

A company's technical staff normally performs value analysis teardown. However, this dramatic visual aid is used as a stimulus for other interested people. Those outside the product development loop, having different paradigms, offer fresh, good ideas that have been conceived from a different perspective. What would a plastics expert, or other material and process specialists, think when looking at a machined part? Entirely new ideas, not only about material but also manufacturing procedures, may emerge. Encouraging such spontaneous comments is accomplished by creating an open access display room in the procurement lobby to be viewed by suppliers and others waiting to meet with buyers. Supplier ideas are encouraged and collected by the technical staff and evaluated at a later date.

End product producers, who are at the front end of competition, place their name and reputation at risk for liability related problems arising from the use of their products. Those who are most directly involved with reducing liability risk represent the most enthusiastic users of the value analysis teardown process. In Japan, consumer goods manufacturers such as automobiles and home electronic appliances have embraced and integrated value analysis teardown as part of their operating culture. But the use of value analysis teardown in parts manufacturing still lacks total acceptance and endorsement.

Most product producers outsource their components manufacture to focus on assembly and test. They are turning more of the parts manufacture to more cost effective supplier experts. This has encouraged the global growth of component manufacturers, which has increased the competitive pressures among those producers. That competition may even be sharper than that among end product producers. The value analysis teardown method offers the same advantages to parts manufacturers as it does to end product producers.

G. Case Study

Streamlining Diesel Engine Development—Siemens PLM Software-1
Siemens.com/plm[3]
Isuzu wanted to significantly reduce the time spent preparing and translating engine model data for use by its multiple analysis programs.

Data Convergence Consumes Valuable Time

Among the leading manufacturers of advanced sport utility vehicles and commercial vehicles, Isuzu had become the linchpin for General Motors' diesel engine development. Isuzu was producing 13 different diesel engine models—from the 1.1 liter 13LB1 industrial engine to the 30-liter model 10TDI truck engine. Isuzu was also developing a next-generation, ultra-clean diesel engine that exceeds stringent exhaust emissions standards around the world, putting this low emissions power plant in the same class as future environmentally friendly gasoline engines.

Continually seeking process improvement, Isuzu management noted that far too much of the development process was spent on data convergence. It took an engineer about three weeks to convert the design geometry to the format required for each of the best-of-breed analysis programs used in the past. Additional time was required to convert and manipulate results files into formats needed to combine them and compare them to physical testing.

I-Deas Unified Environment Eliminates the Need to Translate Data

Isuzu made the decision to implement I-Deas NX Series due to its ability to deliver leading-edge modeling and analysis tools within a single integrated environment. I-Deas is based on the concept of digital master models that are used to evaluate multiple design concepts so that the final product more closely matches customer expectations. I-Deas helps engineers analyze design concepts as soon as they are defined. I-Deas analysis tools utilize the same geometry that is created by the I-Deas modeler. In addition, there is integration among the results files so that, for example, thermal analysis results can be easily combined with finite element modeling results, enabling the easy calculation of overall stresses and deflections due to both mechanical and thermal loading.

Finally, I-Deas correlation capabilities provide a unique tool for comparing dynamic finite element analysis and experimental testing results that eliminates a considerable amount of additional data manipulation that was required in the past.

They reduced the development cycle by two months; engine performance also significantly improved. By moving to I-Deas, Isuzu has slashed eight man-months of time that was previously consumed by data conversion. This savings has been redirected to proactive engineering opportunities. The capabilities of I-Deas analysis tools are in every way equal to the best-of-breed software that we used in the past. The time that we save in data convergence makes it possible to deliver significant improvements in engine performance. With those improvements, Isuzu is taking the engines to market an average of two months faster.

VII. EXERCISES

- Are teardowns ethical?

- At what point does a teardown exercise become unethical? How large or how small a system do we consider?

- Do teardown exercises encourage us to regress to the mean; that is, are we merely copying somebody else's design work?

- How do we avoid copying? What about the overtones of plagiarism, patent violation, and copyright violation?

- How do we set ground rules for the various types of teardowns in order to keep them clean?

- Who should lead the teardown exercise?

- How should the teardown be documented? Does that not leave *evidence*?

- How do teardowns differ from benchmarking?

- Do we ask for permission before doing a teardown?

- Is it ethical to teardown a piece of rental equipment? For example, can we rent or lease a class 8 semitractor and take it apart?

- What happens if we teardown a rental and do not put it back together correctly? Who owns the problem?

- Does the teardown activity have value with military equipment?

- U.S. troops who used the Kalashnikov rifles must have torn them down in order to clean them—why was the technology not considered for U.S. rifles?

- How do we derive a cost reduction from a teardown?

- If we are shocked at the "cheesy" nature of the design we are tearing down, might not that be an impetus to our own creativity? "Hey, we can do better than that lousy design...!"

- How do we choose candidates for teardown? Do we want best-in-class, best-in-world, worst-in-class, or worst-in-world?

- If we see something really ghastly in somebody else's design during a teardown, do we use this information in our marketing? If it were a safety issue, do we let the other company know?

- Do these companies not know that everybody is doing the teardown exercise to see what is new?
- Does the fact that "everybody" does it make it okay?
- Companies say "innovation," yet they copy each other without any shame. What is wrong with this picture?
- What about the statement, "we do not want to reinvent the wheel..."
- How do we organize components during the teardown of an assembly? Manufacturing engineers will probably lay them out as they believe it would be assembled and design engineers will lay the parts out by design block. Which is better?
- What are the criteria for a really good teardown exercise? What would a rubric for teardowns look like? Create one for class discussion.

ENDNOTES

1. Rains, James A., Jr., and Yoshihiko Sato. "The Integration of the Japanese Teardown Method with Design for Assembly and Value Engineering." Lawrence D. Miles Value Foundation. Last modified June 15, 2011. Accessed June 28, 2012. http://www.valuefoundation.org/paper03.pdf.

2. Sato, Yoshihiko, and J. Jerry Kaufman. *Value Analysis Teardown: A New Process for Product Development and Innovation.* New York, NY: Industrial Press, Incorporated, 2005.

3. https://www.plm.automation.siemens.com/CaseStudyWeb/dispatch/ viewResource.html?resourceId=5662. Retrieved September 20, 2012.

CHAPTER 5 – The DoD Approach

I. Rubric for the DoD Approach

Criteria	Level 1 (50–59%)	Level 2 (60–69%)	Level 3 (70–79%)	Level 4 (80–100%)
Analyze how individual stakeholders are affected by economic change	Analyzes how individual stakeholders are affected by economic change using limited critical thinking	Analyzes how individual stakeholders are affected by economic change using some critical thinking	Analyzes how individual stakeholders are affected by economic change using good critical thinking	Analyzes how individual stakeholders are affected by economic change using excellent critical thinking
Analyze the change in the dollar`s value on the DoD work	Analysis of the change in the dollar`s value on the DoD work demonstrates limited comprehension of the impact	Analysis of the change in the dollar`s value on the DoD work demonstrates some comprehension of the impact	Analysis of the change in the dollar`s value on the DoD work demonstrates considerable comprehension of the impact	Analysis of the change in the dollar`s value on the DoD work demonstrates thorough comprehension of the impact
Analyze the power of different stakeholders to make profitable decisions	Analysis of the power of different stakeholders to make profitable decisions provides limited information for each project studied	Analysis of the power of different stakeholders to make profitable decisions provides some information for each project studied	Analysis of the power of different stakeholders to make profitable decisions provides considerable information for each project studied	Analysis of the power of different stakeholders to make profitable decisions provides thorough information for each project studied
Analyze the public vs. private provision of a good or service	Analysis of the public vs. private provision of a good or service provides limited information on both advantages and disadvantages	Analysis of the public vs. private provision of a good or service provides some information on both advantages and disadvantages	Analysis of the public vs. private provision of a good or service provides considerable information on both advantages and disadvantages	Analysis of the public vs. private provision of a good or service provides thorough information on both advantages and disadvantages
Apply the cost-benefit method of inquiry to current projects	Applies the cost-benefit method of inquiry to current projects with limited effectiveness	Applies the cost-benefit method of inquiry to current projects with some effectiveness	Applies the cost-benefit method of inquiry to current projects with considerable effectiveness	Applies the cost-benefit method of inquiry to current projects with a high degree of effectiveness
Compare characteristics of different structures of business organizations	Compares characteristics of different structures of business organizations with limited organization	Compares characteristics of different structures of business organizations with moderate organization	Compares characteristics of different structures of business organizations with good organization	Compares characteristics of different structures of business organizations with exemplary organization
Compare public and private sectors	Compares public and private sectors with limited reference to goods and services produced and employment levels	Compares public and private sectors with some reference to goods and services produced and employment levels	Compares public and private sectors with considerable reference to goods and services produced and employment levels	Compares public and private sectors with thorough reference to goods and services produced and employment levels

Criteria	Level 1 (50–59%)	Level 2 (60–69%)	Level 3 (70–79%)	Level 4 (80–100%)
Demonstrate understanding of the private sector	Demonstrates limited understanding of the private sector	Demonstrates some understanding of the private sector	Demonstrates considerable understanding of the private sector	Demonstrates thorough understanding of the private sector
Demonstrate understanding of the public sector	Demonstrates limited understanding of the public sector	Demonstrates some understanding of the public sector	Demonstrates considerable understanding of the public sector	Demonstrates thorough understanding of the public sector
Describe characteristics of private, public, nonprofit, and volunteer sectors	Describes characteristics of private, public, nonprofit, and volunteer sectors making limited connections	Describes characteristics of private, public, nonprofit, and volunteer sectors making some connections	Describes characteristics of private, public, nonprofit, and volunteer sectors making many connections	Describes characteristics of private, public, nonprofit, and volunteer sectors making all or almost all connections
Describe the role of government interventions	Describes the role of government interventions with limited comprehension	Describes the role of government interventions with some comprehension	Describes the role of government interventions with considerable comprehension	Describes the role of government interventions with thorough comprehension
Evaluate the effectiveness of government legislation and regulatory programs	Evaluation of the effectiveness of government legislation and regulatory programs provides limited information	Evaluation of the effectiveness of government legislation and regulatory programs provides some information	Evaluation of the effectiveness of government legislation and regulatory programs provides considerable information	Evaluation of the effectiveness of government legislation and regulatory programs provides thorough information
Explain the concepts of self-interest and interdependence	Explains the concepts of self-interest and interdependence with limited understanding	Explains the concepts of self-interest and interdependence with some understanding	Explains the concepts of self-interest and interdependence with considerable understanding	Explains the concepts of self-interest and interdependence with thorough understanding
Produce a cost and benefit analysis of this trend for differing stakeholders	Produces a cost and benefit analysis of this trend for differing stakeholders providing limited detail	Produces a cost and benefit analysis of this trend for differing stakeholders providing some detail	Produces a cost and benefit analysis of this trend for differing stakeholders providing considerable detail	Produces a cost and benefit analysis of this trend for differing stakeholders providing thorough detail
Use criteria to make a comparison	Rarely uses criteria to make a comparison	Sometimes uses criteria to make a comparison	Often uses criteria to make a comparison	Routinely uses criteria to make a comparison

II. Questions to Ponder

- What are the constituent costs to the cost of ownership?
- Consider the value of a product or service as viewed from the perspective of cost of ownership.
- Does the DoD approach have too much overhead for your organization?

- What would you measure to gauge the effectiveness of your value engineering activities?

- How does your company manage the short-term improvement and the longer-term value proposition?

- When do you know the product or service is past the maturity phase and into the death phase?

- How do value engineering techniques extend the life phase?

- How does the DoD model reward the suppliers? Why is this important?

III. Cost Improvement Scenario

A. Situation

DoD itself had an unmanned aerial vehicle (UAV) capability that had an obsolete and expensive-to-maintain component that was unique on the planet!

B. Objective

The objective was to completely replace the obsolete computer system, channel controller, and some other devices with an up-to-date UNIX-based computer system.

C. Action

A contractor made a proposal for change, which was approved.

D. Results

The system switched over completely from an outdated mainframe and a unique component to side-of-desk sized minicomputers.

E. Aftermath

Because the architecture of the minicomputers was based on the RS/6000 (IBM) chip set, translation to the PowerPC was relatively straightforward later on. This scenario is a case where the total cost of operation was a major consideration.

IV. Benefits

The benefits of value engineering that the Department of Defense (see Figure 5.1) expects to receive are similar to those that your business or service would also receive—the exception being the war fighting capability.[1] These benefits are as follows:

- Cost reduction
- Communications
- Procedures
- Waste reduction

- Performance
- Efficiency
- Reliability
- Producibility
- Quality
- Effectiveness
- Readiness
- War-fighting capability
- Cycle time

All of these benefits streamline our value proposition making our company good stewards of the environment as well as providing an excellent value proposition for our customers. Equipment such as the tank below Figure 5.1 are costly and failures in the product can have a great consequence.

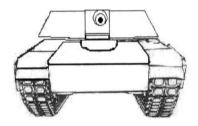

Figure 5.1 Focus on cost is important for DoD—a tank is an expensive weapon system.

The objective of value engineering in the arena of defense contracting is to reduce the government's procurement or ownership costs (these include operational costs, maintenance costs, and training costs—sometimes known as total cost of ownership or TCO) while maintaining required performance. One way we can achieve this objective is by responding to the value engineering clauses in DoD contracts and statements or work. These clauses ask or demand that contractors initiate, develop, and submit *cost-reduction* proposals during the execution of a contract that involves changes to contract requirements. These clauses generally require that the government share with the contractor any cost reduction resulting from a value engineering change proposal (VECP). Value engineering clauses in DoD contracts are insufficient. The clauses allow contractors to question government specifications, statements of work, and those requirements that effectively contribute nothing (with the exception of cost!) to the contract. Furthermore, the government must accept the invitation. Then both parties (government and contractor) work together to capture the actual benefits.

The contractor never has to wait for the government to ask. Contractors can make recommendations at any time during the execution of a contract—it is then the responsibility of the government to respond and approve or reject the proposed savings. This kind of situation applies with nongovernmental organizations (NGOs) and nonprofits also. Here are some examples of value engineering possibilities:

Advances in technology	Incorporation of new materials, components, techniques, or processes (advances in the state-of-the-art) not available at the time of the previous design effort.
Excessive cost	Prior design proved technically adequate, but subsequent cost analysis revealed excessive cost.
Additional design effort	Application of additional skills, ideas, and information available but not utilized, during previous design effort.
Change in user's needs	User's modification or redefinition of mission, function, or application of item.
Feedback from test/use	Design modification based on user tests or field experience suggesting that specified parameters governing previous design exaggerated.
Design deficiencies	Prior design proved inadequate in use (e.g., was characterized by inadequate performance, excessive failure rates, or technical deficiency).
Miscellaneous	Other factors not included in above.

V. Function

Function is defined as the specific purpose or use of our product (be it service or hardware)—describing what we must accomplish. For value engineering studies, we reduce the description of function to the simplest accurate expression. We accomplish this by using merely two words: an active verb and a quantifiable noun (however, note that we are not using the imperative mood per se). "Support weight," "transmit power," and "accumulate charge" are reasonable example expressions of function. We strive that each function is described with terms that are both quantifiable and measurable.

VI. Worth

DoD defines worth as the least expenditure required to provide an essential function and further informs us that this status we establish by comparison. Worth is not affected by the consequence of failure. For example, if a bolt supporting part of a submarine fails, the submarine may sink. Even so, the worth of the bolt is the lowest cost necessary to provide a reliable fastening (not the cost of a submarine).

VII. Cost

Cost is the total amount of funds required to acquire, utilize, and maintain the specified functions (often miscalled Total Cost of Operation or TCO). For the seller, it is the total expense coupled with the manufacture of a product. For DoD, the total cost includes not only the purchase price of the product but also the costs of introducing it into inventory, operating it, supporting it throughout its usable life and disposing of it when it no longer serves a useful, functional purpose. In other words, DoD takes a holistic approach to cost. We believe that when these numbers can be calculated, they should be used. Even when these numbers cannot be rigidly calculated, we can likely glean a general perspective of these associated costs by looking at our historical record as it applies to similar past projects and products.

$$Value\ Index = \frac{worth}{cost} = \frac{utility}{cost}$$

VIII. Value

Value is the relationship of worth to cost in accordance with the customers' needs and resources for particular situations. The ratio of worth to cost is the principal measure of value for DoD. Thus, a "value equation" may be used to derive a value index as follows (per DOD 4245.8-H).

We can increase value by (1) improving the utility of something with no change in cost, (2) retaining the same utility for less cost, or (3) combining improved utility with a decrease in cost. Please note that this does not correspond with Karl Marx's discussions of use value and exchange value as separate entities.

Optimum value is achieved when all utility criteria are met at the lowest overall cost. Although worth and cost can each be expressed in monetary units, it is easy to see that the monetary units fall out of the equation, providing a dimensionless abstraction we call "value."

IX. Effective Value Engineering Programs

An effective and sustained value engineering program will have:

- Top management involvement to ensure implementation and continuing support by middle management

- A key individual to lead the value engineering program—an individual who has substantial expertise in value engineering principles, techniques, and appropriate acquisitions

- A plan to ensure that actions which contribute to a successful program are reflected on and acted on

- Value engineering objectives, goals, policies, responsibilities, and reporting requirements implemented using a project management approach

- Infrastructure to support including tracking of past activities results
- The funds required for administrative and operating expenses such as testing and evaluating proposals
- A comprehensive training and orientation program
- Dissemination of information ("cross-pollination") to communicate successful applications to others who can benefit

DoD expects the following should also be included:

- Close coordination with contract administration (contracting officer and contract office representative) and marketing to ensure proper value engineering contractual participation and marketing follow-through.
- Management attention to ensure that the value engineering discipline is used to earn as much additional income as is feasible.

These ideas are the foundation on which the structure of a strong program may be built.

Other Considerations

Those enterprising souls who commence a new value engineering program or re-energize a quiescent program would be well-advised to select early-in-the-life cycle projects that benefit the most from value engineering. These projects should be ones that exhibit:

- A large-dollar expenditure
- Reasons other than cost (i.e., deficiencies in performance, reliability, etc.)
- Value to system or executive management

As the value engineering program ripens and the opportunities become less obvious (all the "low hanging fruit" is gone), we would use additional criteria to pick our future projects. Here are some considerations:

- No known deterrents such as exorbitant test costs, tooling costs, or implementation schedule requirements.
- A product with excessive complexity.
- A design that utilizes the most advanced technology.
- An accelerated development program.
- An item which field use indicates is deficient in some characteristics such as excessive failure rate or extravagant operating cost.
- An item utilizing older technologies for which modernization appears very promising.

One of the features of value engineering is the revelation of cost improvement opportunities that might otherwise have remained invisible. In our own experience, we have often heard the anguished query: "But!! But! Where will I find any cost reductions?" We know from experience any organization has, at a minimum, hundreds of opportunities for cost savings. Use of the previously discussed brainstorming and mind mapping techniques may help to ferret out some of these allegedly elusive cost improvement ideas. The Defense Department has a phased approach:

Phase	Topics
Orientation	What is the candidate item we wish to study?
Information Gathering	What is it? What is its function? Cost? Worth?
Speculation	Can we perform this function with another device or service?
Analysis	Cost of alternatives? Least expensive?
Development	Does proposed alternative function as expected? Does proposed alternative meet requirements (especially regulatory)? What does this alternative need to make it function properly?
Presentation	Recommendation? Alternatives? Cost? Savings? Implementation plan/schedule?
Implementation	Entire or partial approval with funding? Responsibility for implementation? What actions do we need to do? Completion dates? Requirements for progress reporting?
Follow-through	Did it work? Did we save any money? Would we repeat the exercise? Benefit to others? Proper publicity?

One of the primary purposes of value engineering is to analyze the functions of an item—in short, to define its purpose. Because we must analyze the part or service, we are not reducing cost by arbitrarily performing slash and burn to achieve the lowest cost through some technique such as browbeating our suppliers. Other methods may reduce the intrinsic quality and reliability by cheapening the product as a cost reduction (we have seen cases where these kinds of decisions have led to recall or campaigns— thereby more than obliterating any opportunity for cost reduction). We have also seen where this form of cheapening the product erodes the product quality, which does not go unnoticed with our customer. In the most severe of these cases, we trade off the immediate cost improvement for loss of customers to our organization, or in a state of constant corrective actions for our cost improvement work. The value engineering technique as espoused by the Department of Defense starts with a definition of the mandatory functions and then seeks lower cost possibilities to achieve that *essential* function. Our goal is to reduce superfluous cost without any loss in needed quality or reliability. The approach of deriving the essential functions is applicable to software also and was the core of a significant software engineering book by McMenamin and Palmer called *Essential Systems Analysis* (Yourdon Press, 1984)[2]. This book still stands as a classic in what it takes to separate the essential from the supplemental in any system, be it software, hardware, or a service!

Functional analysis develops a simple and unambiguous definition of function per each part of the product or service under analysis. Such functions are usually classified as either basic or secondary: a basic function is a function that cannot be eliminated without degrading the usefulness of the end item; a secondary function is not *essential* to use the item in its proposed application but is a result of the chosen design solution. Limiting or reducing secondary functions and minimizing the cost of basic functions results in value improvement for the product or service which remains consistent with all requirements. The term "best value" refers to the best relationship between worth and cost. In other words, an item that reliably performs the required basic function at an appointed time and place and which has the lowest total cost represents a "best value."

One peculiarity of DoD cost reductions, is that they need not come from the functional analysis, particularly if the contract demands a specific approach. In general, the DoD prefer "early onset" change proposals to later ones, particularly since an early change stands the chance of garnering more savings through the life of the product or service. Once our product development and tooling actions start, we will have the burden of overcoming these monetary hurdles.

X. Cost Analysis

A. Variance Analysis

Organizational managers have an ongoing burden to provide justification of the variances of actual performance versus budgeted targets (we can use earned value analysis here). We can perform a variance analysis of numerous cost drivers and cost elements when our operational reporting shows our activities are out of tolerance. The purpose of variance analysis is to ensure a more profound understanding of the differences between planned and actual performance. If desired, we can collect this historical data and use it later as a basis for prediction. If we know we have a problem, we are more likely to do something about it.

We can analyze a negative variance in procurement of manufacturing components to ascertain the root cause of the variance. It may be due to the use of excessive quantities of material as operators learn how to build the product, improper understanding of our needs by the supplier, or procurement of components that are more expensive than our costed bill of materials indicated they would be. In general, we desire to act quickly to apprehend the root cause, take action, and avoid having to go back to the customer (especially the government) with a need to re-budget the program!

We might use the following calculations as variances:

- PV—Planned value (BCWS—budgeted cost of work scheduled)

- EV—Earned value (BCWP—budgeted cost of work performed)

- AC—Actual cost (ACWP—actual cost of work performed)

- SV (schedule variance) = EV-PV

- CV (cost variance) = EV-AC

- BAC (budget at completion) = sum of planned values of all work packages of the project

B. Ratio Analysis

We can also use business ratios to assist in detection of adverse directions in our financial, schedule, and quality well-being. If we are going to use ratios, then it would be wise to define them early in the project and make sure our customer comprehends the purpose of these calculations. Overhead can be difficult to calculate, so an indirect approach such as ration analysis can help us determine if we are in a dire situation.

Most of our higher-level ratios will be oriented around return on investment. Examples of some ratios we might use are as follows:

- Capital to income—what is the capital investment versus the anticipated income for this project or cost savings? This calculation is somewhat similar to return on investment.

- Debt to income—how deep do we owe versus anticipated improvement in margins.

- Return on capital—invested capital over expected return (another way to look at return on investment).

- Current ratio—current assets for this project over current liabilities for this project can indicate a make-or-break condition, particularly if we can reduce liabilities.

- SPI (schedule performance index) = EV/PV

- CPI (cost performance index) = EV/AC

- SV% (schedule variance %) = ((EV-PV)/PV)*100

- EAC (estimate at completion) = AC+(BAC-EV)/CPI

C. Trend Analysis

Trend analysis eases the analysis of overhead costs (see Figure 5.2). One of the many uses of this method is to mark anomalous deviations from the "flight plan." With trend analysis, we can detect adverse trends. This also allows concentration on more significant expenses (variable or fixed) or organizations that seem to be disorderly. By isolating indirect costs that need investigation, we have a method for improving overhead control. We can use time series analyses, regression techniques and compare with our variance and ratio analyses.

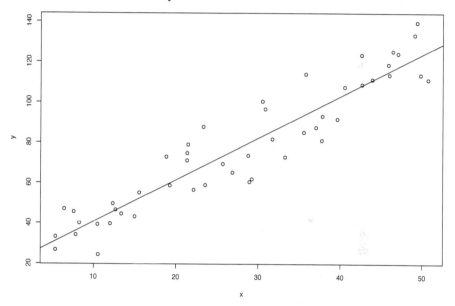

Figure 5.2 An example trendline with a simple linear trend.

D. Management Analysis

Management should use a multimodal approach by considering what is revealed by the variances, the ratios, and the calculated trends. Indirect labor is difficult to calculate, even with activity-based costing. We may have to disaggregate indirect overhead into the myriad possibilities to reveal cost variance in those areas. We may get to the point of analyzing benefits, travel, clerical, and other expenses. We want to ensure we are dealing with a high enough level of management to make painful decisions.

We can use any regression method that makes sense; that is, we can cautiously apply it so long as the data supports the model. The simple, linear regression in Figure 5.2 shows a straightforward, upward trend in the model. We can test our models with goodness-of-fit calculations and even eyeballing the result.

XI. EXERCISES

- If we are providing scientific, engineering, technical systems, most of our costs will be indirect. How are we going to contain cost?

- Does it still make sense to calculate nearly all of our overhead from direct labor? Is this not a throwback to the early part of the 20th century?

- Which ratios would you use to determine if our project is out of control?

- How much historical data do we need to have in order to do trend analysis?

- Does it make any sense to use throughput accounting, a tool from the theory of constraints?

- What are the issues with activity-based costing? At the end of the 20th century, this method was proclaimed to be the solution to costing issues.

- When is the best time to propose a value engineered cost reduction to a customer?

- Do we want to propose cost reductions at the time of product launch?

- How stable does a project have to be before we can assess the situation and see if cost reductions make any sense?

- How long after launch should we begin to analyze product and our processes for cost reductions?

- If our product is overengineered, can we lower the quality or reliability of the product in order to effect a cost reduction? Is this activity even ethical?

- What is the best way to state the business case? Are we selling something every time we propose a cost reduction?

- Should the same team that designed the product or process also be the team that executes the cost reduction? Put together a list of benefits and drawbacks to using the same team.

- How do we deal with absurdities in the customer specification, especially if the customer is the government and dwarfs our enterprise by comparison?

- Who in the project will do the variance analysis, the ratio analysis, and the trend analysis? Does it make sense for it to be the project manager or does this present a conflict of interest?

- Who must be involved in the calculation of overhead? The standard components of overhead are direct labor, materials, and a mysterious value called factory overhead.

- What is the drawback to re-budgeting the project? At this point in our discussion, we should ask ourselves if we have ever seen a project that was re-budgeted.

- Should we not have an environment without fear? In short, if we are afraid to re-budget, what are the repercussions on the project? How would we conduct a budget change negotiation? Which parties must be involved in this discussion? What would be the expected political fallout?

ENDNOTES

1. Acquisition and Logistics, *Value Engineering*. Publication no. DOD 4245.8-H. Washington, DC: Department of Defense, 1986.

2. McMenamin, Stephen M., and John F. Palmer. *Essential Systems Analysis*. New York City, NY: Yourdon, Incorporated, 1984. Still one of the best resources for breaking a system down into its essential components.

CHAPTER 6 – Classical Value Analysis / Value Engineering Techniques

I. Rubric for Classical Techniques

Criteria	Level 1 (50–59%)	Level 2 (60–69%)	Level 3 (70–79%)	Level 4 (80–100%)
Analyze economic conditions that encourage an enterprising workplace	Analyzes economic conditions that encourage an enterprising workplace with limited results	Analyzes economic conditions that encourage an enterprising workplace with some results	Analyzes economic conditions that encourage an enterprising workplace with good results	Analyzes economic conditions that encourage an enterprising workplace with excellent results
Analyze enterprising skills to set goals	Analyzes enterprising skills to set goals with limited objectivity	Analyzes enterprising skills to set goals with some objectivity	Analyzes enterprising skills to set goals with good objectivity	Analyzes enterprising skills to set goals with excellent objectivity
Analyze given scenario	Analysis of given scenario provides limited insight	Analysis of given scenario provides some insight	Analysis of given scenario provides considerable insight	Analysis of given scenario provides thorough insight
Analyze the effect of competition	Analyzes the effect of competition with limited reference to consumer and business behavior	Analyzes the effect of competition with adequate reference to consumer and business behavior	Analyzes the effect of competition with considerable reference to consumer and business behavior	Analyzes the effect of competition with thorough reference to consumer and business behavior
Analyze the impact of the competition	Analysis of the impact of the competition demonstrates limited use of a SWOT	Analysis of the impact of the competition demonstrates some use of a SWOT	Analysis of the impact of the competition demonstrates considerable use of a SWOT	Analysis of the impact of the competition demonstrates thorough use of a SWOT
Analyze the resources that may be needed for a new benchmark	Analyzes the resources that may be needed for a new benchmark with limited results	Analyzes the resources that may be needed for a new benchmark with some results	Analyzes the resources that may be needed for a new benchmark with good results	Analyzes the resources that may be needed for a new benchmark with excellent results
Apply research and critical-thinking skills to evaluate ideas	Applies limited research and critical-thinking skills to evaluate ideas	Applies some research and critical-thinking skills to evaluate ideas	Applies good research and critical-thinking skills to evaluate ideas	Applies thorough research and critical-thinking skills to evaluate ideas
Assess research information	Assessment of research information demonstrates limited use of criteria	Assessment of research information demonstrates some use of criteria	Assessment of research information demonstrates considerable use of criteria	Assessment of research information demonstrates thorough use of criteria

Criteria	Level 1 (50–59%)	Level 2 (60–69%)	Level 3 (70–79%)	Level 4 (80–100%)
Assess the size of the potential target market for the new venture	Assessment of the size of the potential target market for the new venture demonstrates results of limited research	Assessment of the size of the potential target market for the new venture demonstrates results of some research	Assessment of the size of the potential target market for the new venture demonstrates results of considerable research	Assessment of the size of the potential target market for the new venture demonstrates results of thorough research
Compare a number of business plans	Comparison of a number of business plans provides limited information	Comparison of a number of business plans provides some information	Comparison of a number of business plans provides considerable information	Comparison of a number of business plans provides thorough information
Compare a variety of distribution strategies	Compares a variety of distribution strategies with limited information	Compares a variety of distribution strategies with adequate information	Compares a variety of distribution strategies with good information	Compares a variety of distribution strategies with complete information
Compare a variety of job descriptions and requirements	Compares a variety of job descriptions and requirements with limited criteria	Compares a variety of job descriptions and requirements with adequate criteria	Compares a variety of job descriptions and requirements with good criteria	Compares a variety of job descriptions and requirements with excellent criteria
Compare advantages and disadvantages of pursuing continuous growth	Comparison of advantages and disadvantages of pursuing continuous growth demonstrates limited use of critical thinking skills	Comparison of advantages and disadvantages of pursuing continuous growth demonstrates some use of critical thinking skills	Comparison of advantages and disadvantages of pursuing continuous growth demonstrates considerable use of critical thinking skills	Comparison of advantages and disadvantages of pursuing continuous growth demonstrates thorough use of critical thinking skills
Compare different types of business ownership	Is able to list three different types of business ownership	Is able to list different types of business ownership and provide an outline of each	Is able to compare different types of business ownership	Is able to compare different types of business ownership by using specific examples from our community
Compare how marketing is applied and implemented in different economic systems	Compares how marketing is applied and implemented in different economic systems using limited research	Compares how marketing is applied and implemented in different economic systems using adequate research	Compares how marketing is applied and implemented in different economic systems using good research	Compares how marketing is applied and implemented in different economic systems using thorough research
Compare invention and innovation	Compares invention and innovation with limited understanding	Compares invention and innovation with some understanding	Compares invention and innovation with considerable understanding	Compares invention and innovation with thorough understanding

Criteria	Level 1 (50–59%)	Level 2 (60–69%)	Level 3 (70–79%)	Level 4 (80–100%)
Compare levels of service among a variety of competing companies	Is able to describe various levels of service for different companies	Is able to describe different aspects of service levels for different companies	Is able to compare levels of service among a variety of competing companies	Is able to compare levels of service among a variety of competing companies and suggest alternatives
Compare models of venture-planning frameworks	Compares models of venture-planning frameworks using limited criteria	Compares models of venture-planning frameworks using adequate criteria	Compares models of venture-planning frameworks using good criteria	Compares models of venture-planning frameworks using excellent criteria
Compare the channels of distribution	Compares the channels of distribution with limited reference to type of products	Compares the channels of distribution with some reference to type of products	Compares the channels of distribution with considerable reference to type of products	Compares the channels of distribution with thorough reference to type of products
Complete self-assessment and standardized assessment tasks	Is able to complete self-assessment and standardized assessment tasks with limited understanding	Is able to complete self-assessment and standardized assessment tasks with some understanding	Is able to complete self-assessment and standardized assessment tasks with considerable understanding	Is able to complete self-assessment and standardized assessment tasks with superb understanding
Describe characteristics of potential target markets	Describes characteristics of potential target markets based on limited research	Describes characteristics of potential target markets based on some research	Describes characteristics of potential target markets based on good research	Describes characteristics of potential target markets based on thorough research
Determine resources required for benchmarking project	Determines few resources required for benchmarking project	Determines some resources required for benchmarking project	Determines many resources required for benchmarking project	Determines all or almost all resources required for benchmarking project
Determine the ancillary requirements of the new benchmarking project	Determines few of the ancillary requirements of the new benchmarking project	Determines some of the ancillary requirements of the new benchmarking project	Determines many of the ancillary requirements of the new benchmarking project	Determines all or almost all of the ancillary requirements of the new benchmarking project
Develop a benchmarking project plan	Develops a benchmarking project plan with limited effectiveness	Develops a benchmarking project plan with some effectiveness	Develops a benchmarking project plan with considerable effectiveness	Develops a benchmarking project plan with excellent effectiveness

Criteria	Level 1 (50–59%)	Level 2 (60–69%)	Level 3 (70–79%)	Level 4 (80–100%)
Differentiate between required fixed and variable cost items	Demonstrates limited ability to differentiate between required fixed and variable cost items	Demonstrates some ability to differentiate between required fixed and variable cost items	Demonstrates considerable ability to differentiate between required fixed and variable cost items	Demonstrates a high degree of ability to differentiate between required fixed and variable cost items
Evaluate effective customer service techniques	Evaluates effective customer service techniques with limited data	Evaluates effective customer service techniques with adequate data	Evaluates effective customer service techniques with considerable data	Evaluates effective customer service techniques with comprehensive data
Evaluate factors that influence an enterprising workplace	Evaluates few factors that influence an enterprising workplace	Evaluates some factors that influence an enterprising workplace	Evaluates many factors that influence an enterprising workplace	Evaluates a variety of factors that influence an enterprising workplace
Explain how competitors affect a market	Is able to explain in simplistic terms how competitors affect a market	Is able to generally explain how competitors affect a market	Is able to explain clearly, how competitors affect a market	Is able to explain clearly, how competitors affect a market in differing circumstances
Explain the process of market research	Explains the process of market research with limited understanding	Explains the process of market research with some understanding	Explains the process of market research with considerable understanding	Explains the process of market research with thorough understanding
Explain the stages in the life cycle of a business	Explanation of the stages in the life cycle of a business demonstrates limited knowledge	Explanation of the stages in the life cycle of a business demonstrates some knowledge	Explanation of the stages in the life cycle of a business demonstrates considerable knowledge	Explanation of the stages in the life cycle of a business demonstrates thorough knowledge
Generate ideas that match your selected entrepreneurial opportunity	Generates few ideas that match your selected entrepreneurial opportunity	Generates some ideas that match your selected entrepreneurial opportunity	Generates many ideas that match your selected entrepreneurial opportunity	Generates a wide variety of ideas that match your selected entrepreneurial opportunity
Identify common interview questions	Is able to identify few common interview questions	Is able to identify several common interview questions	Is able to identify many common interview questions	Is able to identify all or almost all common interview questions
Identify factors involved in product pricing	Identifies few factors involved in product pricing	Identifies some factors involved in product pricing	Identifies many factors involved in product pricing	Identifies a variety of factors involved in product pricing

Criteria	Level 1 (50–59%)	Level 2 (60–69%)	Level 3 (70–79%)	Level 4 (80–100%)
Identify factors that affect growth and decline of job sectors	Is able to identify factors that affect growth and decline of job sectors with limited accuracy	Is able to identify factors that affect growth and decline of job sectors with some accuracy	Is able to identify factors that affect growth and decline of job sectors with significant accuracy	Is able to identify factors that affect growth and decline of job sectors with masterful accuracy
Identify ineffective leadership skills	Is able to identify 1–2 ineffective leadership skills	Is able to identify 3–4 ineffective leadership skills	Is able to identify 5–6 ineffective leadership skills	Is able to identify 7–10 ineffective leadership skills
Identify ineffective teamwork skills	Is able to identify 1–2 ineffective teamwork skills	Is able to identify 3–4 ineffective teamwork skills	Is able to identify 5–6 ineffective teamwork skills	Is able to identify 7–10 ineffective teamwork skills
Identify investment choices	Is able to identify 2–3 investment choices	Is able to identify 4–5 investment choices	Is able to identify a variety of investment choices	Is able to identify a wide variety of investment choices
Identify positive teamwork skills	Infrequently identifies and encourages positive teamwork skills	Often identifies and encourages positive teamwork skills	Usually identifies and encourages positive teamwork skills	Routinely identifies and encourages positive teamwork skills
Identify your target market	Identifies target market with limited accuracy	Identifies target market with some accuracy	Identifies target market with good accuracy	Identifies target market with excellent accuracy
Produce a revised and final version of your venture plan	Produces a revised and final version of your venture plan that demonstrates limited organization	Produces a revised and final version of your venture plan that demonstrates some organization	Produces a revised and final version of your venture plan that demonstrates good organization	Produces a revised and final version of your venture plan that demonstrates excellent organization
Summarize information gathered	Summarizes information gathered using limited organization	Summarizes information gathered using some organization	Summarizes information gathered using considerable organization	Summarizes information gathered using thorough organization
Use criteria to make a comparison	Rarely uses criteria to make a comparison	Sometimes uses criteria to make a comparison	Often uses criteria to make a comparison	Routinely uses criteria to make a comparison

II. Questions to Ponder

- What are functions? How is value extracted and measured from the function?
- Is there really a homogenous value to a product or service? How does this impact our product or service as a charge to our customers?
- How does benchmarking constructively affect our value engineering activities?
- How does benchmarking impact our product or service requirements?

III. Cost Improvement Scenario

A. Situation

A certain vehicle manufacturer has an ongoing cost and weight improvement project. There are annual cost improvement targets associated with this effort, broken down by vehicle discipline; for example, electrical, cab, and chassis.

B. Objective

The objective was to reduce the cost of the vehicle by a defined percentage across the entire vehicle system. Additionally, we had to accomplish a weight reduction assigned by number of pounds.

C. Action

To meet the cost and weight improvement targets, it was decided to have competitor vehicles be brought in for a series of reviews. One vehicle was considered at a single event with a total of three vehicles for the review. The vehicles selected ranged from the largest market share manufacturer, to an ultra low cost vehicle from outside of this company's immediate market.

The vehicles were brought into a warehouse and disassembled with the constituent parts placed in well-documented areas associated with the appropriate vehicle. To save time, a specialty house was brought in for the disassembly of the vehicles. This company, A2Mac1, provides teardown expertise.

D. Results

The cost improvement targets were met. The use of the ultra-low cost (low-function) Asian vehicle did not provide much fodder for cost improvement. This specific marketplace was not receptive to such a low feature and low specification vehicle.

E. Aftermath

Much can be learned in the actual teardown. Hiring an outside vendor to tear the product down is helpful in terms of hours; however, this comes at the price of losing the knowledge that is obtained from physically performing the teardown by one's self. It is one thing to see how the parts go together; it is another to learn by performing the teardown.

Candidates for teardown should be those from which we believe it is possible to learn. In this case, the vehicle had no basis in the marketplace of the company performing the teardown, producing small impetus for cost improvement. Though the vehicle was most assuredly a low-cost version, not much was gleaned to help the local manufacturer to improve their vehicle cost.

IV. Benchmarking

A. Is Benchmarking Valuable?

One of the criticisms we have heard against benchmarking—checking our process, service, or products against somebody else's—is that the process will ultimately lead to mediocrity as the companies within a given niche all copy each other. We suggest that this canard might more reasonably be leveled against teardowns.

With benchmarking, we are usually setting a standard ("drawing a line in the sand") for improving our own performance *above* that standard. This approach hardly represents a regression towards the mean. In essence, we are saying, "here is a new standard—now let's see if we can beat it," rather than "here is a new standard—let's see if we can meet it." This process is akin to looking around your college class, identifying who gets the best grades, and seeing to it that you do better than they do. The competition (as it were) can be harnessed to provide improvements.

So how does benchmarking really enhance value engineering? If we are able to implement significant improvements to an ineffective or inefficient process, we will see improvements to the bottom line. The best of all worlds occurs when we discover we can actually eliminate portions of our own process. Simply speeding up the process often does not yield satisfactory cost savings.

B. Performance Benchmarking

We use process benchmarking to assess various facets of our processes in relation to the processes of so-called best practice companies, sometimes within a market niche which we define specifically with the intent of making comparisons. By analyzing a specific market niche, our organization develops strategies and tactics for improvements or we can co-opt and then adopt specific best practices, while always endeavoring to increase some component of our own performance. Benchmarking may be a one-time activity, or it can become part of a plan-do-check-act Deming/Shewhart cycle such that our enterprise continually seeks to improve its practices. We are cautious with the term "best practices" because we have seen this terminology used frequently by individuals who have made no effort to ascertain if, in fact, we are looking at "best practices" or "trendy" practices.

Hence, we are going to compare performance measures of target processes with processes from some well-defined group (see Figure 6.1). The well-defined group need not be in our industry; for example, we may be an automotive supplier but we might benchmark paper management and control with Federal Express, UPS, and the U.S. Post Office.

If we are a vehicle supplier, we may measure aerodynamics of some of our competitors' vehicles ultimately in an attempt to improve the vehicles' fuel economy. We may use this information to drive our designs to better performance—or if we already perform better, we will make the market customers aware of this fact.

Obviously, we need to gather some data to determine where we are in comparison to our benchmark organizations. In areas where we are inferior to the benchmark organizations, we perform a gap analysis and determine what it takes to at least achieve the level of performance of the "best practice." In cases where we meet or exceed the benchmark enterprises, we can push even harder by playing to our strengths—one of the paths to setting our own enterprise apart from competitors.

C. Benchmarking Process

A thorough discussion of benchmarking is the book *The Benchmarking Handbook: Step-by-Step Instructions*[1] by Bjorn Andersen and Per-Gaute Pettersen. We have modified their approach a bit, so please do not assume our discussion is a summary of their excellent book.

Benchmarking—Plan

Benchmarking plans do not have to be very complicated; for example, once we have selected a process that we wish to use in order to benchmark our enterprise against the market niche we have chosen, we will then select a cross-functional team to analyze the results of our benchmarking activities. In addition to choosing a team, we will document the process as we go through the steps. Ultimately, our team will also establish the performance metrics of interest in this particular benchmarking activity. Of course, at the end of the process the team will produce a report and recommendation based on the results of the benchmarking activity. We will want to consider the following activities:

- The primary focus of the study
- The purpose or purposes for the benchmark exercise
- The areas and subdivisions for which we will develop questions
- The number of questions we anticipate asking the target firm
- The decision about whether we will look at one or more companies
- The definition of our desired results

Benchmarking—Explore

How do we find our benchmarking market niche? We can either use a preliminary team or the actual benchmarking team of our own enterprise to put together a list of criteria that such a market niche would have to supply. Once we have a set of criteria, we can begin to search for probable partners for doing whatever we want to do better than we do it. If we do not look for partners who do the job better than we do it, then we will simply regress to the mean. The goal during benchmarking is to improve our own processes by either meeting a higher standard based on the benchmark of the market niche or by exceeding that standard.

A simple method for selecting partners out of the pool of partners is to use the approach pioneered by Stuart Pugh. We list our potential partners across the top of the table, establishing column headers. We list our criteria down the first column, creating row names. Once we have constructed this matrix, we can evaluate the criteria against each enterprise using numerical measures, minus or plus signs, or any other character that will indicate the value of our assessment.

Once we have selected our candidate partners, the next logical step is to go ahead and establish communications with these companies. In the case where we are looking at companies outside of our own market, it is less likely that these companies will deny a request for benchmarking. Hence, using noncompetitive partners increases the probability of acceptance of our proposition on their side.

The possibility also exists that by using noncompetitive partners we may be able to more easily implement with our own employees.

Benchmarking—Discover

The benchmarking team will also need to look at our own enterprise. One of the things they need to accomplish is an assessment of what we need to know. Once the team is aware of what they need to know, they can begin to look for resources for this information.

Once the team has catalogued the resources for the necessary information, they can select the methods for access. In addition to that, they will also want to select a tool that allows them to not only store this information but to also retrieve it. This concept suggests the need for a database. Such a database often becomes a bone of contention for several reasons:

- Purely textual databases are inefficient
- We need a good selection of search terms if we use a relational database
- Access should be defined for this source of information
- The underlying database product (e.g., open source, commercial, hybrid, relational, hierarchical, network, object-oriented)

Once we have established the database, which we will use for the benchmarking effort, we can begin to collect data (see Figure 6.1). We will collect data from our own enterprise in order to create a baseline of information against which to compare our benchmarking partners. Once we know our own information, we can go to our partners, with whom we have secured permission, and we begin to collect information about their superior process. When we have completed all of our information and data collection, we then organize this information and we perform some kind of reflective practice; for example, we could do an after action review or a debriefing.

Let's look at some potential questions:

- What are your organization's major market segments?
- How many people are employed by your organization?
- How are they divided amongst the market segments?
- Where are the X and Y departments located within the structure of the organization?
- Describe how X department leadership coordinates with the Y and Z departments and other business units (of course, we ask if they have such a situation!).
- To what extent does the X department leadership and the Y department group collaborate and cooperate? Do they have a collegial ambience?

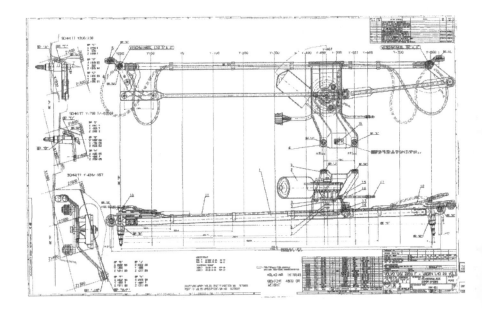

Figure 6.1 Drawing of a wiper system; we can save money even with simple systems.

- To what extent do staffs from the business units and department X collaborate and cooperate? What is their level of collegiality?

- What is the name of your process?

- What method do you use in investigating business processes?

- What method do you use in deriving and developing system requirements?

- Is documentation for this process available and is it available to us?

- Who "owns" this process? (Department or business unit.)

- How do you determine the scope?

- In what scenarios does this process apply?

- How do you acquire information (e.g., surveys, questionnaires, interviews, etc.)?

- How do you align these requirements analyses to your business processes?

- Do you have an explicit and overt approach methodology for eliciting, documenting, and validating requirements and what is it (what are they)?

- Which stakeholders are involved?

- What standards do you apply in classifying requirements? In short, how do you bring in regulatory requirements?

- How long have you executed this process?

- Why did your organization choose this process?
- What were your principal goals in adopting this process?
- What skills used in the process need to function effectively?
- How did you receive executive support for choosing your process?
- What was the business case for choosing this process?
- What skills did staff involved in the process need to function effectively? How did you ensure that staff had those skills?
- What obstacles did you face in implementing your process?
- What kind of results have you experienced with this process?
- Describe your organization's outcomes with this process.
- What are your process strengths?
- What are your process weaknesses?
- How is your enterprise dealing with these lapses?
- What facets of the process work well and why?
- What facets of the process are problematic and why?
- Is there anything you would like to change about your process?

Benchmarking—Evaluate

At this stage, we have stored our information in some kind of bucket, preferably a database. At this point, we can support our information by type or category or we could do something a little more sophisticated and take a look at what we have using database cross tabulation. Cross tabulation allows us to look at summary tables based on our information that may show us unexpected results.

As we poured information into our database, we should already have taken steps to verify that we have good quality information. In some cases, we may have had different people document the same process to determine what was the same and what was different; that is, to compare and contrast. Another item of concern lies with something we might call factors that are peculiar to specific partners. These factors need to be removed or at least understood before we move on. Of course, as we are performing our deep analysis, we are looking for gaps between our enterprise and those of our partners. Another place to look for gaps is between partners. It is possible that one partner may have a stellar subprocess that merits more profound investigation. In short, we wish to establish the causes for these apparent performance gaps.

Benchmarking—Accommodate

Once the team has finished a deep enough analysis that decision can be made, they will identify opportunities for improvement for each partner practice that is clearly superior in performance to what our own enterprise is doing. Having a list of opportunities allows us to set targets: either targets equal to the benchmark or targets better than the benchmark. This phase also requires an implementation plan for each improvement. Part of the reason for using a plan aside from the obvious benefits of more efficient way accomplishing our goals, is the documentation we yield by so doing.

Obviously, once we have an implementation plan we move to execute that plan and use frequent feedback to assure ourselves we are meeting our targets. Depending on the profundity of the modifications to our own price, the monitoring and status updates should be sufficiently frequent that deviations from plan are minimal. Of course, if we discover a defect in the plan, we will make the appropriate corrections and resume our control cycles. Finally, the team will generate a report. Our only question at this point will be whether we wait long enough to ensure that our new process is actually an improvement or whether we issue a follow-up report at some later date.

Benchmarking—Reclaim

If the leadership of our enterprise is visionary, they will have chosen to make benchmarking an ongoing process. That decision suggests that we will modify our benchmarks upwards as our own practice evolves. We may conduct more benchmarking studies in the same market niche or we may choose to look further afield to find other options and increase the opportunities for cross-pollination.

Not only do we continue benchmarking, but we can also look at the benchmarking process as yet another process that is a candidate for improvement. We can either use benchmarking itself as a tool to improve our own benchmarking or we can use other tools to accomplish the same goal (e.g., Six Sigma, lean, FAST, etc.).

Benchmarking—Ethics and Morals

All the time we are benchmarking, we need to ensure that all of our actions are entirely above-board and legal. If even the slightest taint pertains to any potential action, we are far better off eliminating that action rather than walking the fine edge between the illicit and the licit.

We anticipate that a key artifact in a partner relationship will be some kind of nondisclosure agreement. Even if our partners are not in the same market in which we play, they will nonetheless maintain trade secrets. In some cases, we will want to clarify with our partners exactly what we are allowed to coopt for our own use and what remains under their stewardship. It goes without saying that any release of information from our benchmarking efforts to any kind of third-party, including another partner, is simply unacceptable. It also makes sense that if we are deriving a benefit from a partner, then we might also provide some information of our own to our partner companies. We may even find situations where we can respectfully make recommendations regarding their already superior processes.

Clearly, the goal is to clarify the expectations of all parties, eliminate misunderstandings, and ensure privacy. Each of our actions, then, must be honest and completely open. Even our participation in a benchmarking relationship should remain a confidential matter. At no point should we use the fact that we have benchmarked ourselves against a set of worthy partners as a marketing item.

As with all projects, even though both sides may have teams, single points of contact should be established from the start of the benchmarking effort. Having a single point of contact is a reasonably effective method for controlling the flow of information.

Since the processes of our partners are essentially better than our own processes, it makes sense that we behave respectfully toward our partners, including their corporate cultures. For example, suppose we had chosen Federal Express and the U.S. Postal Service. We cannot expect that the cultures of these two organizations are going to be identical or even similar. Yet each organization may have something to offer by way of paper management or logistics or some other critical competence they possess.

In many cases, it may make sense to actually sign a contract with our partners. The contract will explicitly define the scope of activities as well as the limits to communication.

As we go into the facilities of our partners, we should be able to demonstrate a significant level of preparedness. We do not want to waste our time or their time during this process. The partner should also receive any audit documentation that we are going to use during our inspection of their processes: checklist, questionnaires, surveys, and interview guides.

Any commitment that we make to a benchmarking partner, regardless of whether we have a contract with them, should be followed through completely. Any deviation from this ethical goal must be communicated clearly and openly. We must treat our partners as well or better than we treat ourselves. That alone is a huge compliment of benchmarking success.

As with teardowns, some readers may have ethical qualms regarding the use of benchmarking. We should note that in every case we have solicited agreement from our benchmarking partners. These permissions are a key difference between benchmarking and executing a teardown. When we do teardowns, we solicit the permission of nobody. In either case, we are looking for inspiration rather than directly copying the work of somebody else. Just knowing that another group has found a new way to do something may be enough to ignite our own imaginations.

One of the most important things we want to avoid when doing either teardowns or benchmarking is something called regression to the mean. Sir Francis Galton did not choose the word "regression" because he thought it sounded nice. The term is used pejoratively, as a kind of mathematical put-down. Hence, we are trying to grow our product and processes beyond what we see in an teardown or a benchmarking exercise. In the case of benchmarking, we may choose to inform our benchmarking partners of what we did with the inspiration they provided.

We want to remember while benchmarking, that we are not only improving a product or process, but we are also executing value engineering. Consequently, we want ensure that when we present our results and when we make our initial proposal, that we include potential savings and estimates of market value increase. Benchmarking is nonclassical value engineering. With Six Sigma projects, we often came under fire from managers who said "What you do is not a Six Sigma project." We do not care: our purpose is to improve our profit. In essence, then, we are pursuing a pragmatic form of value engineering. As long as we are saving money, we are doing our job— meaning, we also have no negative events attached to any of our value engineering activities (for example, a recall or increased cost of quality).

V. EXERCISES

- How do we avoid letting benchmarking drive us towards mediocrity? Propose a solution to this conundrum.

- Pick a noncompeting firm and create a plan that will drive a process within your own firm to new levels of efficiency and effectiveness.

- Create a presentation that indicates how you will merge your benchmarking plan with other cost reduction initiatives.

- Propose an ethical approach to benchmarking our processes against a competitor. How would you communicate with the other company?

- Put together a short brief on how you make a recommendation for improvement to a partner company.

- Discuss at what point the number of questions is likely to become burdensome for the partner company to answer. Can you find some research to support your statements?

- A look at the questions we have in our text shows how involved the benchmarking process can be and we do not particularly consider these to be low-level questions. How deeply do you go? Write a discrete continuum of five statements from high level to low level that define your purpose.

- How much statistical work is involved in a benchmarking analysis?

- Which departments in your enterprise are most likely to benchmark and why?

- Does it make more sense to select people from different departments to improve diversity and increase the chance of cross-pollination?

- How will you speak with at the target company? Explain how you would achieve some level of diversity with the partner.

- Define an appropriate time to *return* to the target company to see if any changes or improvements have occurred. Describe the steps to achieve permission to do so.

- Research the World Wide Web to ascertain if "boilerplate" templates exist for setting up a benchmarking exercise. If you cannot find such a template, invent at least an outline and explain your rationale.

- How often should the benchmarking team meet?

- For how long should the benchmarking team meet?

- Choose a partner company. Analyze their structure and construct a map of the interrelationships of the various pieces. Dive into, at a minimum, the business unit level. If divisional or departmental information is available, consider using this data also.

- Evaluate the financial standing of the target company chosen in the previous exercise. What numbers will you look at? What numbers will tell you whether you are looking at a good candidate?

- What Web 2.0 tools can help in this exercise? For example, experiment with an online mindmapping tool such as MindMeister.

- Can we speed up the survey process by using online survey tools? Consider what it would take to use SurveyMonkey, a free-to-use online tool.

- Explain how you would use wiki technology to accelerate your benchmarking process and make it easier for your partner to participate.

- Prepare a proposal that demonstrates how working within the "cloud" will be to the benefit of our brother benchmarker and target company.

- Examine the www.zoho.com Web site and see which tools would be relevant to a benchmarking exercise

ENDNOTES

1. Andersen, Bjorn, and Per-Gaute Pettersen. *The Benchmarking Handbook: Step-by-Step Instructions*. London, UK: Chapman & Hall, 1996.

CHAPTER 7 – Classical Techniques

I. Rubric for the FAST Approach

Criteria	Level 1 (50–59%)	Level 2 (60–69%)	Level 3 (70–79%)	Level 4 (80–100%)
Analyze concepts	Analysis of concepts results in conclusions with limited factual support	Analysis of concepts results in conclusions with some factual support	Analysis of concepts results in conclusions with considerable factual support	Analysis of concepts results in conclusions with thorough factual support
Analyze concepts providing details	Analysis of concepts provides limited details	Analysis of concepts provides some details	Analysis of concepts provides considerable details	Analysis of concepts provides thorough details
Analyze given scenario	Analysis of given scenario provides limited insight	Analysis of given scenario provides some insight	Analysis of given scenario provides considerable insight	Analysis of given scenario provides thorough insight
Assess research information	Assessment of research information demonstrates limited use of criteria	Assessment of research information demonstrates some use of criteria	Assessment of research information demonstrates considerable use of criteria	Assessment of research information demonstrates thorough use of criteria
Communicate information about four types of vital signs	Communicates information about the supporting functions with limited clarity	Communicates information about the supporting functions with some clarity	Communicates information about the supporting functions with considerable clarity	Communicates information about the supporting functions with a high degree of clarity
Communicate information accurately	Communicates information with limited accuracy	Communicates information with some accuracy	Communicates information with considerable accuracy	Communicates information with a high level of accuracy
Communicate information clearly	Communicates information with limited clarity	Communicates information with some clarity	Communicates information with considerable clarity	Communicates information with a high degree of clarity
Communicate information effectively	Communicates information with limited effectiveness	Communicates information with some effectiveness	Communicates information with considerable effectiveness	Communicates information with a high degree of effectiveness
Communicate information using an appropriate format	Demonstrates limited ability to communicate information using an appropriate format	Demonstrates some ability to communicate information using an appropriate format	Demonstrates considerable ability to communicate information using an appropriate format	Demonstrates a high level of ability to communicate information using an appropriate format

Communicate information using appropriate style	Demonstrates limited ability to communicate information using appropriate style	Demonstrates some ability to communicate information using appropriate style	Demonstrates considerable ability to communicate information using appropriate style	Demonstrates a high level of ability to communicate information using appropriate style
Communicate information using technology	Communicates information demonstrating limited use of technology	Communicates information demonstrating some use of technology	Communicates information demonstrating considerable use of technology	Communicates information demonstrating expert use of technology

II. Questions to Ponder

- What value analysis/value engineering methods preceded Six Sigma, Lean Six Sigma, and lean manufacturing?
- After studying this approach, does it seem useful?
- What kind of tool can we use to build these diagrams?
- Do we have to use the diagrammatic format?
- How many styles of diagram exist for the functional analysis system technique (FAST)?
- Where can I find more information on FAST?
- When did this kind of value analysis/value engineering commence?
- Is the language usage in this kind of approach useful? Does it really reduce ambiguity or just make things worse?
- How far can we go to reduce ambiguity and why?
- How do we calculate the dollar (euro) value of the cost savings?

III. Cost Improvement Scenario

A. Situation

This particular company used screws to hold their housing together. Screws are difficult on the manufacturing line because they require a special driver as well as a feeder for the screws and we always have the risk of stripping the threads when we tap out the plastic.

B. Objective

Attempt to eliminate as many screws as possible and use clamping as a substitute.

C. Action

The engineers reviewed the design and worked with the customer, since the customer had required the screws in the first place. Negotiations went back and forth and had no end in sight until the supplier offered to share the cost reduction with the customer (sweetening the deal!).

D. Results

Clamps were introduced on the mating portions of the plastic housings and screws were 80% reduced out of the design, significantly simplifying assembly.

E. Aftermath

The reliability engineering group observed no significant increases in returns over a period of several years, suggesting that this change was a robust improvement.

IV. FAST Introduction

FAST[1] is an acronym for functional analysis system technique. FAST allows us to reduce ambiguity in the definition of a functional product or a functional process (and probably for some dysfunctional one also!). Different customers interpret value of a product differently. Characteristics that are common to value are high level performance, capability, emotional appeal, and style relative to its cost (see Figure 7.9). Value is generally expressed in terms of maximizing the function of a product relative to its cost:

Value = (Performance + Capability)/Cost
Value = Function/Cost

Value is not about minimizing cost. Though, for some cases, we can influence the value of a product by increasing its function (performance or capability) and cost as long as the added function increases more quickly than its added cost. The concept of functional worth is important, which is, the lowest cost to provide a given function.

Lawrence D. Miles[2] is the father of modern value analysis and value engineering. His first key concept was the idea of "use function." A product could have use functions or aesthetic functions. Use functions require an action to occur while aesthetic functions please the end customer.

Miles identified three steps related to initial investigation into functions:

1. Identification

2. Clarification

3. Naming

He required functions to be stated in exact sentences. In order to make the process ostensibly simpler, he required a verb and a noun, producing short phrases that look like miniature sentences written in the imperative mood. For example, we might use:

1. Generate torque

2. Control vibration

3. Fasten panel

4. Bill customer

The first example is particularly valuable because we can measure torque with appropriate devices, which suggests that we want to choose nouns we can measure, for example:

1. Volts

2. Amperes

3. Ohms

4. Length (metric or English)

Any scalar value is a good candidate for a functional noun and simplifies the process of measuring cost. Verbs must be precise and describe an action, making the exercise more difficult than it might appear at first glance. With FAST, all functions must be in the verb–noun format (see Figure 7.1).

Miles's second key concept was that of the aesthetic function. Aesthetic functions are specified the same way we specify use functions. For example:

1. Reduce noise

2. Improve visibility (might also be a use function)

3. Minimize duration (in other words, reduce time it takes)

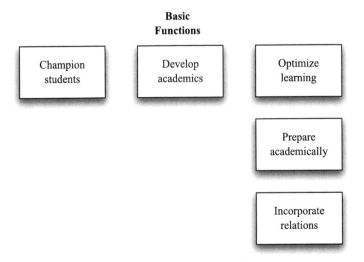

Figure 7.1 Use of verb–noun becomes quite difficult as we dig more deeply.

With both use functions and aesthetic functions, we provide that for which the customer is willing to pay. We might guess that we have some cost opportunities in the aesthetic area, with higher end automobiles being an example of aesthetic function for profit.

Miles also identified the concept of basic and secondary functions. Basic functions are the fundamental reason the customer is willing to buy the product or service. The basic function of an automobile is to transport the customer. The basic function of a shoe is to "protect foot." Secondary functions are those functions for which the designer has the flexibility to find an effective solution. A secondary function supports the basic function. Miles discovered that secondary functions are often a huge component of the total cost of the product.

A simple plan for proceeding through the Miles approach is as follows:

1. Separate the functions (we can use a spreadsheet format to capture our preliminary ideas).

2. Work and rework the two-word descriptions with particular attention being paid to those we might be able to measure.

3. Analyze each function for methods, materials, measurements, manpower, and machines as well as environmental considerations.

4. We can build an Ishikawa diagram for each function. The depth of labor we put into this project will be dependent on the expected cost savings.

5. Estimate the cost of each function.

6. Rollup the costs of the functions to calculate an overall cost for the product or service.

7. Prepare work in a spreadsheet format for cost comparisons.

8. Be patient and diligent.

Miles also recognized that a given product or service might have functions that are dependent on other functions. The solution approach chosen here was list the functions in an appropriate order, which is easy to say and often difficult to execute.

1. Evaluate each function as if it were a simple function.

2. Move on to a dependent function and continue to evaluate.

3. Complete the list by following the logic of the dependencies.

Miles was also highly concerned with accurate cost analyses of products and services. He suggested that function-property relationship (e.g., nomograms and other plots of performance) were readily available to designers. Usually the designer could also find the property-material relationships as well (e.g., tensile strength). Some catalogues provide material-cost information. He declared that we could then work our way back to functional cost from the material cost information.

Finally, Miles stated that costs were really based on comparisons, since "value" is an ambiguous term with no absolute measure. This concept implies that we must understand what is valuable to the customer. In some cases, the aesthetics may be of more importance to a given customer (e.g., they might like the way the painting looks in their house). In cases where the end customer does not see the product, the aesthetics of the product may have minimal importance.

Miles provides a straightforward algorithm for working through the value analysis problem, using the following steps:

1. Identify the functions.

2. Separate functions.

   a. Start with the total or basic function.

   b. Proceed to subconcepts.

3. Group functions into assemblies with well-defined purposes (somewhat similar to what we do when we create an affinity diagram).

4. Recognize the problem at hand.

5. Capture required information (e.g., materials cost).

6. Explore new solutions creatively.

7. Select the best choices, with especial attention on cost.

8. Assess the disadvantages of the best solutions and minimize these, much as we do with robust design.

9. Execute the new set of improved solutions.

10. Eliminate any "show stoppers."

11. Push the project to a decisive conclusion.

Miles used the term "results accelerators," which included:

1. Information from the best source.

2. Dropping of assumptions sufficient to annihilate preconceptions and permit real refinement.

3. Use real creativity rather than copying the previous solution or only "tweaking" the previous solution.

4. Push through "show stoppers."

5. Feel free to use industry specialists (e.g., supplier experts, customer experts, consultants, and contractors).

6. All tolerances should have a cost associated with them (once again, this relates well with robust engineering, where tolerance design occurs at the end of the process).

7. If commercial off-the-shelf products meet the requirements, then use them.

8. Be willing to pay the supplier for their knowledge; after all, they are then functioning as a consultant to our firm.

9. Use the appropriate standards—it makes no sense to ignore a standard and lose money subsequently because we must recall the existing product and redesign the product and production process.

10. Personalize the spending; after all, money spent on wasted time is money that will not be used for a bonus, profit sharing, or any other reward system.

Miles's concepts were brilliant and provided the underpinning for the functional analysis system technique. Snodgrass and Kasi[3] provided further theorizing on the approach. Other individuals have contributed to the body of knowledge related to FAST: Charles Blytheway (Sperry Corporation), Wayne Ruggles (Value Analysis, Inc.), and Theodore Fowler (Value Standards, Incorporated).

Snodgrass and Kasi broke their process into discrete phases:

1. Information

2. Creativity

3. Evaluation

4. Planning

5. Implementation

As with Miles, Snodgrass and Kasi realized that a large part of the problem with our products and services lay within the way people coded their expectations of the functionality of the product or service. They used the same verb–noun concept

Figure 7.2 The first description of what they do is often the most difficult.

proposed by Miles. One of their epiphanies occurred when they realized that users of a product often do not understand the constraints of the product. Again, agreeing with the insight of Miles, they felt that the key concept was the determination in unambiguous terminology of exactly what a product/service was supposed to do.

We can take a look at function identification, which may be the single most difficult step in the process of determining exactly what the product is supposed to do. One issue lies with assumptions that a given function or group of functions must be present, much like the situation with human beings—they do not pay a doctor for a prescription; they pay the doctor in order to feel better. These kinds of assumptions can become limiting concepts; that is, they are illusory constraints. An example of this issue in school counseling occurs when we try to define what a counselor does.

- Do they provide psychotherapy for students?

- Do they reassign students to different classes?

- Do they inform students of poor scholastic performance?

- We suggest that the counselor's basic function is to "champion students" even though this sounds like hand waving (see Figure 7.2).

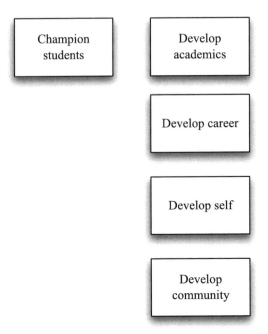

Figure 7.3 Adding the basic functions is nearly as difficult as deciding on the high-level function.

As we define secondary functions, they will explain how we champion students. We will use the counselor example to illustrate how to construct a FAST diagram;

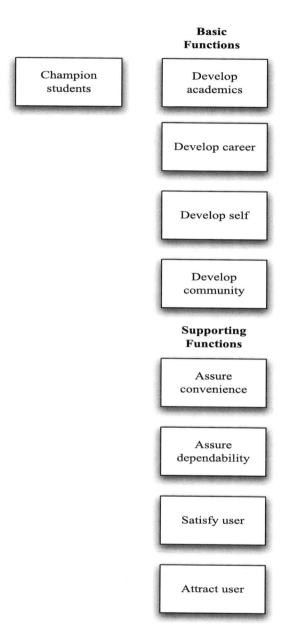

Figure 7.4 The supporting functions may be hard to tie in with the reality.

however, if we were doing a value analysis, we would analyze a specific product.

We can take our identified functions and define them in terms of types. We can define "use functions" as with Miles and we might also define "aesthetic functions," also as with Miles. An alternative form would be "work" and "sell" functions, but the relationship is largely the same as with Miles. Arthur Mudge indicated that work functions use the verb–noun description and that sell functions use passive-verbs/immeasurable-nouns (qualitative descriptions). Snodgrass broke things down into the "task" which, in turn, had primary functions and supporting functions. Supporting functions could be one of four types:

- Assuring convenience

- Assuring dependability

- Satisfying the user or customer

- Attracting the user or customer

Ultimately, it was Blytheway who created what we now know as a FAST diagram, with the "why" of the product or service appearing as we go left on the horizontal diagram and the "how" as we go to the right. Some diagrams show causation in the sense of "when," by using the vertical axis

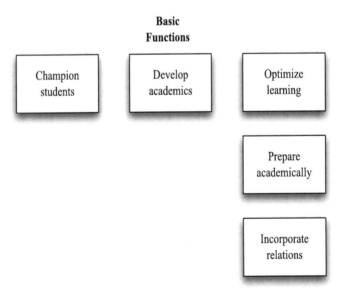

Figure 7.5 Use of verb–noun becomes quite difficult as we dig more deeply.

V. Creating a FAST Model

The FAST model has a horizontal directional orientation described as the how-why dimension. This dimension is described in this manner because how and why questions are raised to structure the logic of the system's functions. Starting with how a function is performed, helps in developing a more specific approach. This line of questioning and thinking is read from left to right (see Figure 7.3).

To abstract the problem to a higher level, *why* questions are raised and are read from right to left. First, the best way to undertake a task is to begin with the goals of the task, then going back to exploring the methods to attain the goals. When the FAST model is used to address any function with the question *why*, the function to its left expresses the goal of that function. The question *how*, is resolved by the function on the right, and is a method to perform that function being addressed. A systems diagram starts at the beginning of the system and ends with its goal (see Figure 7.3). A FAST model, reading from left to right, starts with the goal, and ends at the beginning of the "system" that will achieve that goal.

Second, changing a function on the *how-why* path affects all of the functions to the right of that function. This is a domino effect that only goes one way, from left to right. Starting with any place on the FAST model, if a function is changed the goals are still valid (functions to the left), but the method to accomplish that function, and all other functions on the right, will be affected.

Finally, building the model in the *how* direction, or function justification, will focus the attention on each function element of the model (see Figure 7.4). Whereas, reversing the FAST model and building it in its system orientation will cause the team to leap over individual functions and focus on the system, leaving function "gaps" in the system. One rule to remember is while constructing a FAST model build in the *how*

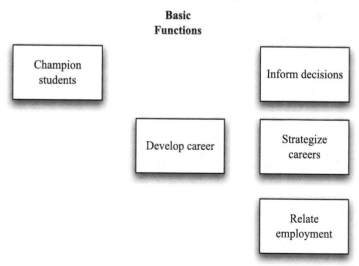

**Basic
Functions**

Champion
students

Inform decisions

Develop career

Strategize
careers

Relate
employment

Figure 7.6 We expand our analysis of the counseling activity.

Basic Functions

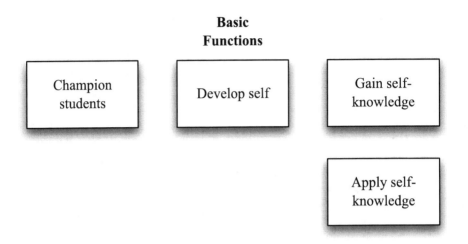

Figure 7.7 We continue our development of the prototype FAST diagram.

direction also test the logic in the *why* direction (see Figure 7.1 and Figure 7.6).

The vertical orientation of the FAST model is described as the *when* direction. This is not part of the intuitive logic process, but enhances the intuitive thinking process. We should note that *when* indicates cause and effect and does not represent time orientation.

Boundaries of the study are represented by the scope lines and are visible as two vertical lines on the FAST model. The scope lines bound the "scope of the study," or that aspect of the problem with which the study team is concerned. The left scope line determines the basic function(s) of the study. The basic functions will always be the first functions to the immediate right of the left scope line. The right scope line identifies the beginning of the study and separates the input function(s from the scope of the study.

The objective or goal of the study is the "highest order function," located to the left of the basic function(s and outside of the left scope line. Any function to the left of another function is a "higher order function." Functions to the right and outside of the right scope line represent the input side that "turn on" or initiate the subject under study and are known as lowest order functions. Any function to the right of another function is a "lower order" function and represents a method selected to carry out the function being addressed.

Functions that are to the immediate right of the left scope line represent the purpose or mission of the product or process under study and are called "basic functions." The basic function will not change once it has been determined. If the basic function fails, the product or process will lose its market value. All functions to the right of the basic functions portray the conceptual approach selected to satisfy the basic function.

The concept describes the method being considered, or elected, to achieve the basic function(s).

The concept either represents the current conditions (as is) or proposed approach (to be). It is always good to create a "to be" rather than an "as is" FAST model, even if the assignment is to improve an existing product. The "to-be" approach provides an opportunity to compare the ideal product to the current product, and thus resolves questions on how to implement the differences.

An "as is" model will limit the team's attention to incremental improvement opportunities. To trace the symptoms of a problem to its root cause and to explore the ways to resolve a problem, an "as is" model is extremely useful. It is useful because of the dependent relationship of functions that form the FAST model.

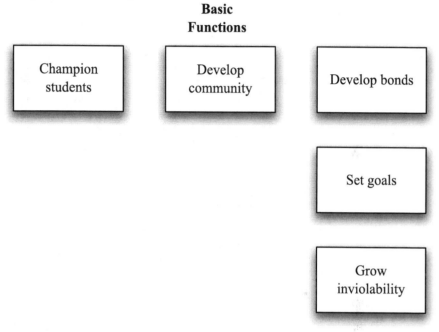

Basic Functions

Champion students

Develop community

Develop bonds

Set goals

Grow inviolability

Figure 7.8 The process becomes a little easier once we have some practice converting to verb–noun statements.

Any function on the *how-why* logic path is a logic path function. If the functions along the *why* direction lead into the basic functions, then they are located on the major logic path. If the *why* path does not lead directly to the basic function, it is a minor logic path.

Changing a function on the major logic path will alter or destroy the way the basic function is performed. Changing a function on a minor logic path will disturb an independent (supporting) function that enhances the basic function. Supporting functions are usually secondary and exist to achieve the performance levels specified in the objectives or specifications of the basic functions or because a particular approach was chosen to implement the basic functions.

Independent functions describe enhancements of a function located on the logic path. They do not depend on another function selected to perform that function. Independent functions are located above the logic path function(s), and are considered secondary, with respect to the scope, nature, level of the problem, and its logic path.

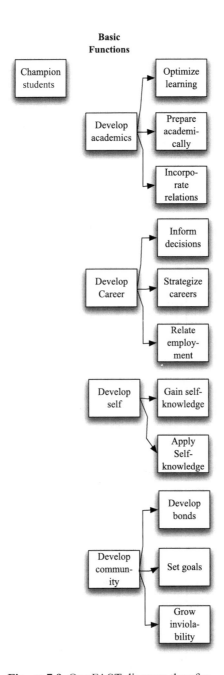

Figure 7.9 Our FAST diagram thus far.

Let's take a look at our "school counselor" example. We will walk through the stages of developing the FAST diagram as well as adding some commentary to make it clear why we made the decisions we made. Our first step is to define the highest order function, which we consider to be "champion students." All other functions will be subordinate to this high order function.

We can take a hint for the next step by looking at the American School Counselor Association (ASCA) national model, with some minor modifications:

In Figure 7.4, we added the Snodgrass-style supporting functions to the basic functions, which in turn, are subordinate to the high-order function. What we have is some difficulty aligning the counseling concepts as we understand them with the standard Snodgrass nomenclature. We would like to note that we are using the ASCA Standard National Model as a basis for our example and any failures in interpretation belong to us! We have changed some of the wording to reflect the demand for the verb–noun approach.

The noun–verb requirement cramps our style, as well it should. The entire purpose of this approach is to flush out the fluffy language often used in ambiguous descriptions. Do not take this comment as a condemnation of the national standard. We are building a FAST model, not critiquing the ASCA model!

Using the verb–noun format and endeavoring to eliminate ambiguity is a huge component of the FAST effort. These actions are very similar to the difficulties we run into when writing a requirements specification (if we are the writer) and deciphering the requirement specification (if we are the supplier or contractor). We think the exercise is worth the effort. The "verb–noun" approach was a major insight by Lawrence Miles and provides us with a tool and a filter for the removal of indeterminacy in our use of language.

The way we present this example is but one formulation of the FAST approach. In some diagrams, we will see a critical path identified that takes off horizontally from the basic function. We are trying to avoid producing a simple hierarchy chart of supporting functions because that is not really what a FAST diagram is designed to be. We will continue our analysis.

School counselors still provide career guidance to students, much as they did in the days when they were known as "vocational counselors." Of course, term "vocational" comes from the Latin word for "calling."

We took the national model idea of social skills and came up with "develop community" which is not quite the same thing. However, we must align with the verb–noun requirements and that is one way to do that.

In Figure 7.9, we can see how our diagram is developing. The next step will involve developing each box further to the right as we more carefully explicate the "how" of each "why." As we indicated, we are not building a hierarchy chart of derived behaviors. Consider for a moment the difficulty of the exercise. In this example, we are dealing with a topic that we see described most often in qualitative terms. We also see this in the verb–noun boxes we have developed so far. The ideal is to come up with nouns that we can measure; however, it may not always be the case that we can easily find a way to achieve measurable results. We should have no bias towards qualitative data. One example of the benefits of qualitative approaches is the Kastle-

Meyer test for blood, which is an extremely quick test conducted with phenolphthalein and hydrogen peroxide and which only tells us whether the brown substance is blood or not. If not, we presumably waste no more time on the sample; if yes, we move on to the next step. We can construct our FAST diagrams, at least in part, with high-value qualitative information with no shame. Our goal is comprehension, especially in the case of cost reductions. We are not performing this exercise as some kind of religious ritual that allows for little or no latitude in performance. On the other hand, we do not want to completely obliterate the spirit of the technique. We recommend that the practitioner proceed with sound judgment and work through his or her own FAST diagram more than once and also submit it for review by peers and others.

If we take a look at Figure 7.10, we see the continuation of "optimize learning" as

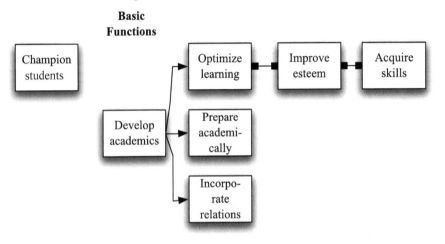

Figure 7.10 We begin to deepen our concepts.

we break that particular thread into components further defining the "how." We can go as far to the right as makes sense until we reach some point, perhaps, where we have an "assumed" function. We really only cared about those functions we can derive as "hows," and in the other direction, those functions we can derive as "whys."

What about our supporting functions? Figure 7.11 shows how we have expanded on the supporting functions recommended by Snodgrass. We think the expansion makes reasonable sense. Some FAST diagrams will never show much expansion of the supporting functions, but we think this approach adds more information and, hence, supplies value to the user. Office accessibility, feedback, training, and safe havens are items we can measure quantitatively. As we mentioned, a basic function dealing with self-development may have to use qualitative values. Either way, we learn more about our school counselor function.

We could continue this exercise to even deeper levels, but we suspect the example has presented most of what we need to know about FAST diagrams. The Snodgrass and Kasi book is available as of this writing at http://wendt.library.wisc.edu/miles/milesvestudies.html. It is free to download and represents a complete analysis of how

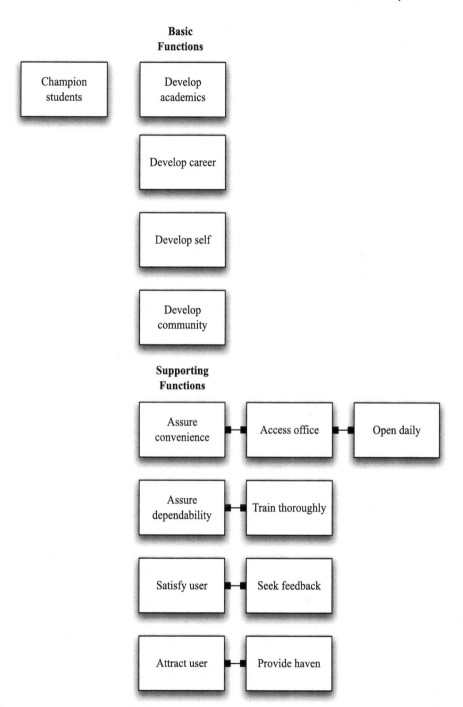

Figure 7.11 We see in this figure how the supporting functions can be developed.

a standard FAST diagram would be constructed. We also recommend a free download of Lawrence Miles's book *Techniques of Value and Analysis and Engineering* at http://wendt.library.wisc.edu/miles/milesbook.html. The Miles book is more than 350 pages in length, and it contains many examples as well as Miles's particular approaches to problem solving. Because of the soundness of the reasoning in both books, they remain current; they are also current because the ideas contained therein are timeless. Additional papers by Miles and others can also be found at the Wendt library Web site at the University of Wisconsin at Madison. While other practitioners tout Six Sigma, Six Sigma Lean, and lean manufacturing (as do we), these works are exceptional in their clarity, logical thinking, well-ground methodologies, and power to effect financial improvement.

VI. EXERCISES

- Choose a sample product such as a pencil or a cupcake and develop a FAST diagram to represent this product. Present your results.

- Is the FAST approach too complicated for regular use by individuals without substantial training?

- Can we derive benefits from questioning why our product has certain features?

- The FAST approach is often used to achieve cost reductions by removing unnecessary or obsolete features. How would we use the FAST approach to add new features that may result in increased sales but do not really yield a cost reduction?

- Do the original design documents present any value for product analysis?

- Can we use the FAST technique with processes? Provide at last five example processes.

- In fact, can we use the FAST technique to analyze the FAST technique? Explain how this would be done and support your answer with an example.

- If the FAST technique is so good, why do not we use it all the time? In fact, why do we not use it during requirements analysis?

- How does FAST relate to regulatory requirements? If the FAST analysis indicates the regulatory requirement has no meaning, how would we handle this situation?

- How high a level can we use the FAST approach? For example, would we use it to analyze the purpose and costs of a battleship or an aircraft carrier?

- How low a level might we go to analyze a given product? Where do we stop? Explain your criteria.

- Is the FAST technique itself sufficient documentation to implement a product change?

- If the FAST technique does not provide sufficient documentation to proceed with the change, what other documentation do we need?

- How do we maintain configuration management of a FAST analysis?

- Using the Internet, search for software tools that specifically support FAST analysis. Be prepared to produce a short presentation to your peers that describes the benefits and costs of using such a tool.

- If no tools available for FAST analysis, how would we convert an existing tool to support this methodology?

- We have seen the FAST technique used to support a more logical approach to the creation of a failure mode and effects analysis. How can we do this?

- How would we use FAST with Six Sigma, Lean Six Sigma, and lean manufacturing in a hybrid approach? Specify the phase or phases of these methodologies where we could use the FAST technique.

- Write a two-page essay describing how we might use FAST to improve the project management process.

- Is it possible to use FAST with controversial topics? For example, what would be the verb–noun substitute for the word "marriage?" How about "abortion?" (Yes, these are emotional terms.) Can we remove the emotional overtones of any of these terms or are they so shrouded with position-taking, religious viewpoints and philosophy that we have no hope of ever coming to the table with some rational definitions?

ENDNOTES

1. Crow, Kenneth. "(1) Value Analysis and Function Analysis System Technique." *New Product Development Solutions*. Last modified 2002. Accessed November 23, 2011. http://www.npd-solutions.com/va.html.

2. Miles, Lawrence D. *Techniques of Value Analysis and Engineering*, 3rd Edition. Washington, DC: Lawrence D. Miles Value Foundation., 1989.

3. Snodgrass, Thomas J., and Muthiah Kasi. *Function Analysis: The Stepping Stones to Good Value*. Madison, WI: University of Wisconsin, 1986.

CHAPTER 8 – Saving Money with Six Sigma Projects

I. Rubric for Six Sigma Projects

Criteria	Level 1 (50–59%)	Level 2 (60–69%)	Level 3 (70–79%)	Level 4 (80–100%)
Analyze measurements	Analysis of measurements demonstrates limited use of critical thinking	Analysis of measurements demonstrates some use of critical thinking	Analysis of measurements demonstrates considerable use of critical thinking	Analysis of measurements demonstrates thorough use of critical thinking
Apply designed experiments (DOE)	Applies DOE with limited success	Applies DOE with some success	Applies DOE with considerable success	Applies DOE with excellent success
Apply mathematical skills in a spreadsheet analysis for various tasks	Applies mathematical skills in a spreadsheet analysis for various tasks with limited accuracy	Applies mathematical skills in a spreadsheet analysis for various tasks with some accuracy	Applies mathematical skills in a spreadsheet analysis for various tasks with considerable accuracy	Applies mathematical skills in a spreadsheet analysis for various tasks with thorough accuracy
Apply the steps of the Six Sigma process	Applies the steps of the Six Sigma process with limited effectiveness	Applies the steps of the Six Sigma process with some effectiveness	Applies the steps of the Six Sigma process with considerable effectiveness	Applies the steps of the Six Sigma process with a high degree effectiveness
Choose the most appropriate production method by conducting a test run	Rarely chooses the most appropriate production method by conducting a test run	Sometimes chooses the most appropriate production method by conducting a test run	Often chooses the most appropriate production method by conducting a test run	Always or almost always chooses the most appropriate production method by conducting a test run
Communicate information effectively	Communicates information with limited effectiveness	Communicates information with some effectiveness	Communicates information with considerable effectiveness	Communicates information with a high degree of effectiveness
Conduct an accurate cost analysis of final product or process	Conducts an accurate cost analysis of final product or process with limited success	Conducts an accurate cost analysis of final product or process with some success	Conducts an accurate cost analysis of final product or process with considerable success	Conducts an accurate cost analysis of final product or process with excellent success
Create process control charts	Creates process control charts with limited clarity	Creates process control charts with some clarity	Creates process control charts with considerable clarity	Creates process control charts with excellent clarity
Demonstrate organizational skills with teams	Demonstrates limited organizational skills with teams	Demonstrates some organizational skills with teams	Demonstrates good organizational skills with teams	Demonstrates excellent organizational skills with teams
Demonstrate planning skills	Demonstrates limited planning skills	Demonstrates some planning skills	Demonstrates considerable planning skills	Demonstrates excellent planning skills
Describe conditioning processes that change physical and mechanical properties	Describes conditioning processes that change physical and mechanical properties with limited information and understanding	Describes conditioning processes that change physical and mechanical properties with some information and understanding	Describes conditioning processes that change physical and mechanical properties with considerable information and understanding	Describes conditioning processes that change physical and mechanical properties with thorough information and understanding

Criteria	Level 1 (50–59%)	Level 2 (60–69%)	Level 3 (70–79%)	Level 4 (80–100%)
Describe five major areas of a Six Sigma project (DMAIC or DMADV when using DFSS)	Description of five major areas of a Six Sigma project provides limited information	Description of five major areas of a Six Sigma project provides some information	Description of five major areas of a Six Sigma project provides considerable information	Description of five major areas of a Six Sigma project provides thorough information
Describe how to optimize productions systems	Description of how to optimize productions systems provides limited information	Description of how to optimize productions systems provides some information	Description of how to optimize productions systems provides considerable information	Description of how to optimize productions systems provides thorough information
Develop a bill of material that indicates specifications and quantity	Develops a bill of material that indicates specifications and quantity with limited clarity	Develops a bill of material that indicates specifications and quantity with some clarity	Develops a bill of material that indicates specifications and quantity with considerable clarity	Develops a bill of material that indicates specifications and quantity with excellent clarity
Develop a line organization chart	Develops a line organization chart with limited effectiveness	Develops a line organization chart with some effectiveness	Develops a line organization chart with considerable effectiveness	Develops a line organization chart with a high degree of effectiveness
Develop an appropriate flow chart for major areas of activity	Develops an appropriate flow chart for major areas of activity providing limited detail	Develops an appropriate flow chart for major areas of activity providing some detail	Develops an appropriate flow chart for major areas of activity providing considerable detail	Develops an appropriate flow chart for major areas of activity providing thorough detail
Develop engineering reports that communicate specifics of the product or process	Develops engineering reports that communicate specifics of the product or process with limited effectiveness	Develops engineering reports that communicate specifics of the product or process with some effectiveness	Develops engineering reports that communicate specifics of the product or process with considerable effectiveness	Develops engineering reports that communicate specifics of the product or process with excellent effectiveness
Evaluate information using supporting factual details	Evaluates information using few supporting factual details	Evaluates information using some supporting factual details	Evaluates information using many supporting factual details	Evaluates information using a wide range of supporting factual details
Explain and apply the principles of dimensional metrology	Explains and applies the principles of dimensional metrology with limited success	Explains and applies the principles of dimensional metrology with some success	Explains and applies the principles of dimensional metrology with considerable success	Explains and applies the principles of dimensional metrology with excellent success
Explain the activities associated with industrial relations	Explanation of the activities associated with industrial relations demonstrates limited knowledge	Explanation of the activities associated with industrial relations demonstrates some knowledge	Explanation of the activities associated with industrial relations demonstrates considerable knowledge	Explanation of the activities associated with industrial relations demonstrates thorough knowledge
Explain the factors associated with human costs	Explanation of the factors associated with human costs demonstrates limited understanding	Explanation of the factors associated with human costs demonstrates some understanding	Explanation of the factors associated with human costs demonstrates considerable understanding	Explanation of the factors associated with human costs demonstrates thorough understanding

Criteria	Level 1 (50–59%)	Level 2 (60–69%)	Level 3 (70–79%)	Level 4 (80–100%)
Monitor production process	Monitors production process with limited effectiveness	Monitors production process with some effectiveness	Monitors production process with considerable effectiveness	Monitors production process with a high degree of effectiveness
Prepare a flow chart depicting the responsibilities and duties of group members	Transfers flow chart concept to new procedures with limited effectiveness	Transfers flow chart concept to new procedures with some effectiveness	Transfers flow chart concept to new procedures with considerable effectiveness	Transfers flow chart concept to new procedures with a high degree of effectiveness
Raise quality performance	Raises quality performance with limited success	Raises quality performance with some success	Raises quality performance with considerable success	Raises quality performance with a high degree of success
Use a number of quality control processes	Rarely uses a number of quality control processes	Sometimes uses a number of quality control processes	Often uses a number of quality control processes	Always or almost always uses a number of quality control processes
Using the problem solving model assess and alter projects and designs	Uses problem solving skills to assess and alter projects and design with limited effectiveness	Uses problem solving skills to assess and alter projects and design with some effectiveness	Uses problem solving skills to assess and alter projects and design with considerable effectiveness	Uses problem solving skills to assess and alter projects and design with a high degree of effectiveness

II. Questions to Ponder

- What is the cost of quality?

- How does variation affect our product or service cost?

- How does our organization understand and control our process variation?

- Think of a time when product variation had a negative cost consequence for your organization.

- Consider how we balance quality control versus our enthusiasm to achieve the cost reduction. How do we maintain this balance?

- Are the Six Sigma phases of define, measure, analyze, improve, and control cast in iron?

- When is the Six Sigma approach inappropriate?

- How do we merge lean manufacturing practices with Six Sigma?

- What is design for Six Sigma?

- How do we know a best practice is actually a best practice?

- How do we ensure we are really saving money for the company?

- How do we factor in the cost of training versus the benefit of our cost reduction?

- How much training do we really need?

- What can we do if we want to institutionalize our improvements?
- Who needs to be involved in the institutionalization of improvements?
- How do we choose a legitimate trainer to educate our green belts and black belts?
- Is Six Sigma last year's or last decade's fad approach to saving money?
- Is there a point at which we stop our Six Sigma initiative and move on to something else in good conscience? How will we know if and when we have reached that time?
- What is the best follow-on choice to Six Sigma?

III. Cost Improvement Scenario

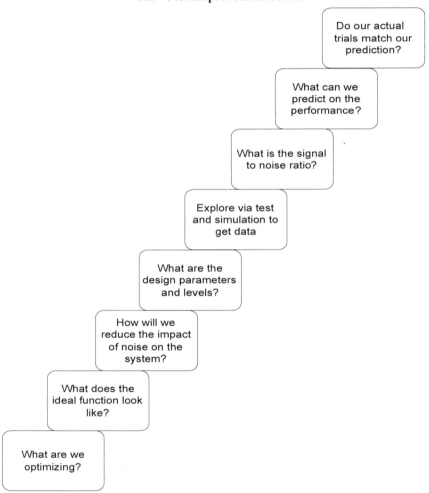

Figure 8.1 Standard steps for parameter design.

A. Situation

The goal was to remove the use of "X#" designators on printed circuit boards (PCBs)—these boards could not be sold to the customer with this "experimental" designation; hence, the company was wasting money when the time came to change over.

B. Objective

Save hundreds of dollars on prototype boards and change the culture of acceptance of mediocre schematic release.

C. Action

The printed circuit board team was ordered to drop the "X#" designation over their own carping: "What will the customer think when they get revision M?" The idea that the company probably had design incompetence if they were at revision M never entered their minds.

D. Results

Boards were produced without the "X#" designator. The customer never said anything, which is not surprising given that, in most cases, they never opened the product to see the revision of the PCB.

E. Aftermath

Once the manager of the PCB layout team moved on to other responsibilities, they reverted back to the "X#" designator. This result was the product of lack of sustainable control on a legitimate cost reduction.

IV. What Is Six Sigma?

In one sense, Six Sigma is the marriage of quality management with cost reductions and value engineering. The methodology also follows a distinct and easy to remember algorithm. The tools to be used by the practitioner are well known and well documented. This approach has been available since roughly the middle of the 1980s. Motorola, General Electric, and AlliedSignal used Six Sigma initially. These companies used Six Sigma to save billions of dollars.

Since Six Sigma focuses heavily on the bottom line, the chances of achieving significant value engineering are extremely high. All Six Sigma projects must be vetted before a committee that usually contains representatives from the finance department. This step alone helps to ensure that the selected projects will indeed save money for the enterprise. More mature organizations will use the project review committee to also prioritize projects; this prioritization does not necessarily mean that smaller projects will disappear in favor of larger ones, but rather, that high leverage projects are the order of the day.

V.   How Does Six Sigma Relate to Value Engineering?

Six Sigma has its own approaches to managing projects. It does not correspond exactly with what we call traditional value engineering. We do not consider the situation particularly relevant. Far more important is the availability of a powerful tool and proven methodology to help us affect the bottom line by implementing validated cost reductions, profit improvement, and even cost avoidance.

When one of us was the primary Six Sigma project champion, we often heard complaints that some of the projects were not really Six Sigma projects but something else. We think that this kind of carping about details is counterproductive. We know of at least one individual who felt that some of the projects actually represented lean manufacturing. Who cares? The goal of lean manufacturing, Six Sigma, and value engineering is to save money, improve the bottom line, and improve the chances for survival of our companies.

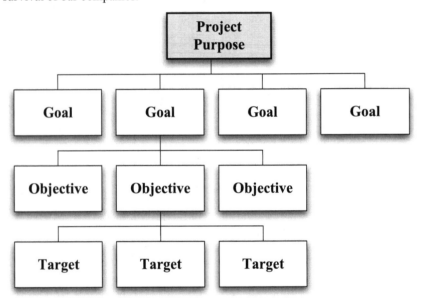

Figure 8.2 We can derive goals, objectives, and targets from our project purpose.

VI.   The Phases of Six Sigma

For Six Sigma projects that do not involve design engineering, we have five phases for each project: define, measure, analyze, improve, and control. We often find that the define phase is sometimes the most difficult part of the entire project. It is during this phase where we set the project scope (see Figure 8.2), which not only tells us what we are going to do but also informs us about what we are not going to do with regard to the project. In some cases, we will iterate back-and-forth between a given phase and the next phase of a Six Sigma project as we learn more about what we are trying to do. Sometimes during a *define* phase we are able to go ahead and do project costing. However, we find it more common that Six Sigma teams will have to venture into the measure phase in order to develop enough information that costing becomes realistic. During the measure phase of a Six Sigma project, we will collect data within the scope that we already established in the define phase. We approach these projects with some caution because we do not want to consume substantial resources before we have even established the cost basis for the project. That is why many Six Sigma implementations have an individual known as the project champion. The project champion will function as mentor, facilitator, and guide for the project team.

The Six Sigma analyze phase is often where we first see the use of statistical tools. We do not always need to use statistics but we should know enough about statistics to know when they are needed. Again, we may go back and forth among phases as we learn more about our project during this analyze phase. Sometimes, we will discover information that was not so obvious when we started the project. As always, we can go to the project champion for advice and counseling regarding our next steps.

As with any of the value engineering approaches, the analyze phase will often consume the most time and resources. The analyze phase combined with the measure phase often consumes well over half the project time. Not only will we carefully select our tools during this phase, but we will also use some intuition as we attempt to see what the data we have collected can reveal to us—let the project, product, or service speak to us.

The improve phase is the point at which we take the information we have gleaned during the analyze phase and we use other tools to improve the existing situation— nearly always with an improvement to the bottom line. Again, it is very common to use statistical methods during this phase, but it is not a requirement. One of the most powerful statistical tools is the designed experiment, which will tell us which are the most important factors, how they relate, and allow us to perform some optimization to achieve maximal results.

The control phase is an innovation with the Six Sigma approach. By applying control methods, we move our improvements towards sustainability. Product or process controls allow us to see if we have really improved the situation but they also allow us to maintain that improvement. Without these controls, it is likely that our service or product will revert back to what it was before we implemented the improvement.

VII. Choosing Six Sigma Projects

How do we choose Six Sigma projects? Basically, we look initially for opportunities for improvement. Not every opportunity will yield a significant improvement to the bottom line. This concern for the bottom line is one of the factors that separates the Six Sigma approach from total quality management; in other words, all Six Sigma projects should be bottom-line related but not all TQM projects have a financial impact.

In any plant, office, or business, we believe hundreds of opportunities for improvement and value engineering are readily available if we only have eyes to see them. Sometimes we can take a systematic approach and list every work cell, every known issue, and every suspected issue. At other times, we may look and listen for complaints because complaints are clearly opportunities for improvement. Either way, we need to let our employees be aware of what we are trying to do and the benefits that all the savings will provide to them. If the employees see a benefit, they generally are more likely to assist in an initiative like Six Sigma.

VIII. Costing Six Sigma Projects

We can cost Six Sigma projects in the same way we would do costing for any other project, including product development. In short, we will develop a work breakdown structure that defines the deliverables for the project and we will follow that with a bill of resources that define the people and tools we need in order to proceed with the project. These two simple steps are often enough to apply some simple cost estimates relating to consumption of resources. Our next step, then, would be to ascertain the level of savings we expect to see from our project. Different organizations will require different ways of stating how we achieved our savings; for example, they may ask us to provide an annualized value for our project savings or they might choose some other quantum of time.

As with all value engineering projects, our cost analysis needs to be realistic. Chief financial officers will want to see true cost reductions rather than cost avoidances. The situation occurs because a cost avoidance does not really affect the bottom line. We have seen CFOs accept profit improvements when the project removed a set of old parts that were an eyesore as well as yielding income. We have found that explaining through cost reduction and profit improvement to employees is often prone to misunderstanding. Another source of problems occurs when we make a process change that we know improves a production line or service delivery but we cannot prove that our change affects the bottom line because we already have excess capacity. When this situation occurs, it suggests that the project should not have been accepted in the first place. Of course, an executive may choose to override immediate financial considerations to yield a long-term improvement.

IX. Using Design for Six Sigma

Design for Six Sigma takes a Six Sigma concept into the design arena. The tools are somewhat similar, but we begin to see designed experiments and other statistical tools during the product development portion of the program. The idea of design for Six Sigma is to improve the product before launch rather than waiting for disgusted customer feedback to improve the product after launch. If we eliminate a substantial amount of product returns, we save money. For a project like this, we would have to go do historical data in order to demonstrate that we had made an improvement over previous releases. Hence, costing of design for Six Sigma can be more difficult than the cost for standard Six Sigma.

Our phases for design for Six Sigma are similar to those for standard Six Sigma: define, measure, analyze, design, and verify. We know of other acronyms for design for Six Sigma and its phases, but the general idea is that we are reducing the haphazard approach often used during product development and substituting a more systematic method of product development.

One of the other considerations with design for Six Sigma is the concept of customer delight. We know we can measure the cost of returns but how do we measure the cost of customer dissatisfaction? In many cases, we may be able to go to our marketing group and get an estimate on the cost of customer dissatisfaction, both in lost business and in lost new business. This estimate may be the best we can do in this situation but it should at least give us an order of magnitude idea for the value of such an intangible concept.

One of the principal tools in any approach to design for Six Sigma is the use of the designed experiment. To execute a designed experiment, we must know what we are trying to accomplish, the factors involved, a means of measuring effects, and some knowledge of some statistical tools. Two of the primary tools we use when designing experiments are analysis of variance or ANOVA and the general linear model when it is appropriate. In general, our goal is to design a robust product; that is, a product that is as immune to extraneous stimuli as we can design it. The designed experiment will reveal which factors are significant and subsequent mathematical analysis will show us how to increase the robustness of the product. Once we have gone as far as we can go in the robustness exercise, we can then assess the steps we need to take with regard to tolerancing. This approach originated with Taguchi and it is rational and appropriate to this day. While we may not choose to use the Taguchi form of designed experimentation, the steps of concept exploration, parameter design (see Figure 8.1), and tolerance design are all useful and reasonable.

X.   Rational Expectations from Six Sigma

In our experience, the first three to four years of a Six Sigma initiative yield savings of approximately 3% of revenue. After about four years, we have eliminated nearly all of the obvious and easy to accomplish projects. Then, we expect the savings to drop by roughly half. These estimates are based on experience, so they are empirical but not scientific.

Once we have picked the easiest of all possible projects, we then can look to other techniques to perform value engineering in both design and manufacturing. We can use the hybrid form Lean Six Sigma or we can go straight to lean manufacturing. We favor Lean Six Sigma because the Six Sigma approach provides a nicely organized algorithm for proceeding through the project, people already understand the bottom line approach, and we have a wealth of statistical tools we can add to what is normally used on lean projects.

If we use the ASQ Six Sigma Black Belt body of knowledge as a starting point, we can provide a structure survey of what we need to know in order to proceed to value \ engineering through Six Sigma. We have been part of successful Six Sigma programs; hence, we can verify many of the thoughts from the body of knowledge based on real occurrences.

Enterprise-Wide Deployment

One of the "secrets" of successful Six Sigma lies with enterprise-wide deployment. If we do not have the support of management, we will fail. We observed a successful Six Sigma program falter when management took off on a tangent by trying to implement a lean initiative based on weak data and unproven theories. We have nothing against the lean approach; however, we think the most successful method lies with merging both methodologies into the hybrid version called Lean Six Sigma.

The idea of continuous improvement has been around at least since the 1920s with the advent of work by Joseph Juran. By the 1930s, we were seeing publications from Walter Shewhart and W. Edwards Deming. After the war, the Japanese rebuilt their industrial base, in many cases, with consultative assistance from these individuals and homegrown concepts from Ishikawa (see Figure 8.3), Taguchi, and Ohno, among others. In the United States, we saw work from the Crosby brothers and others. In the 1980s, after the failure of some Total Quality Management (TQM) approaches, we saw the advent of Six Sigma: project-based, bottom line–focused, with a strong toolbox. In some ways, we might consider Six Sigma to be the result of what we learned from TQM.

From the very start, Six Sigma projects were required to focus on the monetary value to be yielded by the changes wrought by the project. We did not have to guess at value—we had to calculate that value in some agreed upon currency. No longer were we trying to improve quality everywhere; we were endeavoring to improve quality where it had the most impact on the enterprise.

Management may choose to set goals for specific departments (closer to TQM) or they may allow Six Sigma to sprout as a kind of grass roots movement within the enterprise. Often, the initial financial effect occurs from the procurement (purchasing) department, since they have the ability to leverage suppliers for lower prices. This approach is fine so long as the department does not cut corners on the engineering

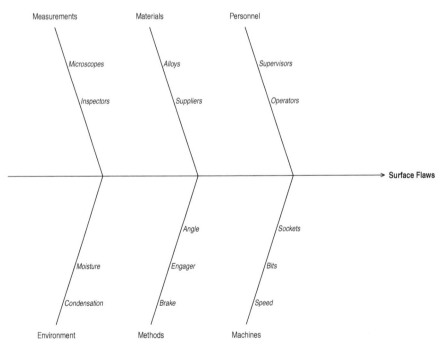

Figure 8.3 The Ishikawa diagram can help us plan as well as solve problems.

change process. Production or manufacturing may have some obvious bottom-line affecting improvements, often in the area of process improvements (the removal of a subprocess from the procedure rather than simply increasing throughput of individual processes). The design group may use Design for Six Sigma (DFSS) or more traditional value engineering techniques to remove costly subprocesses by designing them out (e.g., selective soldering uses expensive robots). The marketing department may be able to streamline processes and improve other processes that involve both customer and supplier.

As we noted, as the Six Sigma initiative matures, we may evolve into Lean Six Sigma, which melds the concept of waste reduction with that of quality improvement. A good way to proceed into Lean Six Sigma is the traditional kaizen approach of hundreds or thousands of small improvements—the continuous movement towards improvement then becomes a part of the corporate culture.

Service enterprises can use Six Sigma and Lean Six Sigma to improve processes. Obviously, we still want oversight from a mature committee to ensure that we are receiving a financial return on our efforts. For example, a department store may choose to use designed experiments to determine the effects of location, product placement, employee placement (cash registers), and other factors on the sale of products. The service department at an auto dealership might use Lean Six Sigma to reduce customer wait times and to standardize work (not just standardize the bill!).

Leadership

For Six Sigma or Lean Six Sigma to be successful, we need top-level management involvement (see Figure 8.4). We know this approach is real because we have seen an enterprise "jump tracks" by ignoring Six Sigma and moving toward a particular version of lean manufacturing as they chased the will o' the wisp of cost savings. When they chose to do this change, the saving from Six Sigma evaporated. The drawback was that this particular lean implementation did not use rigorous costing and, hence, the savings were nebulous at best.

Executive leadership drives middle management, which in turn, drives low-level management and rank-and-file employees. The trick to making this approach work is educate the employees at all levels about the benefits of improving company margin and how it affects the stability of the enterprise. Furthermore, we may need to issue reassurances about downsizing—having surplus capacity is a very good place to be in if we are aggressively pursuing markets.

The executive leadership may take on the additional and specific responsibility of being a project champion. The purpose of a champion is to remove organizational roadblocks so that the project can continue to move forward. The champion can have tremendous influence on the success of the project. Furthermore, the champion must have sufficient organization leverage to effect hurdle removal.

What can affect the ability of a Six Sigma or lean team to progress? Sometimes an organization will evolve a set way of performing certain processes, so much so that nobody sees the inefficiencies in the process anymore. An example of this situation occurs when we see a configuration management document that requires twenty or

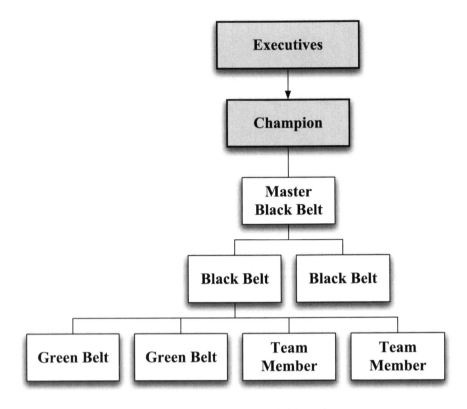

Figure 8.4 A typical (and overrated) Six Sigma belt hierarchy.

more signatures to proceed; in this case, we are seeing confusion between need-to-know and need-to-approve. Other hurdles may be cultural and also remain undetected, lurking in assumptions and prejudicial beliefs. Elsewhere in this book we briefly discuss an assumption surfacing technique (SAST), but any team activity that brings assumptions and prejudices to light is usable to improve the climate for change.

We may discover other roadblocks in the form of inadequate resources. We have seen CEOs indicate that Six Sigma is self-supporting; therefore, no money is needed to initiate the program. This belief makes no sense! Yes, Six Sigma returns cash to the corporation, and often, quickly; however, seed money is usually needed to train the employees in the methods of Six Sigma. The same applies to lean and Lean Six Sigma also.

We must maintain configuration management for the duration of all projects, lean or Six Sigma. Configuration management is the overarching concept by which we maintain a level of change control. In some situations, we may find we must reverse a change and proper documentation will help us to get there. In general, a company should already have a configuration management system in place for routine changes. Nonroutine changes are potentially riskier and the need for management can be significant. Software development should *always* use a software configuration management tool (e.g., subversion) to maintain revision control and the ability to backtrack. Hardware changes, drawing changes, and documentation changes can also fall under the configuration management system. Enterprise-level tools are available to support configuration management; however, for smaller companies, we can use a database or even a paper system so long as we use it rigorously.

We see words like "transformation" and "organizational change" bandied about in management magazines and general audience management tomes. Do we really want "transformation" as such? The word "transformation" means to "mold or figure" across but it contains overtones of revolutionary change. We favor the more gentle approach of traditional kaizen, where thousands of small changes apply. Moreover, traditional kaizen is the golden path to cultural change in the corporation. Instead of advertising pabulum about revolutionary change, we make change revolutionary. We change the effect by affecting our manner of change. Do we really desire to "drive" employees with a macabre metaphor of bestial brutality?

A Six Sigma project must be managed as a project and must be accepted by an oversight committee. We can apply the same mentality to kaizen events (a term we deprecate) so that they proceed promptly and with minimum wasted effort. The general goal is to ascertain the projects with the greatest impact, which is not always easy to do, particularly when our costing ventures into the region of intangibility. In some cases, we may accelerate a process but be unable to positively identify the financial benefits. In those cases, we should look for projects that provide obvious cost benefits and only go to the more nebulous projects if and when it makes sense.

Perhaps one of the most overplayed parts of the Six Sigma approach is the use of the terms

- Green belt
- Black belt
- Master black belt
- Process owner

How can a process owner be a "process owner" when they do not normally own the paraphernalia of production? While the belt designations were intended to demarcate levels of training, they sometimes ended up representing yet another hierarchy, producing resentment and rancor at the "lower" levels of the hierarchy. We need to clarify what "belts" really mean in the sense of levels of training at the outset of our Six Sigma initiative. We have seen green belt projects return more immediate and larger monies than anything seen with a black belt project.

A. Enterprise Process Management and Metrics

If we retain our focus on the flow of revenue and value of margins, then we should gain a more mature understanding of the relationship of our suppliers to ourselves and of ourselves to our customers. Somewhere in this stew of competing goals, we should make the effort to establish financial fairness among all of these stakeholders—simply beating suppliers down to improve costs may lead to an increase in defective products or the supplier going out of business.

We would also like to note that any system of metrics can produce a distorted impression of the bottom line of our business. We know from our accounting training that determining actual profit is a complex task.

Some of our metrics will include factors we measure that directly relate to efficiency, quality, and reduced waste; for example, here are some "critical to" areas of concern:

- Critical to quality (CTQ)

- Critical to cost (CTC)

- Critical to process (CTP)

- Critical to safety (CTS)

- Critical to delivery (CTD)

- Critical to reliability (CTR)

- Critical to assembly (CTA)

- Critical to customer (CTC or CTCust)

- Critical to materials (CTM)

It is possible to get silly with "critical to" ideas; the reason for CTX is to remind developers and producers that these issues are important and should not be overlooked. Each one of them has a set of metrics related to significant factors, particularly financial metrics; for example, CTR might include the total cost of returns.

We can also include some level of benchmarking in our measurement activities (see Figure 8.5). We can compare ourselves to another department within our own company (collaborative), a noncompeting but efficient organization outside of our

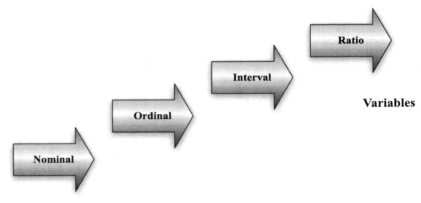

Attributes

Figure 8.5 The four measurement scales, from categorical type to absolute zero, same interval type.

enterprise (collaborative), or against a competitor (competitive benchmarking, when such knowledge is ethically available). We want to avoid a regression to the mean; that is, we do not want benchmarking to lead to copying that results in a common mediocrity. Hence, the general goal of benchmarking is to elevate us by "competing" against an organization that performs better than ours does. We need to be careful when using terms like "best practices" and ensure that we have proven that these practices are indeed the best through designed experiments or other objective means.

Other tools for measurement include the balanced scorecard, estimates of customer loyalty, key performance indicators, and others. None of these is deadly if used with caution and awareness of the potentially distorting effect of using only a subset of metrics. For example, a key performance indicator should be defined to be "key" as the result of a designed experiment or as the product of some other ANOVA generating statistical calculation. The analysis of variance (ANOVA) will generally give us an idea of which factors are significant. Again, we proceed with caution, because it is possible that a concatenation of lesser factors may add up to a large influence on results.

We have a host of financial measure, a small subset of which is useful to our Six Sigma and Lean Six Sigma projects: cost of quality (COQ), net present value (NPV), and return on investment (ROI). Additionally, we might perform cost/benefit analyses, trade-off analyses, and other more complex analyses to ascertain the value of our projects.

We can calculate cost of quality using items from the following table:

General cost	Specific cost	Characterization	For example
Conformance	Prevention	Does not happen	• Planning • Training • Quality management system • Use of customer-required documents
	Appraisal	Audit	• Testing • Inspection • Setups • Test equipment • Routine audits • Special audits
Nonconformance	Internal failure	Defects caught	• Rework • Scrap • Supplier returns
	External failure	Defects at customers	• Warranty • Recall • Campaigns • Liability • Customer satisfaction

We can use our net present value (NPV) equation to help us make choices. If we set NPV to zero and solve, we get the internal rate of return. Both methods are satisfactory for a given project, but may not be useful when comparing projects nor do they really consider the cost of capital. We do not really expect our Six Sigma projects to be massive, multiyear burdens.

The simplest calculation of return on investment (ROI) involves simply looking at how much we have invested (outgoing) and how much we received (incoming). This simple method may be good enough for a quick project. The more complex versions of ROI, involving arithmetic mean and geometric average rates of return, may not be worth the extra effort to calculate.

To perform a cost/benefit analysis, we might take the following steps:

1. Define the project or projects

2. Analyze comprehensively all involved ("stakeholders")

3. Analyze costs

4. Predict benefits

5. Predict any subsequent costs

6. Quantify in terms of capital (money)

7. Use NPV, IRR, or payback

8. Verify robustness of model by modifying numbers; that is, a sensitivity analysis

9. Select most robust project with the highest rate of return

If a cost/benefit analysis yields a robust project with a low rate of return or a non-robust project with a high rate of return, we may have to start over again or drop the project.

The simplest trade-off analysis is the Pugh concept selection approach, named after the late Stuart Pugh, who created it. Basically, we create a matrix where the column headings reflect our design choices and the rows are attributes of each design choice. We set the value of our existing design choice to be zero and at the intersection of each row and column, we indicate whether it is better or worse than the existing option using simple symbols: "++," "+," "0," "-," "--." Of course, we can substitute numerical values for the symbols to give the illusion of increased precision, but often the symbols are adequate. At the bottom of each column we sum the "+" and "-" values to indicate our preferred choice. Perhaps, the trickiest part of the exercise is avoiding "jiggering" the choice by overemphasizing the positive qualities of a favored design choice.

Team Formation

Team Types and Constraints
A formal team is often a team appointed by managers. This kind of team may even have a written team charter that spells out the goals of the team. In general, we would not expect a team to become a real team simply because they have been so designated.

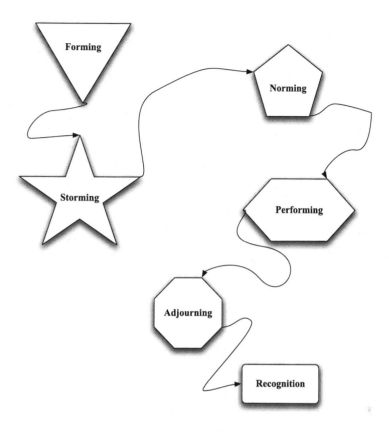

Figure 8.6 One well-known model of group evolution.

Informal teams can arise when a group of people realizes they have a common goal. Note that the common thread in all teams is that they have a purpose. Some informal teams may arise from social networks. Another term often used is "ad hoc teams," which are teams formed on the spur of the moment to satisfy an immediate need. Unless the participants know each other well, they may never cohere into a functional team (see Figure 8.6).

Virtual teams exist when all or some of the members are not collocated. In these cases, the use of technologies such as e-mail and videoconferencing become a necessity. These technologies can reduce, but may not eliminate, the need for face-to-face meetings. Like any other form of team, a virtual team will be as strong as the relations among the members and their understanding of the common goal.

Cross-functional teams have members from various enterprise functions; for example, a cross-functional engineering team could have mechanical, electrical, metallurgical, and software engineers working towards a common goal. The usual weakness of cross-functional teams lies in the fact that the members are more familiar with their functional peers than they are with team members from other functions. The tension between team leaders and functional managers may negatively influence the ability of the team to ever become a cohesive unit.

The idea of self-directed work teams (SDWT) really came to the fore in the 1990s when Kimball Fisher published *Leading Self-Directed Work Teams*[1]. Most of Fisher's text is given over to showing how management can implement what he also calls "high performance teams." The following is a list of the steps he recommends for implementing self-directed work teams:

- Understand SDWT by investigating it
- Accept SDWT by preparing for it
- Make SDWT work by directing the implementation
- Sustain SDWT by managing the transition
- Continuously improve SDWT through a well-considered maturation process

Note the idea of continuous improvement fits in well with the Six Sigma approach to quality. Furthermore, Six Sigma Black Belt teams are often self-directed work teams with highly dedicated members, formally elucidated for management but informally formed in reality. Moreover, cross-functional and virtual approaches are possible also.

Team Roles

Leaders and Followers

In social networks, the vertices of influence often become obvious through the number of connections these individuals have. Informally, they are probably leaders. Even in self-directed work teams, some level of leadership attains and some SDWTs may use a round robin leadership, where each participant on the team occupies the decision-making spot for some prearranged period of time. In some cases, individuals are content to be followers. They prefer to remain in their comfort zone—this situation is not always negative, for a person may realize that the leadership role is outside their level of competence or maturity.

The Six Sigma model uses the following approach: executive leadership provides resources, Champions argue the business case and remove obstacles, Master Black Belts direct Black Belts and work on large-scale problems, Black Belts may direct Green Belts and certainly work on significant problems, and Green Belts work on more tractable problems. These roles are not absolutely required in the manner stated, but they provide a convenient way to keep track of the deployment of the Six Sigma initiative.

Six Sigma deployment officers should use the belt system with some caution. Green Belts, for example, can often turn in projects that affect return on investment now and not later to the greater benefit of the enterprise. The Green Belt role is extremely important, especially when a company is starting to deploy Six Sigma. Green Belt projects allow for early and significant achievements, which reinforces the entire deployment and project process.

Other roles may exist within the team framework, for example:

- Timekeepers help to maintain the tempo of the meetings and can provide a service by time-boxing the meeting (time-boxes are strictly delimited times;

when the end of the box is reached, the meeting is over, period).

- Facilitators help to keep the meeting participants focused on the purpose of the meeting and they can assist the timekeeper with tempo issues.

- Data gatherers go out to the location of the data, virtual or real, and accumulate the data into tables, trees, or whatever format makes sense.

- Data manipulators take the data from the data-gatherers and proceed to analyze the data using spreadsheets, statistical software, and other tools.

- Functional managers are the owners of a given function and the team may need the functional manager's support, especially if we are speaking about a cross-functional team.

- Project/program managers often work in a matrix environment, where the base staff reports to both a functional manager and a program manager—they drive programs to a predefined conclusion.

Team Member Selection

We can look at the required skill sets and derive them from the definition of need for this particular team occasionally, special skill sets may require outside consultation, perhaps in the form of an advisor or mentor. One example would occur if we require someone who has the statistical knowledge to use short-term statistical process control or even nonparametric statistics. We also have to consider the possibility that the use of a special skill set on our team may have a negative effect on the individual's regular job. Because of this, we need to consider our team relationships and the effect each team member has on their home positions.

We do not expect Six Sigma teams to exceed seven members. The reason for this is very simple: at five members, we have more than 120 possibilities for arranging our team members. As we increase the number of members on our team, we become victims of a stochastic explosion (the combinations increase factorially).

We also want to make sure that we have a high level of commitment from team members. In return, we must provide sufficient empowerment, tools, and support to ensure the success of the project. Anything less, is a betrayal of the team.

When we launch a team, one of the first orders of the day is to ensure that the team understands its purpose. Once the purpose of established, we can proceed to a discussion of team goals, which we will derive from the team purpose. We have already mentioned the word commitment, but this word has deeper meanings; for example we need to know how long the team will last, what character traits we wish to see, and whether or not the individuals involved are stakeholders.

At this point in the evolution of our team, we will define responsibilities and delivery schedules. Behind all of this activity must be a high level of management support and team empowerment. By empowerment, we mean the team must have the capability to accomplish the task that they and we have defined. The team will also have to share relevant information, focus on interests, be open to inquiry, and even be willing to discuss issues often considered out of limits.

We can help see to it that our teams remained motivated by reinforcing the achievement of team goals. In some cases, we may reward subtests also. We know that early successes will reinforce later success. The goal here is to avoid hopelessness and discouragement.

One of the most common models for the life cycle of a team involves six phases:

- Forming
- Storming
- Norming
- Performing
- Adjourning
- Recognition based on results

We have already noted that team size is a factor in team communications. If we have distributed teams, we may have challenges with time zones, languages, geography, cultures, and other distractions related to any one of those or combinations of those factors. We expect the team to spend regular time reflecting on the purpose of the team, which can be encapsulated in a document called the team charter. In this team charter, we can also document communications protocols and build a table to reflect the various relationships. We might also note that communication is what arrives at the receiving end and is not at all what the transmitter sends. Because of this situation, we may need some level of handshaking similar to that seen in computer communications protocols, allowing us to do some level of verification of messages to ensure clear indication. To continue our information theory metaphor, we might also add channels for communication; for example, we can use e-mail, voice mail, face-to face speech, or even paper documents. Obviously, some level of care will be required to ensure we are not making things worse by adding communications channels.

We would like to note that there are often pitfalls that can be managed when communicating with team members; for example, when we have a meeting we should expect to document an agenda, an action plan, a schedule, and provide detailed minutes of the meeting itself. These documents provide a reference for subsequent use when we awaken to the fact that we are, as a group, confused. Just as we have ground rules for our team, we should also have ground rules for our meetings. Any meeting worth holding should have an agenda and minutes at a minimum. If we are fortunate enough to have a facilitator present, we can move off-topic commentary to a parking lot board and remain on task, driving our meeting to significance. Additionally, a facilitator can reduce clashes among egos. We may also wish to invite our team champion to some of the meetings; however, we need to be careful that we do not become overly dependent on the power and status of the champion.

Team Dynamics

Setting goals is one way to help focus a team; for example, the participants should ask:

- What is this meeting about? (Ultimate goal question)

- What are we supposed to accomplish? (Ultimate results questions)
- Why did they ask me? What is my contribution to be?
- How will the group work? What are the ground rules?

Individuals may volunteer for roles, which can then be approved by the group. Roles can rotate from meeting to meeting if the team agrees to this method of assuring equity. A role does not grant any special authority to a participant; rather, it offers specific obligations and responsibilities. Obligations of a role are available for any participant to exercise, but only team member in that role may exercise responsibilities.

The leader or facilitator can make clear what the responsibilities of each role are to be. The responsibility is wedded to the role. Alternatively, the team can arrive at the responsibility matrix through consensus.

Agendas guide meetings and help keep them on track; hidden agendas interfere with meetings. A good written agenda can help counteract hidden agendas. The well-crafted agenda should include:

1. The agenda topics, if appropriate

2. A brief explanation of each item and its importance

3. The individual responsible for each item

4. The duration of each discussion, and

5. The action needed for each item that requires action.

When coaching, a team member is in an instructional mode. The team member can gently use some expert knowledge to instruct (with dignity) another team member in how to perform a specific function more optimally.

A mentor is not necessarily a team member and their role is more advisory than instructive. Frequently, a mentor is a more senior individual who has been around the block a few times.

The facilitator stands outside the team and helps them decide how to decide (consensus, majority rules, multivoting, leadership). They also see to it that all issues raised have been addressed, using a "parking lot" board as a temporary holding area. A facilitator can help the team decide on the next step. Moreover, they can summarize results, agreements, and next steps.

An overbearing or dominant team member (1) wields a disproportionate amount of influence, (2) consumes a disproportionate amount of "air time," (3) sees silence as an invitation to talk, (4) inhibits the group from building a functioning team, and (5) discourages participation by other members, who then find excuses for missing meetings.

Ways to deal with dominating participants include having the leader engage others, refocusing the discussion, and using a timekeeper, who can keep dominators in check by asking, "Who has the floor?"

In the case where one or two members rarely speak, problems may occur if the quiet ones are not encouraged to participate. This behavior invites dominators to dominate.

Solutions to reluctance can include deliberately checking around the group, creating activities that rely on participation (trainer games), recording ideas, and testing whether the team is satisfied with the procedures.

Some team members may express personal beliefs and assumptions with such confidence that other team members assume they are hearing facts (or groupthink rears its ugly head). Solutions to opinions include testing comprehension, bringing in the experience of others (asking for suggestions), and deliberately asking for more information. The demagogic use of beliefs, assumptions, and opinions can lead to groupthink, which is a disposition of group members to go along to get along with the majority. In many cases, members will not speak against the majority even when they possess serious qualms about decisions. Silence can become a deadly form of acquiescence. However, silence does not obviate responsibility. For example,

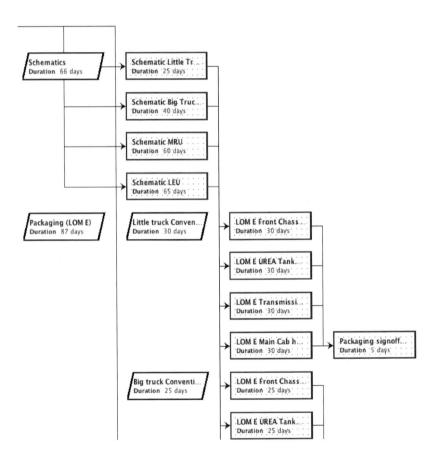

Figure 8.7 A snapshot of a network diagram from a project management tool.

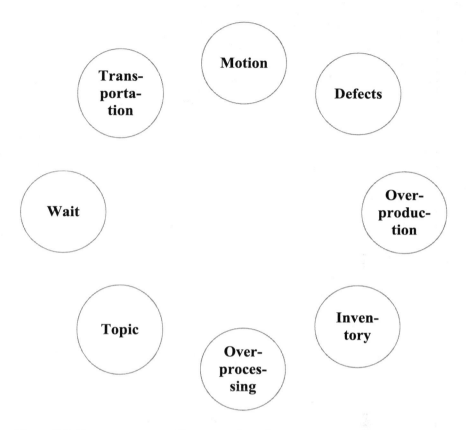

Figure 8.8 The seven wastes of lean manufacturing.

witnessing the creation of a concentration camp while feigning ignorance of its purpose does not eliminate one's responsibility for its existence—an extreme example, but illustrative of the depths of perniciousness involved with groupthink.

Time Management for Teams

The agenda can be a powerful tool for time management rather than the annoyance we often perceive it to be. The typical components of an agenda are:

- Purpose
- Schedule
- Location
- People and roles
- Equipment needed
- Sequence of events

The agenda allows the meeting leader to control the course of meeting, keeping

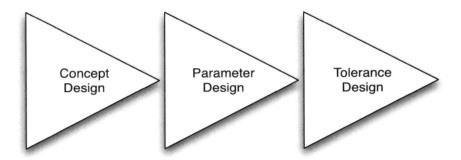

Figure 8.9 An overview of the robust design process.

it on track instead of deviating into irrelevant topics and personal information. The agenda identifies participants and special actors. The special actors will perform functions such as:

- Time-keeping,
- Facilitating,
- Recording (secretary), and
- Directing.

We emphasize the use of the genders in particular because the tool allows us to save one of our most precious resources—time. We can also use agenda control to keep the meeting from devolving into ad hoc chaos. We also suggest that the Six Sigma teams transmit as much information before a meeting as possible; the most common tool is probably e-mail. Moreover, if we are going to call a meeting, we also expect prompt, punctual attendance by participants. We also recommend that the meeting moderator verifies that any required documents and hardware are available and functional; for example, it is a waste of everyone's time if the moderator spends 20 minutes getting the projector to work with the laptop computer. We also want to make sure as project managers that we are not piling meeting on meeting, nor are we spending one or two hours per meeting when 15 minutes will do the job.

Nominal Group Technique, Multivoting

The term brainstorming may mean many things. The way we use it here is a situation where a group will meet and work to generate or create ideas in the following way:
- Gather in an amicable setting
- Lay down ground rules
  - How much time is available
  - Attempt to generate some given amount of ideas
  - If public and oral, no criticism of ideas during generation phase
  - We should capture ideas anonymously by using self-stick notes or

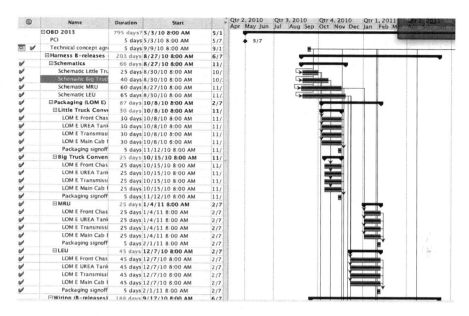

	Name	Duration	Start		Qtr 2, 2010 Apr May Jun	Qtr 3, 2010 Jul Aug Sep	Qtr 4, 2010 Oct Nov Dec	Qtr 1, 2011 Jan Feb M	
	⊟OBD 2013	795 days?	5/3/10 8:00 AM	5/1					
	PCI	5 days	5/3/10 8:00 AM	5/7	◆ 5/7				
	Technical concept agr	5 days	9/9/10 8:00 AM	9/1					
	⊟Harness 8-releases	203 days	8/27/10 8:00 AM	6/7					
	⊟Schematics	66 days	8/27/10 8:00 AM	11/					
	Schematic Little Tru	25 days	8/30/10 8:00 AM	10/					
	Schematic Big Tru	40 days	8/30/10 8:00 AM	10/					
	Schematic MRU	60 days	8/27/10 8:00 AM	11/					
	Schematic LEU	65 days	8/30/10 8:00 AM	11/					
	⊟Packaging (LOM E)	87 days	10/8/10 8:00 AM	2/7					
	⊟Little Truck Conve	30 days	10/8/10 8:00 AM	11/					
	LOM E Front Chas	30 days	10/8/10 8:00 AM	11/					
	LOM E UREA Tank	30 days	10/8/10 8:00 AM	11/					
	LOM E Transmissi	30 days	10/8/10 8:00 AM	11/					
	LOM E Main Cab t	30 days	10/8/10 8:00 AM	11/					
	Packaging signoff	5 days	11/12/10 8:00 AM	11/					
	⊟Big Truck Conven	25 days	10/15/10 8:00 AM	11/					
	LOM E Front Chas	25 days	10/15/10 8:00 AM	11/					
	LOM E UREA Tank	25 days	10/15/10 8:00 AM	11/					
	LOM E Transmissi	25 days	10/15/10 8:00 AM	11/					
	LOM E Main Cab t	25 days	10/15/10 8:00 AM	11/					
	Packaging signoff	5 days	11/12/10 8:00 AM	11/					
	⊟MRU	25 days	1/4/11 8:00 AM	2/7					
	LOM E Front Chas	25 days	1/4/11 8:00 AM	2/7					
	LOM E UREA Tank	25 days	1/4/11 8:00 AM	2/7					
	LOM E Transmissi	25 days	1/4/11 8:00 AM	2/7					
	LOM E Main Cab t	25 days	1/4/11 8:00 AM	2/7					
	Packaging signoff	5 days	2/1/11 8:00 AM	2/7					
	⊟LEU	45 days	12/7/10 8:00 AM	2/7					
	LOM E Front Chas	45 days	12/7/10 8:00 AM	2/7					
	LOM E UREA Tank	45 days	12/7/10 8:00 AM	2/7					
	LOM E Transmissi	45 days	12/7/10 8:00 AM	2/7					
	LOM E Main Cab t	45 days	12/7/10 8:00 AM	2/7					
	Packaging signoff	5 days	2/1/11 8:00 AM	2/7					
	⊟Wiring (8-releases)	188 days	9/17/10 8:00 AM	6/7					

Figure 8.10 Gantt chart snapshot is easy to understand. Dark bars are rolled-up tasks.

other written devices
- We might facilitate group with an experienced individual to keep the exercise on track

Ideas generated using these approaches can be submitted for either the nominal group or the multivoting technique, which we next describe. The idea with these approaches is to convert the clearly subjective choice approach into something resembling objective decision making.

Steps for Nominal Group Technique and Multivoting
Nominal Group Technique
This technique helps build consensus and buy-in. Here are the steps:

1. Select items of concern from a brainstorming exercise (or other source).

2. Write all items on a flip chart, white board, adhesive notes, or 3x5 cards.

3. Eliminate duplicates.

4. "Publish" final list of items.

5. Have each member rank the items on a piece of paper or a 3x5 card.

6. Combine the rankings and score.

7. You have a democratically chosen a list of priorities!

Multivoting
Multivoting is a participative technique that, although democratic, puts people on the spot by moving them gently toward a decision. One form goes as follows:

1. Select items of concern from a brainstorming exercise or other source.

2. Identify voting criteria to eliminate crossed purposes and misunderstandings.

3. Give each member a stock of points to distribute as they see fit.

4. Do not allow more than 50% of any stock to be placed on any one item.

5. Allow voting with points to occur.

6. Tally the results.

7. We have selected a list of priorities.

How do we measure and reward our teams? We measure the performance of the team against the goals, the objectives, and the targets. These goals, objectives, and targets can be reflective of schedule, cost, and quality. In general, we do not want to punish teams because that behavior is ultimately counterproductive. What we want to do is create what is called an operant in behavioral psychology; namely, the event of belonging to the team and achieving is related to response or behavior provided by the team members. Positive achievements will tend to reinforce the desired behavior and we can expect to see that behavior occur more often. We think the idea of having a celebration at the end of the process, and sometimes during the process, is also a form of operant. People like recognition, people like achievement, and people want to have a good time.

B. Define

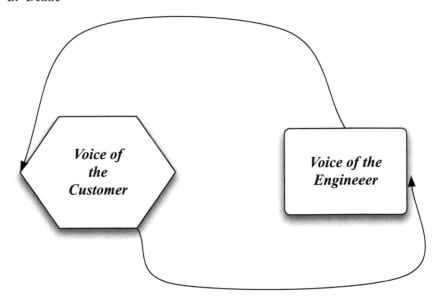

Figure 8.11 Just as the customer informs the engineer, the engineer informs the customer.

The voice of the customer is often overused phrase in marketing literature (see Figure 8.11). However, if we do not listen to what the customer has to say about the product we are developing for them, then who does have some kind of say? Is not the job of the supplier engineer to override the desires of the customer; the engineer may inform the customer in cases where a safety issue or an extremely costly decision has arisen. We see this relationship as a two-way street: the customer informs the supplier, and the supplier has the duty of updating the customer.

Customer identification and segmentation would generally be performed by our marketing organization. In some cases, the question will be what kind of customer can our company support? If we are a small firm ourselves, then we may be doing a very large customer a disfavor if we do not have the capacity to produce a quality product in sufficient quantities for them. This situation applies whether we are talking about internal customers or external customers. In some Lean Six Sigma implementations, we may also see demand segmentation, which is when we use the variability in demand from specific customers to determine how we are going to apply our manufacturing technologies to producing the desired product.

Part of the two-way street we have at the customer uses customer feedback. We can gather this kind of data using surveys, focus groups, interviews, our own observations, and information supplied by third-party services. One of the most significant issues when dealing with feedback of this kind revolves around how we determine the validity and reliability of the information received. In short, we do not want to proceed the same way that Coca-Cola did when they introduced new Coke. Consequently, it is likely we will use several approaches and compare our results as a system of checks and balances to offset internal enthusiasm for specific product.

If we are lucky, customer requirements will be spelled out in a customer specification. Even then, we will need to flow down requirements in such a way that we end up with detailed requirements for which it makes no further sense to decompose endlessly. We can also use somewhat more exotic techniques such as quality function deployment matrices and the Kano model for customer satisfaction. We need to remain cognizant that no customer specification is a truly complete document; in fact, we will need to go back and forth with the customer in order to clarify ambiguities, expand on derived requirements, and make recommendations for improvement. While we are analyzing the requirements, whether we generate the specification or the customer generates the specification, we need to give focus on cost, schedule, and quality. The first two, cost and schedule, are generally easy to measure; the measurement of quality should be the result of a dialogue between the supplier and the customer such that all values generated have meaning for both parties.

If we have been in the business for a while, we can generate some amount of requirements in advance of any kind of specification because of the nature of our business; that is, if we are a vehicle instrumentation supplier, we already know we will most likely be using stepper motors to drive the gauge pointers and, hence, we should be able to spell out some level of needed requirements for the stepper motors well in advance of any specification document. If nothing else, such work will tell us what we need to know and we can go looking for that information in the requirements specification. When we do this kind of activity, we are using our experience as leverage to improve our requirements elicitation.

We have referred to the project charter when discussing how we manage our team. Our project charter is a document that defines an overview of the project for quick assessment by all interested parties. This document should also address the business need for the project as well as providing the high-level details necessary to move forward. In essence, the charter authorizes project, provides a list of names for the team, and gives a top-level description of the required work. An alternative to the project charter is a more detailed document called the statement of work. For U.S. government contracts, the statement of work is usually a required document and has its own military standard. For most Six Sigma projects, however, a statement of work is really overkill and probably does not add enough value to be included in the project documentation.

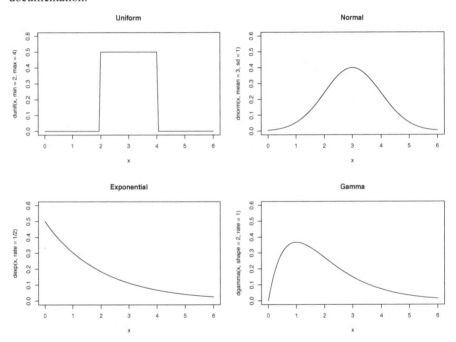

Figure 8.12 A look at some probability distribution functions.

We will also develop a project plan. The project plan is usually not part of the project charter because the plan tends to be too detailed for inclusion. We may express the project plan using project management software such as Microsoft project. We need to be careful to ensure that we do not burden the project with the same level of detail we would use for a major complex product launch. If we do choose to use project management software, we will most likely represent task using a Gantt chart, since these charts need less explanation than the more complex PERT charts and network diagrams. If needed, we can also generate a work breakdown structure to ensure that we do not lose any required and derived deliverable items. Once again, we need to be careful to avoid excessive burdens on the Six Sigma project.

Additional project documentation can include such items as spreadsheets for financial calculations, storyboards for explaining our project management, gate review documents, management review documents, and every presentation we put together about the project. Further documentation would include whatever records we would normally compile as part of the configuration management process.

Problem Statement

Develop and evaluate the problem statement in relation to the project's baseline performance and improvement goals. When we do not have a clear definition of the project goals, we would expect any accomplishment to be a relatively random event. We want to define project scope, which must include timing, quality, cost, and features content even if we are modifying a service and not a product per se. An unplanned change in scope is often called scope creep (see Figure 8.14). Scope creep can be a positive item if we keep it under control and know exactly what we are doing, which includes assessing the effect on costs, schedules, and quality. Scope creep will sometimes occur because we learn something about our project as we proceed through the project; in fact, we have seen some projects make a significant detour due to the amount of information they acquired during the measurement and analysis phases of the Six Sigma project. We can control scope creep using the following items: the project charter, a well-defined change management plan, an endorsement from the project champion, approval from a steering committee, and some method for

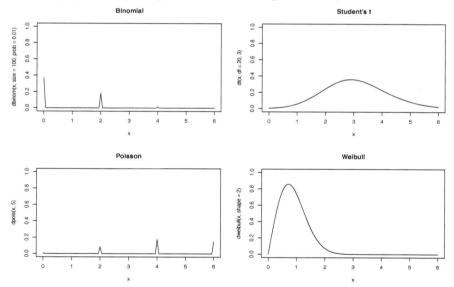

Figure 8.13 More probability distributions.

validating the change.

Goals are necessary in the sense that we use them to keep us on track toward project success. We can break goals into objectives, and objectives into targets. The words really do not matter as long as we understand why we are breaking our project down into more detail pieces. In some cases, the greater level of detail allows us to use binary approach to project management wherein a task or a target is either finished or it is not. If we are using project management software, this binary approach makes it easy to present management with schedule information such as percent complete. Our goals, objectives, targets must be reviewed frequently, in part because we wish to determine if they are still relevant. In a sense, if we can measure our goals, and we

Figure 8.14 Scope creep can be a boon or bust depending on how we control the change.

increase the likelihood that they are relevant; we might even call this evidence-based goal analysis.

Although the use of goals is a common technique in many management books, they should be more than slogans to impress managers. One of us use the motto "Never send garbage to a customer" to simplify the quality approach for the staff. It is similar to the approach of Ford Motor Company in the 1980s with "quality is job one."

In order for project performance measures make any sense, we need to baseline the project so that our measurements will let us know if we have made an improvement, mostly by comparing the baseline to subsequent changes. In effect, the baseline is a project snapshot. Some measures we might use are the following:

- Project budget variance

- Project schedule variance

- How many get reviews we have completed

- Accomplishment of customer due dates and internal due dates

- Milestone completion

- Resource consumption, both materials and hours worked

- Capital expenses

- Supplier on-time delivery

- Prelaunch inventory control

- Progress in prototype development

Although projects can become complex, they really have a small number of project

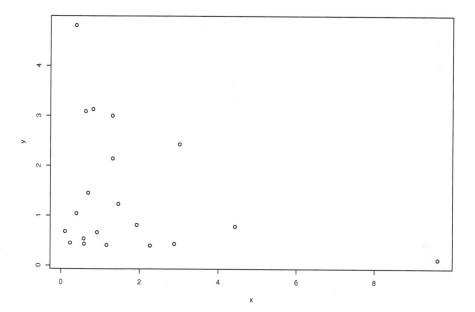

Figure 8.15 Scatter charts show the correlation (not causation) between two factors.

states:

- Below budget
- On budget
- Over budget
- Delayed budget
- Temporarily out of money
- Awaiting expected financing
- Account closed
- Unknown
- Account closed forever

For the schedule, we have the following:

- Ahead of schedule
- On schedule
- Behind schedule
- Suspended, but may return
- Stopped, and will not return
- Schedule started

- Completed
- Unknown (out-of-control)
- Aborted and will never return

In addition to these schedule and budget states, we could reduce an analogous set of conditions for the quality of the product. Schedule, budget, and quality are the three fundamental attributes of a product launch or a project in process as part of a Six Sigma initiative.

C. Measure

What are process characteristics? These are the input and output variables that tell us how well or how poorly our process functions. We use the SIPOC diagram as a starting point for describing our process. This diagram gives us the following information:

- The stakeholders in the form of suppliers and customers
- An explicit list of inputs
- An explicit list of outputs
- A process description that tells us how we transform the inputs into the outputs

If we have a process diagram, then what kind of items can we measure? On a manufacturing line, we will look at work in progress, work in queue, takt time, cycle time, throughput, and production test time. If we are evaluating a service, we may use some of the same metrics we use for manufacturing line or we may adapt them; for example, how long is a customer waiting in a queue?

When we build our process map, we can use several tools: value stream maps, process maps, spaghetti maps, and circle diagrams. Value stream maps help us to find wasted time and lost dollars. The process maps look much like a flowchart; we can use process maps to look for unnecessary processes. A spaghetti map can follow either material released to manufacturing line with the product release to shipping or both. Sometimes the spaghetti map resembles its own name because our manufacturing material is traveling all over the plant. Circle diagrams can show us which items are related to a specific process.

Sampling can be both a blessing and a curse. It is a blessing because sampling often reduces the cost of assessing whatever items at which we are looking. It is a curse because achieving a representative, unbiased, and homogeneous sample is not always easy to do. In some cases we will use the method called stratified sampling, wherein we randomly gather data from a set of bins, much as we would gather random samples from different drawers of a filing cabinet. Pure random sampling is often difficult; for example, we might do things as seemingly silly as selecting items after closing our eyes and turning around. With systematic sampling, we will choose a sample part where we have observed sample behavior after some specific number of pieces of material have passed by. Regardless of the technique we use, we must remain cognizant of the potential for bias in the data.

Data collection does not have to be expensive—simple check sheets on paper can be enough for some projects. We may already be collecting data on the particular area or item of interest. If not, we can begin our measurements on paper; one approach would be to use coding—that is, we measure the deviations from some meaningful value rather than the absolute values. This approach will often simplify our data collection as well as sometimes making it obvious what is going on. Coding is also useful for short-term data collection and is a technique used for short-term control charts in statistical process control. Perhaps the most important component of data collection is the data collection plan that defines exactly how we will collect data. One component will be the level of randomness desired in our data, given that randomness is difficult to prove and even more difficult to achieve.

We can measure both continuous and discrete data—sort of. In fact, almost all data is measured discretely, but some data is modeled continuously. An example would be the data we see on an oscilloscope measurement of an electronic signal. The oscilloscope samples the data sufficiently quickly to give the illusion of continuity; the mathematical lower limit for such sampling is the Nyquist frequency, which is roughly twice the frequency of the measure data. The twice the frequency rule of thumb may not apply if our data has a great deal of noise (random variation).

While measuring, we want to ensure that our tools are accurate (the mean is where it should be) and precise (the variance is minimized). The usual method is to perform a repeatability and reproducibility study on the measure tools to establish which factors contribute the most to variation. When we do a study, we try to ascertain the level of variation of our measuring tools, the level of variation caused by our employees, and the level of variation caused by any other factors such as the procedure itself.

As far as measurement systems go, we can measure just about anything, even categories that are ordinarily considered to be subjective; for example, therapists will use a scale called subjective units of distress. As long as everybody understands the meaning of the measurement system, we think such an approach is appropriate. We can also measure a variety of values that give us some idea of the performance of our departments: marketing, sales, engineering, research and development, supply chain management, customer satisfaction, and finance. Frequently, we will want to use paired indicators: we would pair number of lines of code created by software engineers versus the number of anomalies generated by that particular body of code. In this way, we end up with a check on the initial measurement; thus, retaining the integrity of our system.

Metrology is the science and art of maintaining our calibration system. We want to know that the measurements we take are both accurate and precise. The capability of a specific measuring device is given in terms of a reference standard, another device or piece of measuring equipment to which we compare our tool. We also have to consider how often we are going to check ourselves against standards, with an eye to system integrity as well as cost savings. For example, we have seen antennas calibrated annually when, in fact, they often only need calibration every three to four years, depending on the type of antenna. In addition to the actual measurements, we need to consider the integrity of our calibration supplier; in some cases, we have seen suppliers

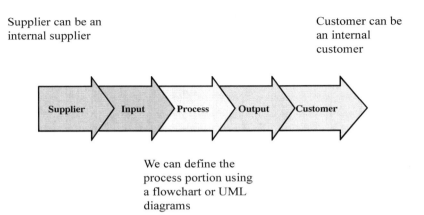

Supplier can be an
internal supplier

Customer can be
an internal
customer

We can define the
process portion using
a flowchart or UML
diagrams

Figure 8.16 This simple representation of a SIPOC diagram is the first step towards understanding our processes.

who did not know the proper method to calibrate a specific device, it still managed to produce a document indicating that the device has been calibrated. The situation implies that the laboratory or calibration manager must possess enough knowledge to

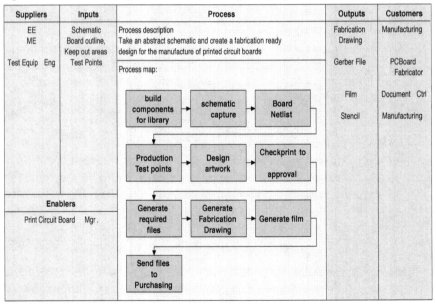

Figure 8.17 A more complex SIPOC diagram may help us define process improvement.

understand the supplier documentation.

Six Sigma and Lean Six Sigma are well known for their use of statistics. The use of statistics does not have to be complex unless there is a clear need for that level of complexity. When we talk about population, which are the totality of whatever we are looking at, we use the term parameters. When we talk about samples, which are a subset of the population and hopefully randomly gathered, we use the term "statistic." We may also look at the arithmetic mean for the geometric mean, variance, standard deviation, the median, and the range. Whenever we use these terms and calculations we need to be sure we understand the nature of the presumed underlying distribution. We know, for example, that the variance for a normal distribution is not calculated the same way we calculate the parents for a gamma distribution.

A major interest is a concept called the central limit theorem. The central limit theorem indicates that if we are studying the means of samples the resulting probability distribution function is that of a normal distribution. Since it is very common in manufacturing to take samples and calculate the means of those samples, it becomes very easy to use the rich body of data available for the normal distribution. When not using the means of samples, we must assess what kind of distribution we seem to be studying.

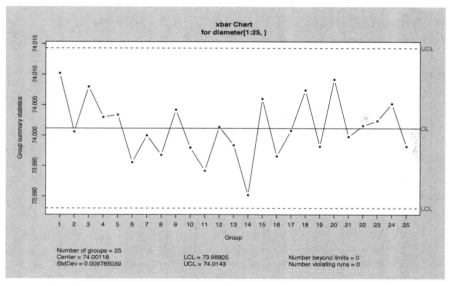

Figure 8.18 A sample XBar-R control chart.

We often see a term called "central tendency." We assume a central tendency for certain probability distribution functions: normal, t, logistic, and beta (under specific conditions). We can use the appropriate formula to calculate the mean once we know the distribution. Regardless of the distribution, we can always assess a value for the median, which simply says we have as many data points below a specific value as we have above a specific value. The median exists even for seemingly exotic distributions such as the Cauchy distribution, which has no moments (no mean, no variance, no standard deviation). The median is also more stable in value than the mean. We measure dispersion using the variance, the standard deviation (the square root of the variance), and the range. We recommend that measures of centrality always be paired with measures of dispersion—using the idea of paired indicators.

We find it difficult to think of a case where using graphical methods with statistics would not add value. The human eye and brain will often see the appropriate pattern more quickly than we can prove it with numerical techniques. We will also use graphical methods to present our data to others, since it simplifies understanding and provides a powerful argument. Statistical software can generate box-and-whisker plots, run charts, scatter diagrams, histograms, probability distribution plots, and a host of other diagrams.

Sometimes we will use the term descriptive statistics for those analyses where we want to know something about our sample or population, but we are not going to draw any inferences about those. In situations where we are going to draw inferences, we use inferential statistical analyses, which imply some level of test being used with the results. Not surprisingly, we need to use some level of care when drawing inferences from the data; for example, medical results are frequently given in the form of odds ratios, which is not the same thing as a straight probability statement.

The idea of probability generally refers to the frequency at which an event occurs. One of the fundamental concepts of probability is that of independent, which occurs when each event has no effect on any other event; for example, when we flip an honest coin the resulting head or tail is independent of any previous head or tail. We also know that some events are not independent and rely on some kind of precondition. The probability that something will not happen is the complement of the probability that the same thing will happen. A mutually exclusive event is one that removes the possibility of another event occurring. All statistics are derived from theories of probability. In general, we recommend that the Six Sigma practitioner have a basic idea of probabilities and be able to use the statistics appropriately. We are not recommending that the Six Sigma practitioner necessarily become a statistician.

In general, we see two kinds of probability distribution functions: discrete distributions and continuous distributions. The two most common discrete distributions are the binomial distribution and Poisson distribution. A set of common continuous distributions would include the normal distribution, the χ-squared distribution, the F distribution, and Student's t distribution. If we are doing reliability analyses, we might expect to see the gamma distribution or the Weibull distribution. Our favorite support text for analyzing probability distribution functions is *Six Sigma Distribution Modeling* by Andrew Sleeper[1].

Probably one of the most commonly used distributions is the normal distribution, not so much because of his most common distribution, but more likely because it is one of the best understood; in addition to which, it is also the distribution that occurs when we plot the means of samples. We see the binomial distribution when we have either/or choices, and interestingly, the binomial distribution begins to look like a normal distribution as a sample size increases. The Poisson distribution is often used to model arrival rates and is generally the tool of choice when analyzing situations that can be modeled as queues. We use the χ-squared distribution most commonly to ascertain whether a given distribution makes sense when modeled against the data (goodness-of-fit). Student's (William Gossett) t distribution is used with small samples and converges on a normal distribution at about 30 pieces. The F distribution is used to assess the relation of variances and sees much used in designed experiments.

We may also see a hypergeometric distribution (discrete) when the fact that we have removed a sample piece affects the calculation of the probability of the next piece; for example, removing a specific card from a deck of cards without replacement. This situation is also an example of a nonindependent probability calculation. We see the exponential, lognormal, and Weibull distribution in reliability engineering. These probability distribution functions are extremely flexible (along with the gamma distribution) and tell us something about what is going on based on their shape.

Process capability is one of those concepts well beloved by managers. The process capability indices attempt to compress a significant amount of quality information into two numbers. We use Cp to assess our actual distribution (normal) versus the required values; we use Cpk to assess the centering of our distribution between the tolerance specifications. These numbers can be useful when they are paired. We know of one situation where some gauge overlays (the part with the numbers and tick marks) had a satisfactory Cp but a terrible Cpk—it turned out the designed overlays were linear but the requirement was nonlinear! In the automotive industry, we may also see Pp, Ppk, and Cpm as other indices for long-term assessment of process performance. Because we anticipate process drift, we expect the Pp and Ppk values to be lower than Cp and Cpk.

If we are going to identify process capability but we know that our data are not normal, we can use percentages and the median in an analogous way to the mean and standard deviation we use with the more common indices. Alternatively, we can use some kind of transformation to convert our data to normality. Personally, we do not like the transformation approach, much preferring to explain what we are doing with the median and the percentages. One of the trickiest parts of using process capability indices is to avoid treating them as if they were a magic number. We must understand what these numbers really mean.

In order to calculate process capability and disease, we will not run a process capability study. Before we run the study, we should be able to prove to ourselves that our process is not statistical control; that is, the process is not chaotic. As with the statistical process control, we need to have the sampling plan, we must verify stability, and we should understand the level of normality of the data.

In some Six Sigma organizations, we will see a set of metrics with different terminology than traditional quality management: defects per million opportunities, defects per unit, rolled throughput yield, followed by percent defective and parts per million. For each of these, we can construct a cross-reference table so we can report our values in a format understood by upper management.

D. Analyze

Correlation is pretty much as the words sound: we attempt to establish a relation between two or more variables. Correlation is never the same as causation, except by accident. All we can say is that a given variable changes this way when another variable changes that way. We usually call one variable the independent variable and the other variable the dependent variable; however, the choice of words can give us the illusion that we are dealing with causation when, in fact, we are not. A typical regression analysis will provide us with a value that indicates how well the model predicts the observed data. Once again, need to be sure to understand that the prediction is by no means an indication of causation.

Figure 8.19 The result of a successful 5S effort is tidy storage, easy access, and visual system.

Regression analysis is one of our most important tools. We can use it to compare the reaction of one variable to another without implications causation. We can also use multivariate regression and the general linear model as a means for studying multiple factors simultaneously. In general, when we build a regression model we will also analyze for residuals; that is, the difference between the prediction of a model and the actual data. If we are doing a time series—that is to say, data over some duration—then we sometimes find that the residuals are more interesting than the actual data with regard to model building. Regression analysis can also be applied to nonlinear models; however, these models are substantially more complicated and difficult to understand.

Multivariable analysis can be accomplished using statistical tools such as principal components, factor analysis, discriminant analysis, multiple analysis of variance, and the general linear model itself. We can also use a much simpler graphical approach called "multivari studies." With this approach, we look at any fact that is measured as a variable and assess a variety of factors that are generally representative categories;

what is nice about this approach is that anomalies are relatively easy to detect because the human eye is so good at detecting patterns. Also in these studies, we will typically consider variation in terms of position on a product, cyclical behaviors, and temporal variation (changes over time).

We can also do the same thing with attributes that we have done with variables

Backsliding improvements

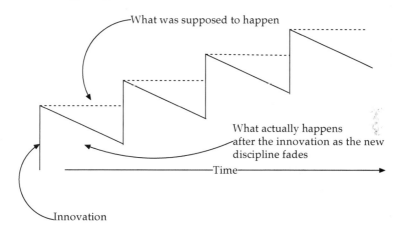

Kaizen's improved version

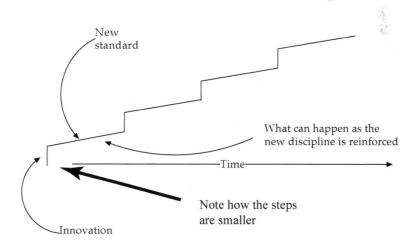

Figure 8.20 True, traditional Kaizen reduces risk and inexorably produces improvement.

using tabular formats for analysis; for example, a contingency table is a quick way to assess data that has categories such as male and female and smoking and nonsmoking.

Additionally, we have other forms of regression; for example, logit, probit, binary regression, and others. Some of these are relatively exotic for use in Six Sigma projects. In general, the more peculiar regressions find use in situations where we are assessing medical or biological data.

Here is some contingency table data using the R language (a powerful language for statistical work):

```
> binge=rbind(c(1630,1684),c(5550,8232)) # gives us the table
> binge
     [,1] [,2]
[1,] 1630 1684
[2,] 5550 8232
> chisq.test(binge)
```

Pearson's Chi-Squared Test with Yates' Continuity Correction
data: binge
X-squared = 86.8062, df = 1, p-value < 2.2e-16

```
> fisher.test(binge)
```

Fisher's Exact Test for Count Data
data: binge
p-value < 2.2e-16
alternative hypothesis: true odds ratio is not equal to 1
95 percent confidence interval:
1.329404 1.550380
sample estimates:
odds ratio
1.435615
The data above corresponds to the contingency table below:

Drinking issue	Men	Women	Total
Yes	1630	1684	3314
No	5550	8232	13782
Total	7180	9916	17096

Note how this data is, in fact, count data. We can definitely say we see a difference between the drinking issue of men and women.

Hypothesis Testing

Hypothesis testing is one of the more powerful tools we use in statistics. Basically, we will compare the results we get for either the mean or the variants were both using statistical tables relevant to the type of test we are conducting. As one might expect, we do have errors; for example type I errors occur when we throw away good parts and type II errors occur when we ship bad parts. Of the two kinds of errors, the type II error is more dangerous because it is so much harder to detect. Sometimes we except a given level of type I error as a cheaper alternative to ever sending a bad part, particularly when we are manufacturing safety-oriented products.

When we do hypothesis testing, we need to consider sample size and have some means for establishing the appropriate distribution for the data. Even though we may establish some level of significance during hypothesis testing, it is not always the case that the information we gain is significant in the real world. This detestable term significance is the complement of the term confidence. When we state a confidence interval, we are stating the probability that the single value we have calculated occurs within this region, sometimes called a "confidence band."

Here is a very small sample of a t-test (hypothesis test with exact sample size) in the R language:

```
> data=c(26,31,23,22,11,22,14,31) #this is the data
> m=mean(data)
> m
[1] 22.5 ## this is a result
> stdev=sqrt(var(data))
> stdev
[1] 7.191265 ## this is a result
> length(data)
[1] 8 ## this is a result
> t=(m-40)/(stdev/sqrt(length(data)))
> t
[1] -6.883 ## this is a result
> ## use pt to get p-value
> ## if pt < 0.05, reject null hypothesis
> pt(t,df=length(data)-1)
[1] 0.0001174466 ## this is a result
> #### REJECT the null hypothesis
```

Note that when we "reject" the null hypothesis, in effect we are saying the difference is statistically "significant" at some level (here, that level is 0.05).

We also need to be aware that when dealing with a continuous probability distribution, we do not really generate point estimates, we generate interval estimates. We can only make a true point estimate with a discrete distribution. Do not ever confuse the idea of confidence interval with the idea of a tolerance interval. A tolerance interval is something that we specify; a confidence interval is something that we calculate.

A common test for comparing means is the t-test; for example, we might compare two collections of sample parts. If we wish to compare the variance, the most common test is F test. Many other tests exist such as the χ-squared test, often used for goodness-of-fit.

The example R code that follows shows how to take a look at outlier values; that is say, data that is visually "out of line" with the rest of the data.

```
> out <- read.table("Outlier example.csv",header=FALSE)
```

```
> out
> mean(out)
  V1 # name of an untitled column
196.575
> quantile(out$V1) # note how we access column!
  0%    25%    50%    75%    100%
  1.00  54.75  103.50 199.50 2631.00
> IQR(out$V1)
[1] 144.75
> boxplot(out) # generates our graphic
> fivenum(out) # generates 'hinges' instead of true quantiles
[1]    1.0  54.5  103.5  200.0  2631.0
# lower hinge is median of lower half of data
# upper hinge is median of upper half of data
# easier to calculate
> sevenfive = quantile(out$V1,c(0.75))
> sevenfive
  75%
199.5
> twofive = quantile(out$V1,c(0.25))
> twofive
  25%
54.75
> top = sevenfive + 1.5 * (sevenfive - twofive)
> top
  75%
416.625
> [out>top]
[1]  700  438  700 2631 1148  951  479  465
```

Analysis of Variance (ANOVA)

We use analysis of variance most commonly as a method for determining the most significant factors in multiple factor analysis. In fact, we will nearly always see an analysis of variance following a designed experiment.

We can analyze categorical data with contingency tables. Categorical data is often called "count data" because we usually have some count expressed as an integer.

Nonparametric Tests

Nonparametric tests exist because sometimes we want to analyze our data but we have no clue as to the underlying probability distribution function. Many of the nonparametric tests still allow us to draw inferences about the data. In a sense, these tests are weaker than parametric tests but still represent a mathematical miracle. Some of these nonparametric tests include Mood's Median, Levene's test, Kruskal-Wallis, Mann-Whitney, and many more.

Failure Mode and Effects Analysis

We mention the failure mode and effects analysis in several places in this book. The technique is well documented by the automotive industry action group. In essence, we built a table, or matrix, and begin to assess potential failure modes. There are two

	Standard Order	Run Order	Point Type	Block	A:A	B:B	C:C	D:D	Response 1
1	12	1	1	1	1	1	-1	1	
2	10	2	1	1	1	-1	-1	1	
3	13	3	1	1	-1	-1	1	1	
4	5	4	1	1	-1	-1	1	-1	
5	9	5	1	1	-1	-1	-1	1	
6	16	6	1	1	1	1	1	1	
7	7	7	1	1	-1	1	1	-1	
8	8	8	1	1	1	1	1	-1	
9	11	9	1	1	-1	1	-1	1	
10	15	10	1	1	-1	1	1	1	
11	1	11	1	1	-1	-1	-1	-1	
12	14	12	1	1	1	-1	1	1	
13	2	13	1	1	1	-1	-1	-1	
14	4	14	1	1	1	1	-1	-1	
15	3	15	1	1	-1	1	-1	-1	
16	6	16	1	1	1	-1	1	-1	

Figure 8.21 The array is our "recipe." We record the results in the last column.

primary automotive tools that illustrate the connection between inspection and testing. Those are the design failure mode effects analysis (DFMEA) and the process failure mode effects analysis (PFMEA). These tools facilitate critical reviews of either the design or the processes that produces the designed product (production processes). We use this tool to critique a particular design or process function using failure modes, causes, effects, and some estimated values. The risk priority number is the product of

	Standard Order	Run Order	Point Type	Block	A:A	B:B	C:C	D:D	E:E	F:F	G:G	H:H	J:J	K:K	L:L	Res
1	9	1	1	1	1	1	1	-1	-1	-1	1	-1	1	1		
2	2	2	1	1	-1	1	1	-1	1	1	1	-1	-1	-1	1	
3	11	3	1	1	1	-1	1	1	-1	1	-1	-1	1	-1	1	
4	6	4	1	1	-1	-1	-1	1	-1	1	-1	-1	1	1	1	
5	5	5	1	1	1	1	-1	1	-1	-1	1	1	1	-1	1	
6	5	6	1	1	-1	-1	1	-1	1	-1	1	1	1	1	-1	
7	7	7	1	1	1	-1	-1	-1	1	1	1	1	-1	1	1	
8	10	8	1	1	-1	1	1	1	-1	-1	-1	1	-1	1	-1	
9	4	9	1	1	1	1	-1	1	1	1	1	1	1	-1	-1	
10	3	10	1	1	-1	1	1	-1	1	1	1	-1	-1	-1	-1	
11	12	11	1	1	-1	-1	-1	-1	1	-1	-1	-1	-1	-1	-1	
12	1	12	1	1	1	1	1	1	-1	-1	-1	-1	-1	1	-1	

Figure 8.22 This form of designed experiment can look at 11 factors in 12 runs!

estimation of the severity, probability and detection of a particular failure. The higher the RPN, the greater the risk to the product design or process. Recommended actions are often testing actions to determine if the estimates of severity, probability and detection are valid or to determine another way to achieve the function. In any case, the results of the DFMEA or PFMEA have an impact on the design verification testing and production validation testing.

Figure 8.23 The SWOT tool is simple and easy to use.

Item and Function Description

In most failure mode and effects analysis (FMEA) formats, this item occurs in the first column. It is as simple as defining the item under failure mode analysis. If we are developing an electronic or mechanical DFMEA, the item may refer to a drawing, a schematic, or a layout diagram. Entering the item alone is probably not sufficient: the "description" should also have a definition of the function of the item. Because it is the function that fails and not the item, we have to list each function separately from every other function while making it clear that they relate to a specific item.

Cause

If we can accept that failure modes are always the product of unplanned behavior at the outputs, then the causes come from one of two sources:

1. Unplanned behavior at an input, or

2. Incorrect behavior at a transformation

When we are dealing strictly with hardware, we can expect that most of the causes will fall into the class of input or inputs mated with an output or outputs. In some cases, however, we can treat the hardware as a form of program, where the input triggers a set of "internal" behaviors that progress to an output. The collection of "internal behaviors" constitutes a transformation. In the DFMEA layout, we should create a new "row" for each cause. This suggests that in the FMEA method of analysis all untoward effects ultimately resolve down to one cause—this understanding is a weakness of the FMEA method. If it is clear to us that multiple causes, independently or in combination, lead to a failure then we can use another tool—the fault tree—to analyze the failure mode.

Severity

The concept of severity in the DFMEA is significant for several reasons:

•   We use it to calculate a "significance" using a combined value called "RPN"

•   We can designate items that present safety issues—which should receive analysis regardless of their RPN

•   We establish a baseline against which we can compare our action results

•   We start off with a list recommended by SAE J1739

We should note that the SAE J1739 list is *not* the final word on severity. MIL-STD-1629A, for example, uses the MIL-STD-882 (Safety and Hazard Analysis) four category classification system to judge severity: Category I = Catastrophic; Category II = Critical; Category III = Marginal; and Category IV = Minor. The government recognizes that Categories I and II are significant regardless of their occurrence or detection and requires that these items be explicitly called out. SAE set up the J1739 format for a granularity of 10 categories and this is probably the most common arrangement. The DFMEA may elaborate on the definitions contained in the standard. If these documents are subject to customer review, all parties should agree on the meanings in the severity categories.

Occurrence

In the DFMEA, "occurrence" relates the frequency of a failure mode and uses a scale from 1 to 10. SAE J1739 recommends a set of ranking criteria in a relatively straightforward table. However, the DFMEA team can set any standard they want; for example, in some cases the criteria for establishing occurrence are simply unavailable. In many cases, the team will *not* have empirical data to support their estimates, especially if they are working on a new product. Another case occurs in a situation where the DFMEA becomes a tool for software. With a given software version and a given failure mode, the event will occur in all products that have that software. In most cases, it makes more sense to simply set the occurrence value at "5" and eliminate it from the calculation.

Design Controls

For a Design FMEA, design controls are typically one, some, or all of the following:

- Reviews
- Computer-aided tools
- Testing
- Inspection
- Standards

The point is that we control designs by performing a collection of "best practices" which we believe result in better designs. In some cases—inspections, for example—we know empirically that the design control does in fact lead to a more defect-free design. When the design control is a test, the FMEA team should call out the specific test document or test that is relevant to the particular failure mode. This way, the DFMEA becomes not only an anticipatory tool, but also a means for specifying test cases. The related test document should show how the test cases flow from the DFMEA to the test description. Reliasoft Corporation has created software called xFMEA that will generate a test document from the D- or PFMEA.

Detection Description

The detection description or detection value provides a way to subjectively evaluate the capability of a design control to detect a defect in the product.

Risk Priority Number (RPN)

This value is the product of the severity, occurrence, and detection values determined after "actions taken":

RPN = severity x occurrence x detection

The higher the RPN, the more significant the failure mode. It is also important to remember criticality, which ties in most strongly with the idea of severity. For example, safety issues are significant regardless of the final RPN.

Recommended Actions

In a design FMEA, recommended actions usually revolve around design modifications that lower the RPN value. It is also possible that the team may come up with NO recommendations. Recommendations may also be procedural; that is, the problem may be so intractable that the team recommends the problem be handled in the instruction manual for the product or a data sheet.

Responsibility and Target Completion Date

This column tries to establish ownership of issues as well as define a time at which the problem will come to resolution. Where there is no ownership, nobody does the design and detection work necessary to improve the product and the FMEA fails! Where there is no completion date, we have no way to audit the FMEA to determine if the engineer ever took the recommended action. Again, the FMEA fails!

Actions Taken

This column implies that either the FMEA team or the responsible engineer or engineers have taken the steps necessary to improve the product. If the "box" is empty, then, presumably no action has occurred and the product does not improve. This portion of the FMEA can also serve to record decisions to *not* act and point to an external document that defines that decision. Remember, the FMEA is a tool to help us work better, not a bureaucratic go-through-the-motions waste of time. We have seen the FMEA treated like a checklist item many times in order to provide documentation for a Production Part Approval Process (PPAP) notebook. Doing this kind of paper-wrestling misses the point! The technique is potentially a massive money-saver because we are terminating problems before they really become issues. The "actions taken" section helps document the activities we actually did in order to make a better product.

Sev, Occ, and Det

After we take action, we recalculate the severity, occurrence, and detection values. All of the comments made in previous sections still apply. If we have done our job well, the new values should be decidedly lower than the old.

Final RPN

This value is the product of the new severity, occurrence, and detection values determined after "actions taken":

RPN = severity x occurrence x detection

When creating an FMEA, we need to remember that the work is a team effort. No absolute RPN values exist. The team will have to decide ahead of time what values are to be considered significant. Additionally, all severity values in the range of eight to ten should be reviewed for criticality; in other words, they may not happen often and they may be readily detectable, but their potential for large-scale damage is enough to merit special attention.

Anticipation

One of the most significant benefits of the FMEA lies in the anticipation of failure. This does not mean we are compiling self-fulfilling prophecies—it means we are taking deliberate and systematic efforts to manage problems and risks before they can become problems and risks. And we capture our efforts in a compact format useful for quick study and conducive to terse descriptions.

Problems

If and when problems occur, the black belt can return to the FMEA to see if this particular problem had already been considered. If not, then update the FMEA; if yes, then wonder why the issue was not dealt with from the beginning.

Documentation
The FMEA can also serve as documentation that appropriate failure anticipation has been taken by the firm. That is, should we have to go to court during a litigation, a well-formulated FMEA can serve as evidence that we have worked diligently to design or manufacture a high quality product.

Product Improvement
The design FMEA is a tool for product improvement. When created with the right attitude, it can serve as a large quality function deployment (QFD). Theoretically, if every potential failure mode has already been considered, then they should have all been dealt with during the action phase of the FMEA.

Process Improvement
The Process FMEA is a tool for process improvement. When created with the right attitude, it can be used to eliminate all significant line problems from the very beginning. Any process can be analyzed, including front office business processes.

Additional Analysis Methods

When planning during Six Sigma projects, or any other project, we might perform an activity called a gap analysis. The gap analysis allows us to set a baseline that we might call the "as is-is state" and as our project evolves we can compare ourselves to an already defined future state. Another way to do this that has been used successfully by Royal Dutch Shell is the activity called scenario planning. With scenario planning, we tell rational stories about the future based on some categories: a better future, an okay future, a moderately bad future, and a very bad future. When planning based on scenarios, our goal is to make any of our decisions robust to all of these scenarios; that is, it should not matter which scenario occurs because our decision is robust.

Root cause analysis is an approach based on the assumption that if we remove a reputed root cause, we also eliminate the consequent effects. In many cases, this approach is not particularly deadly in the realm of reality. However, we need to consider situations where we have a set of conditions that predispose our machine towards failure followed by a precipitating event. We may feel moved to consider the precipitating event to be the root cause; however, we should also consider the collection of events that predisposed our part to fail. When using root cause analysis, several methodologies exist: from Toyota, we have the five whys; we can use the Pareto chart; or, if we are an automotive company, we might choose to use the eight disciplines approach. The choice of methodology matters less than whether we have attained some level of knowledge about the set of contingencies that produces the undesired effect. Once we have comprehension, we can save our knowledge and pass it on to other engineers and company employees.

If instead of root cause analysis, we are trying to eliminate problems before they happen, we can use failure mode and effects analysis or fault tree analysis. Failure mode and effect analysis uses a simple matrix format that is well defined by the automotive industry action group. Fault tree analysis is more involved, and generally requires special tools, a lot of teamwork, and substantial amounts of patience.

E. Improve

The predominant tool used in Six Sigma for improvement is called the design of experiments (see Figure 8.21 and Figure 8.22). This approach allows us to modify all contributing factors at the same time so that we can observe the change in the effect. We use a collection of matrices, or arrays, as recipes for modifying the contributing factors. We use the analysis of variance to determine which factors are highly significant. Once we know the significant factors, we may be able to use multiple variable regression techniques to build a model such that we can optimize these contributing factors to achieve the most beneficial effect. What we want to avoid is the one factor experiment, because this type of experiment only changes one variable at a time and will never show us any of the combined effects. In fact, we have no way of discerning when we have these combinations.

In this particular book, we will not provide a detailed explanation of designed experiments, but we suggest the reader take advantage of one or several of the many monographs available. We consider this technique to be extremely important not only during the design phase but once we are manufacturing the product.

Once we start a design experiment, we should push through to the end of the recipe. If we try to change our experimental recipe while in the middle of gathering data, we will most likely gather results that have minimal meaning. Yes, we know some tools are available to deal with the situation said, but this adds a lot of complexity without adding much value. When using design experiments we can expect to learn a new lexicon of terms; for example:

• *Blocking* to remove or reduce the effects of nuisance variables

• *Interactions*, which are combinations of contributing factors

• *Randomization*, which removes sequence bias

• *Sample size*, which controls the power of our results

• *Error*

• *Treatment* or the modification of a contributing factor

• *Response* or the modification of the effect

Waste Elimination

Waste elimination is a key concept in lean manufacturing—that does not mean it cannot be used in Six Sigma or Lean Six Sigma. We have already discussed the seven traditional wastes. Other important concepts are the following:

• Pull systems grab material as needed rather than pushing them through the system based on a production plan

• Kanban cards or light are signals that a piece is complete and we are ready for the next piece

• 5S is a system for cleaning up our work areas which, once complete, will let us know something is awry when we detect untidiness

- Standard work provides a baseline for measuring performance and standardizes approaches to manufacture and assembly
- Poka-yoke is effectively mistake-proofing our designs
- Cycle-time reduction occurs when we reduce the amount of time it takes to build or assemble a product (also works for services)
- Continuous flow happens when we have no stoppages
- Single-minute exchange of die (SMED) is an approach to reducing the setup times required for equipment (e.g., adding the component reels to a surface mount machine)
- One-touch exchange of die (OTED) is an aggressive technique for shortening time over SMED as well as reducing the amount of movement required

Kaizen is a concept of continuous movement. This was spelled out over twenty years ago, we implement kaizen by forging ahead with tens and perhaps hundreds of small projects. Part of the reason for this lies in the fact that small changes are more likely to produce long-term cultural modification. Unfortunately, during the last 20 years we have seen an alternative form arrive that is called the "kaizen blitz." The idea behind the kaizen blitz is that we can pick an area in our plant or office and over a period of a few days we can focus entirely on that area and cause massive transformation. We are less concerned with the improvements that occurred during a kaizen blitz and more concerned about the sustainability of the improvement. Obviously, we favor the older, slower, and more sustainable approach with its delayed gratification rather than the immediate gratification of the kaizen blitz.

Another technique is known as the "theory of constraints" or "constraints management." The fundamental idea of this concept is that a process is constrained by its slowest subprocess. In general, we apply the theory of constraints by seeking out constraints, elevating their importance, looking for other solutions to the constraint, and doing whatever we can to eliminate that particular sub process as a constraint. This multi step process goes on forever. Constraints will shift; as we fix one constraint another subprocess will then become the constraining item. The theory of constraints is relatively easy to understand and just as easy to implement. While it is not always the optimal approach, it is nearly always a good approach. We should also note that kanban-controlled manufacturing lines have generally already timed themselves in synchrony with the constraint. Even though we have attained synchrony, we have not necessarily improved the performance of the line; hence, the use of the theory of constraints.

We can try other techniques to prove line flow; for example, we might use a genetic algorithm to find the fittest approach for a particular scenario. While this method can work, it is certainly more difficult to implement than the theory of constraints.

We have all sorts of options for improving our processes; for example, we have already mentioned the possibility of using simulations during design and during testing. Why not simulate the process? If we have a high-quality simulation, the verisimilitude should be adequate to allow us to make an informed decision about the quality of our improvement. If we do not have simulation capability, we can run pilot tests, we can execute small-scale designed experiment, and we might even use benchmarking. In effect, we are saying there is really no excuse for avoiding process improvement.

We can also analyze our designs, our processes, and/or test for feasibility. One simple way to do this is to analyze the strengths, weaknesses, the opportunities, and the threats (SWOT, see Figure 8.23) present in whatever it is we are trying to do. At the risk of using another acronym, we can do a PEST analysis: political, environmental, social, and technological factors. It really does not matter what the acronym is—it matters whether or not we put the time and the effort into checking our ideas.

F. Control

We hesitate to write this section because what is often called control is more like the illusion of control. In spite of this, we do have some statistical tools that can help us sustain our progress. One of the most potent tools is statistical process control. Basically, what we are doing here is collecting the means of samples, plotting the results, and looking to see whether we have meaningful variation or random variation. These charts allow us to see the difference.

Engineering process control occurs when we take statistical process control and make modifications to parameters based on what we see. In engineering process control, we will always use a gain to make the adjustment in order to avoid what is called tampering. The reason for this is that tampering will often drive the process out of control, whereas using a gain will help us to process within control.

We only show one kind of control chart in this book because the full range of control charts is outside the scope of this book (if you want more details read *Six Sigma for the New Millennium,* 2nd Edition by Kim H. Pries).

We have never seen a case where intelligent application of statistical process control has not provided some level of value to the practitioner. At a minimum, we will know more about our process and its stability. If we are lucky, we may detect an assignable cause amidst the forest of random variation and be able to do a process improvement.

Other Control Tools

Total productive maintenance is most commonly seen in lean manufacturing initiatives. The purpose of total productive maintenance is to reduce the amount of unplanned machine downtime to a minimum. In order to achieve this goal, we want to practice 5S as well as a well-considered program of machine maintenance. Sometimes, our program of machine maintenance is not necessarily based on the calendar; for example, we know of a custom surface mount machine where the operators knew the belt was due for replacement by feeling "hairs" on the sides of the belt. Of course, this approach required the operator to check the belt on a daily basis. The key point here is that, regardless of the method we choose for scheduling, we minimize the unplanned downtime of the machine.

A visual factory is the name for an approach to increasing efficient behaviors, whether it is in the office or in an actual factory. The general idea is that we are able to discern the state of whatever is going on by simply looking. We have used this technique on manufacturing lines, in laboratories, and in the office. We have also seen the technique used to great advantage in high school classrooms, where students immediately know where to store the tools they have been using in class. On the manufacturing line, we use visual methods to indicate flow rate, performance against quota, and whether we have an emergency challenge. We can also use visual methods in the stock room to indicate a need to release more material to the floor or to restock the warehouse itself.

A control plan is a document we use to specify our processes in enough detail that the people who execute the process know what to do regardless of the circumstance. A typical automotive control plan bears a relationship to the failure mode and effects analysis document but is not oriented around failure modes. One of the more interesting fields in a typical control plan room is that for reaction plan; that is, what do we do when the desired behavior of that particular operation is not happening. In project management, we call this contingency plan and it is a powerful tool for saving time and money.

Sustain Improvements

We use the control portion of the Six Sigma sequence to help us sustain improvements. However, this in itself may not be enough to accomplish the objective. We will want to capture lessons learned in a format that is readily extensible by the employees that need to understand these lessons. We have used the term "stupidity cycle" to describe what happens in the enterprise when employees who remember the last set of fiascoes leave the corporation and we see a resurgence of the same mistakes made previously. One of the most difficult tasks when capturing lessons learned is determining the method we will use to store our lessons; for example, do we use the database or do we use some kind of free-form indexing engine? If the lessons are not readily available to the employees, the employees will simply ignore them.

We could also potentially sustain our improvements by creating training plans that incorporate behaviors that manage the situation that produced the lesson. We think this approach is one of the best ways to incorporate lessons learned for new employees. It is more of a problem when we deal with experienced employees that may have forgotten the last batch of catastrophes. Even so, we can certainly use training to sustain improvement and new processes.

We can also capture our lessons learned in our business documentation in the form of standard operating procedures and work instructions. Again, the use of these documents is potentially easier with new employees than it is with experienced employees.

We also recommend scheduling some kind of ongoing evaluation of our policies and procedures to ensure that they are current and that they are still adding value to the enterprise. We can do this by making this kind of evaluation part of our culture and also by formally scheduling these evaluations. We may even consider the cyclic process used in constraints management to determine if a policy or procedure has become a meaningless constraint on improvement. These evaluations can become a tool also for overcoming the syndrome we call "not invented here." This situation occurs when we think we always have to create our own tools instead of buying them; hence, the buy or build decision becomes institutionalized.

G. Design for Six Sigma (DFSS) Frameworks and Methodologies

Design for Six Sigma is the standard approach used to drive the enterprise from the roughly four or five sigma that we are able to achieve in manufacturing to an honest Six Sigma. The sequence for design for Six Sigma is similar to that for the regular manufacturing Six Sigma: design, measure, analyze, design, and validate. An alternative version is defined, measure, analyze, design, optimize, and validate. Yet another version as ideation, design, optimization, and validation. The sequences and their names really matter less than what it is we do with the product. For example, we can use the robust design sequence to produce a product that minimizes product returns and virtually eliminates recalls. The statistical methods used in design for Six Sigma are very similar to those used in the manufacturing version of Six Sigma. The only significant difference we would expect to see in a design for Six Sigma project is a much more frequent use of designed experiments as a tool for study and optimization. By itself, a design experiment does not produce an optimized result; we take the data from our designed experiment and we use another tool such as a genetic algorithm to produce an optimized result. Our favorite support book for design for Six Sigma is *Design for Six Sigma Statistics* by Andrew Sleeper[2].

Design for X is the design counterpart to critical to X (CTX); in other words, we will design for cost, manufacturability, test, maintainability, quality, and reliability. Different enterprises will choose those factors they wish to emphasize. Many times, our design choices will be based on design constraints; for example, our product may have to fit into a cavity of a specific size. In this design, this requirement becomes a constraint on what we can do with the product. Constraints are not necessarily something that is bad in design, for constraints are often the wellspring for creativity and invention. We use the "designed for…" terminology as a means of emphasizing our priorities to our design teams.

"Robust design" is a design approach founded on the work of Taguchi. The first phase involves concepts assigned, and follows most standard approaches to developing concepts, selling them to management, and seeking customer approval. The next stage is called "parameter design" and it uses designed experiments to ensure that the design team makes choices that are resistant to extraneous environmental influences. In most cases, parameter design will consume the greatest amount of time of the three phases. By the time we are finished with parameter design, we should be close to a finished product. The third and final phase is called "tolerance design" because this is the stage where we apply tolerances to those parts of the design that require them. Tolerance design occurs last because this is the most expensive part of the robust design process (see Figure 8.9) and we wish to minimize the amount of tolerancing we must do in order to make the product satisfactory.

XI. EXERCISES

• Match Porter's five forces with descriptions of their impact on organizations.

- Identify the strategic characteristics of Porter's five forces model.
- Match assessments of a market position with the Porter's forces they represent.
- Recognize examples of proactive strategies associated with an analysis of Porter's five forces.
- Recognize the strategic goal of portfolio architecting.
- Recognize examples of the elements of set-based design.
- Sequence activities associated with a TRIZ approach to problem solving.
- Identify how TRIZ benefits a DFSS initiative.
- Recognize the structure of the conceptual phase of modern systematic design.
- Recognize the key characteristics and benefits of critical parameter management.
- Choose the best concept and take it into the next step of a Pugh analysis in a given scenario.
- Identify key characteristics of Pugh analysis.
- Sequence the steps in a Pugh analysis.
- For a real set of design choices (or something you really want), build a Pugh concept selection matrix—be prepared to defend your choice.
- Explain why you might find the belt hierarchy to be both annoying and offensive.
- Come up with at least five reasons why Six Sigma might not be an optimal choice.
- What are the benefits of using the lean approach, as opposed to Six Sigma?
- Is Lean Six Sigma a meaningful conflation of improvement methodologies or is it yet another method for making money for consultants?
- When does it make sense to use the project approach and when does it make sense to just simply make the change that gives us the cost reduction?
- How do we put all of our changes in a configuration management system?
- Where would we use statistical process control?
- What are the key concepts involved in the use of engineering process control? Why would we choose engineering process control over statistical process control?
- When do you think we should avoid using the designed experiment method? When do you think we must use the designed experiment method? Defend your choices.
- How do we avoid adding to the cost of attaining the cost reduction and yet use a project approach to control our progress? In other words, how do we avoid a top heavy, expensive, and self-negating project approach?
- What is the optimal size for a project team? Defend your comments based on

your experiences with team-based projects.

- What are some of the difficulties with using a measurement system? For example, how could we mislead ourselves using a balance scorecard? Do all measurement systems produce distortions? What are the inherent contradictions in all measurement systems?

- If measurement systems produce difficulties, then what alternatives do we have? Be prepared to defend your statement.

- Why do we baseline our projects before we start?

- How do we know we have made an improvement when we finish our Six Sigma project?

- Provide at least five methods or approaches that support the idea of improvement sustainability.

- What are the best ways to eliminate problems before they happen? Is there really any one way?

- Every problem always has one root cause. Argue for or against this statement, supporting your comments with examples from your experience.

- What open source tools are available to analyze designed experiments? What is the quality level of these tools?

- What is the advantage of using a commercial designed experiment tool?

- Research "response surface methodology." What is the advantage to using this advanced form of designed experiment? What are potential disadvantages of using this approach?

- What is the problem with only two levels in designed experiments? And what is the problem when we choose to examine more than two levels per factor? What kind of trade-offs do we have to make?

- Is the designed experiment approach too complicated to use for ordinary people? What kind of training do we need in order to use this powerful technique for improvement?

- How do we implement the DOE concept on a day-to-day basis? What are the advantages to doing so?

- Does analysis of variance (ANOVA) tell us all we need to know?

- What are some good ways to optimize once we have DOE results?

- How stable is our result? Should we have a campaign of ongoing DOE replications?

ENDNOTES

1. Sleeper, Andrew D. *Six Sigma Distribution Modeling*. Six Sigma Operational Methods. New York, NY: McGraw-Hill, 2007.

2. Sleeper, Andrew D. *Design for Six Sigma Statistics: 59 Tools for Diagnosing and Solving Problems in DFSS Initiatives*. Six Sigma Operational Methods. New York, NY: McGraw-Hill, 2006.

CHAPTER 9 – Saving Money with Lean Manufacturing

I. Rubric for Lean Manufacturing

Criteria	Level 1 (50–59%)	Level 2 (60–69%)	Level 3 (70–79%)	Level 4 (80–100%)
Analyze and explain autonomation (jidoka)f	Analyzes and explains autonomation with limited knowledge and understanding	Analyzes and explains autonomation with some knowledge and understanding	Analyzes and explains autonomation with considerable knowledge and understanding	Analyzes and explains autonomation with excellent knowledge and understanding
Analyze standard work	Analysis of standard work in terms of functionality demonstrates limited understanding	Analysis of standard work in terms of functionality demonstrates some understanding	Analysis of standard work in terms of functionality demonstrates considerable understanding	Analysis of standard work in terms of functionality demonstrates thorough understanding
Apply the kanban method	Applies the kanban method with limited effectiveness	Applies the kanban method with some effectiveness	Applies the kanban method with considerable effectiveness	Applies the kanban method with a high degree of effectiveness
Apply the waste identification and removal approach to their enterprise	Applies the waste identification and removal approach to their enterprise with limited effectiveness	Applies the waste identification and removal approach to their enterprise with some effectiveness	Applies the waste identification and removal approach to their enterprise with considerable effectiveness	Applies the waste identification and removal approach to their enterprise with a high degree of effectiveness
Choose suitable materials and processes	Chooses suitable materials and processes with limited effectiveness	Chooses suitable materials and processes with some effectiveness	Chooses suitable materials and processes with considerable effectiveness	Chooses suitable materials and processes with a high degree of effectiveness
Choose the most appropriate production method by conducting a test run	Rarely chooses the most appropriate production method by conducting a test run	Sometimes chooses the most appropriate production method by conducting a test run	Often chooses the most appropriate production method by conducting a test run	Always or almost always chooses the most appropriate production method by conducting a test run
Communicate information clearly with a visual factory	Creates a visual factory with limited clarity	Creates a visual factory with some clarity	Creates a visual factory with considerable clarity	Creates a visual factory with a high degree of clarity
Implement Total productive maintenance (TPM)	Total productive maintenance demonstrating limited use of technology	Total productive maintenance demonstrating some use of technology	Total productive maintenance demonstrating considerable use of technology	Total productive maintenance demonstrating expert use of technology
Conduct pilot runs, analyze results, and modify as needed	Conducts pilot runs, analyzes results, and modifies as needed with limited effectiveness	Conducts pilot runs, analyzes results, and modifies as needed with some effectiveness	Conducts pilot runs, analyzes results, and modifies as needed with considerable effectiveness	Conducts pilot runs, analyzes results, and modifies as needed with a high degree of effectiveness

Criteria	Level 1 (50–59%)	Level 2 (60–69%)	Level 3 (70–79%)	Level 4 (80–100%)
Demonstrate good housekeeping practices	Rarely demonstrates good housekeeping practices	Sometimes demonstrates good housekeeping practices	Often demonstrates good housekeeping practices	Routinely demonstrates good housekeeping practices
Designs cells and one-piece flow	Creates cells and one-piece flow with limited design skills	Creates cells and one-piece flow with some design skills	Creates cells and one-piece flow with good design skills	Creates cells and one-piece flow with excellent design skills
Demonstrate planning skills	Demonstrates limited planning skills	Demonstrates some planning skills	Demonstrates considerable planning skills	Demonstrates excellent planning skills
Demonstrate setup process reduction required to manufacture products	Is able to demonstrate correct preparation process reduction required to manufacture products with limited success	Is able to demonstrate correct preparation process reduction required to manufacture products with some success	Is able to demonstrate correct preparation process reduction required to manufacture products with good success	Is able to demonstrate correct preparation process reduction required to manufacture products with excellent success
Describe customer demand pace (takt time)	Describes customer demand pace (takt time) with limited detail and examples	Describes customer demand pace (takt time) with some detail and examples	Describes customer demand pace (takt time) with considerable detail and examples	Describes customer demand pace (takt time) with excellent detail and examples
Describe continuous improvement (kaizen)	Description of continuous improvement (kaizen) provides limited information	Description of continuous improvement (kaizen) provides some information	Description of continuous improvement (kaizen) provides considerable information	Description of continuous improvement (kaizen) provides thorough information
Describe how to optimize production systems	Description of how to optimize production systems provides limited information	Description of how to optimize production systems provides some information	Description of how to optimize production systems provides considerable information	Description of how to optimize production systems provides thorough information
Develop a value stream map	Develops a value stream map with limited effectiveness	Develops a value stream map with some effectiveness	Develops a value stream map with considerable effectiveness	Develops a value stream map with a high degree of effectiveness
Develop an emergency action plan	Develops an emergency action plan with limited effectiveness	Develops an emergency action plan with some effectiveness	Develops an emergency action plan with considerable effectiveness	Develops an emergency action plan with a high degree of effectiveness
Identify value added/nonvalue added work	Identifies value added/nonvalue added work with limited success	Identifies value added/nonvalue added work with some success	Identifies value added/nonvalue added work with considerable success	Identifies value added/nonvalue added work with a high degree of success
Handle waste products effectively	Rarely handles waste products effectively	Sometimes handles waste products effectively	Often handles waste products effectively	Routinely handles waste products effectively

Criteria	Level 1 (50–59%)	Level 2 (60–69%)	Level 3 (70–79%)	Level 4 (80–100%)
Lay out patterns to minimize waste of materials	Lays out patterns to minimize waste of materials with limited success	Lays out patterns to minimize waste of materials with some success	Lays out patterns to minimize waste of materials with considerable success	Lays out patterns to minimize waste of materials with a high degree of success
Using the problem solving model to implement mistake-proofing	Uses problem solving skills to implement mistake-proofing with limited effectiveness	Uses problem solving skills to implement mistake-proofing with some effectiveness	Uses problem solving skills to implement mistake-proofing with considerable effectiveness	Uses problem solving skills to implement mistake-proofing with a high degree of effectiveness

II. Questions to Ponder

- How does 5S keep costs under control?
- What are the benefits of standardization?
- How does mass produced custom product or service impact the value proposition?
- What does kanban bring to our organization's efficiency and cost?
- Does your company have a long-term design or service improvement program?
- What approach to cost improvement works best and when?
- Are there benefits to an ad hoc cost improvement activity?
- Does your company recognize time improvement as a cost improvement activity?

III. Cost Improvement Scenario

A. Situation

A fast-food restaurant has a turnover in management. The new manager notices that during peak periods of demand, the assembly of the food and placing the food into the distribution cabinet is slower than the demand from the customers. In the present kitchen layout, the cook produces batches of food and then moves closer to the food cabinet where the cook then wraps and places the food into the cabinet. This consumes time and is so obviously inefficient the entire food making and delivery process appears awkward. Even under the most moderate of customer volume, a single cook cannot handle the demand given the build and delivery process.

B. Objective

The objective is streamline the kitchen and sandwich build area in a way that will allow one person to both build and deliver the food to the food cabinet and customer efficiently for moderate customer volume. The build will more closely resemble a single part flow and not the large batch build that presently exists. The sandwich building area needs to be closer to the delivery to the cabinet and in such a way that allows for easy transfer from the build area to the cabinet.

C. Action

A further study of the work performed in the kitchen during busy times and the excess movement becomes even clearer. The table where the build takes place and the cabinet are too far apart. The electrical layout in the kitchen requires another plug to add to accommodate the multiple electrical appliances. Addition of the electrical outlet allows the cabinet to be closer to the build station. With these two key elements close together, a single cook situated between these two stations now can build the sandwiches as single pieces and quickly. The final touch was to move the product wrapping material on a shelf in front of the cook. In this way, the cook is centrally located to the raw product, the build station and the wrapping components. This means easy access for each step of the build and delivery to the customer. The new layout amounted to a work cell area that previously was a discontinuous work line.

Figure 9.1 Storage of small electronic components so we do not mix or lose the parts.

D. Results

The kitchen staff did not immediately embrace the new kitchen layout. The manager demonstrated the new way of moving in the work area. With the areas, the cook needs access in a central location eliminating the excess movement from the process. It is possible to access materials, build the sandwich, and then wrap and deliver to the cabinet where the cashiers pick the food up and deliver to the customer. It becomes very easy for a single cook to build and deliver the product under relatively high customer volume. The limitation was then the cooking area itself, specifically the grill and ovens. This limitation cannot be resolved.

E. Aftermath

Eventually, the cooks see the new way of working as an improvement in delivery. The speed of execution and ease of access means reduced stress upon the kitchen staff. The benefit was even more evident in the breakfast rush of the restaurant. Where the previous kitchen arrangement required two people just to build and another to cook; now it was possible to have one person build most of the time and only under heavy customer volume, would there be a need for two and almost never three kitchen personnel.

Figure 9.2 Orderly maintenance of connections and wire harness repairing components reduces time to fix.

IV. What Is Lean?

Initially, we can view the lean approach as a means by which we reduce waste. That seems easy enough. What kinds of waste? The seven wastes are the following:

212 Reducing Process Costs with Lean, Six Sigma, and Value Engineering Techniques

- Transportation
- Inventory
- Motion
- Wait
- Overprocessing
- Overproduction
- Defects

We deal with the seven wastes elsewhere in this book.

A more sophisticated concept is that of "pull" versus "push." Hagel, Brown, and Davison[1] identify the evils of push as:

- Scarcity mentality
- Elites decide
- Hierarchical organizations
- People to be molded
- Bigger is better = economies of scale
- Forecast demand
- Central allocation of resources
- Meet demand

Pull, on the other hand, involves:

- Finding
- Connecting
- Innovating
- Reflecting

They also discuss loosely coupled modularity, an ideal for software since the days of Yourdon and Constantine's[3] early work on structured software. The general idea of pull is that we ask for what we need and our desire percolates back through the system to fulfill this need. Rather than forecasting demand, we wait for demand to happen and then pull what we need through the system. At the same time, we achieve the drum-buffer-rope effect used in the Theory of Constraints. We need to ensure that we have continuous flow (or close to it) with minimal interruptions. This goal implies that we also have a flow of information in addition to the flow of material.

In a fully activated pull system, we might have thousands of suppliers who can meet our needs at hundreds of locations (or thousands...). Each cell only needs two pieces of information: what cell our work came from and what cell our work is going to.

V. Production Organization or 5S

One of the features of lean implementation is the use of 5S, which we define to be:
- Sort—getting things cleaned up and organized (see Figure 9.1 and Figure 9.2)
- Set in order—organize, identify and arrange everything in a work area
- Shine—regular maintenance
- Standardize—make it easy to maintain—simplify and standardize
- Sustain—retaining our success

Sorting indicates we will sort everything in each work area. We retain only what is necessary. Materials, tools, equipment, and supplies that are infrequently used should be stored separately. Items that are unused should be discarded. Do not keep things around for just in case situations. We should also beware of the sunk cost fallacy: we paid money for this unused item and now we have to keep it forever. As a result of the sorting process, we eliminate or repair malfunctioning equipment and tools. Obsolete equipment/materials and other unused items disappear. Our goal is to clean up our work areas enough, we can see our way to the next step. Also, clean areas send a warning flag when something is out of order. Clutter is nearly always the result of fear or the lack of decision making or both.

In our next phase, we organize, rearrange and identify everything in a work area for the most efficient and effective retrieval and provide all tools, equipment, and materials with their own specific locations. Commonly used tools should be close to where we will use them. Storage areas, cabinets, and shelves should be properly labeled with the name of the tool. We should clean and paint floors to make it easier to spot dirt, waste materials, mislocated documents, and dropped parts and tools. Outline areas on the floor or on tool boards to clearly indicate where things go. In an office, provide bookshelves for frequently used manuals, books and catalogs. Label the shelves and books so that we easily identify them and return them properly. Systematic organization goes beyond simple work areas. Our facilities should also be systematically organized. For example, various kinds of pipes can be color-coded by the type of fluid, liquid or gas, that flows through them.

Regular cleaning allows us to use the power of the routine task to maintain what we have achieved with the first 2 S's while making the job easier to do because we never allow our "stuff" to become disorganized and chaotic as it was before the initiative began. Our approach can be considered a more active variant of inspection. While inspecting our work areas, it is easy to also clean/reorganize the machines, tools, equipment and supplies. Routine inspection makes it easy to spot lubricant leaks, equipment misalignment, breakage, missing tools and diminished levels of supplies. We can fix problems when they are small (this is part of the Taoist principle of *wei wu wei*). The power of the routine task avoids downstream fiascos.

We should standardize the practices from the previous steps, which will help make them a part of the corporate culture. Our new standards will help people work into new habits and they will be especially useful with new employees. We can try to use labels, signs, posters, and banners, although our experience suggests these often become visual noise quickly.

Our final step involves training as well as standards maintenance. As with Six Sigma, we will need a "control" phase to monitor our results as we move on from the initial work. We will continue to educate our employees about maintaining standards. We must also keep our staff up-to-date with any changes in the program or that affect the program.

VI. Lead Time Reduction

Lead time reduction refers to the steps we need to take to reduce machine setup times, a common issue in manufacturing. We also note that lead time reduction can apply to other processes; for example, insurance claim handling, handoffs, and decision making.

The goal is to reduce the setup time out of the scheduling equation so that we have maximum flexibility at minimum cost. If our setup is extremely time-consuming and forces us into batches, we lose this flexibility and make our production scheduling more complex.

Lead time reduction can also be applied to the product development process. For example, we may find ways to optimize our requirements elicitation—improving our present form of elicitation and improving our response times. Rapid prototyping parts as well as simulation activities may help reduce our organization's typical time to produce the product. Additionally, automation of our testing may improve our time to test the product and therefore improve the product development cycle time.

VII. Kanban

A kanban is a production schedule signaling method. The most famous approach uses sets of physical cards. To successfully implement production kanban, we must follow some simple rules:

- Never pass on defective products to the downstream process
- The downstream process withdraws only what material is needed and when needed
- Produce the exact quantity withdrawn by the downstream process
- Level the production (avoid batching per se)
- Kanban cards can be used to tune the process
- Ensure the process is robust and reasonable

The kanban card is a critical component of this approach that uses physical cards to signal when to move materials within a manufacturing or production facility or to move materials from a supplier to the plant. The Kanban card is a message (i.e., a semaphore) that signals consumption of the product, part, or inventory such that when the semaphore is raised it will trigger the replacement of that specific product, part or inventory. Depletion drives demand. Kanban cards should simply signal the need for more materials, service, or process. Sometimes kanban is used in stockrooms to physically indicate the reorder points for material.

We have used the kanban approach in a commercial laboratory. We found that the nonelectronic/electrical workstations had excess capacity. The best way to use this resource was to have the "resource" pull the work. The electrical testing was more labor intensive, although we had some success with kanban here as well.

VIII. Demand Segmentation

Demand segmentation is a method whereby we "segment" our product demand by looking at the amount of variation using a simple statistic called the coefficient of variation (which is simply the standard deviation of our sample group or the mean of our sample group—the inverse of the signal to noise ratio). While the method is simple, it does have a few caveats:

- Our calculation for a standard deviation assumes a normal distribution
- The mean must exist (we are not looking at a Cauchy distribution)
- We must have enough data to support the calculation
- We must prove we are looking at a normal distribution
- We cannot use the standard normal distribution (because the mean = zero)

We harp on the distribution requirement because we have seen a plant manager use this method in a situation where the customer only made one order in a calendar year—yet this individual used a spreadsheet to calculate mean and standard deviation. Not only was the distribution not normal, there was simply insufficient data to make much of any calculation regarding variability of demand. We need to use common sense when we make these calculations because the spreadsheets are not going to protect us from ourselves!

IX. Production Scheduling

Lean production scheduling is generally a by-product of lead time reduction on machine setups. If the setup time becomes vanishingly small, then the setup becomes a nonfactor in production scheduling (see Figure 9.7). In general, "batching" then becomes anathema. We normally batch to distribute the cost of the setup across more product. The main defects of batching are as follows:

- The effects of a mistake are at least the size of the batch
- We have less scheduling flexibility
- We spend little time improving the process

Of course, batching has some advantages such as uniformity of production for the length of the run, allowing the machine operators to become extremely proficient at assembling that product.

The point of leveling production scheduling is to make the most intelligent decision that reduces wasted time (cost), bad product (cost), and customer dissatisfaction (probable cost).

X. Inventory Reduction

Excess inventory for "just-in-case" scenarios is often a case of opportunity cost. Reducing inventory means we reduce our carrying cost; in essence, we are not consuming money for something that will not be consumed in the near future. Inventory reduction is part of the reason we want to demand segmentation or some other method of analyzing our demand.

XI. Lean Six Sigma

We think the path of the future is the wedding of Six Sigma with traditional lean practices. This approach brings the highly disciplined, algorithmic approach of Six

Sigma to Lean, provides portions of the Six Sigma body of knowledge, and takes some of the automotive company idolatry out of the equation.

A. Lean Six Sigma Overview

Lean Six Sigma is a fortuitous combination of two 21st-century value engineering methodologies. We believe, based on our experience, that this approach takes the best characteristics of both philosophies and merges them into an even more powerful tool to increase the value of the enterprise.

B. Lean Six Sigma Goals

The initial value we derive from Lean Six Sigma is twofold: first, we apply a known methodology to a loose collection of tools and, second, we focus clearly on the value engineering aspect of LSS by emphasizing the bottom line for projects.

As we already know from Chapter 8, Six Sigma was a profit-oriented offshoot of the Total Quality Management movement that addressed issues with broken programs by reinforcing the need for consideration of profit improvement. Lean, on the other hand, is generally considered to have originated with the Toyota automobile company, although large components were prefigured by

- Training Within Industry (TWI), transmogrified into Kaizen, continuous improvement, and employee relations in addition to training
- 5S, another partial offshoot of TWI
- Standard work from TWI
- Quality at the source from Juran and Deming
- Just in Time, from Ford

In Japan, the primary Lean progenitors were:
- Taiichi Ohno, Toyota
- Shigeo Shingo, various, including Toyota
- Genichi Taguchi
- Kaoru Ishikawa

These gentlemen benefited from visits from Juran, Deming, and others from the United States; however, they also provided substantial and imaginative solutions to production, human relation, and management problems on their own. Taguchi, for example, provided a unique approach to using designed experiments and proselytized his methods tirelessly.

As with standard, Six Sigma, the overall LSS initiative will go nowhere without the involvement and support of upper management. The "belt" system is toothless without the influence of the executive corps. Simply put, the executives set the tone for what is important to the enterprise and, in spite of top-down and bottom-up tools such as Hoshin planning, the rank and file will generally follow their lead, especially when it means ignoring another "flavor of the week" company improvement initiative. Once we have this crucial support, we can institute the system of Champions, Master Black Belts, Black Belts, and Green Belts if desired. We recommend the approach because it provides sufficient structure that accountability is simplified.

Given that LSS is a hybrid format, we suggest that realistic savings, based on experience, should run at least 5% of revenue, particularly if neither of these programs has been implemented separately/independently. The overarching goal should be overhaul of the enterprise environment insofar as we can prove we are increasing value and enhancing profit.

C. LSS Project Management

All projects must be linked to enterprise goals, particularly the goal of profit improvement. We have seen some goals that related to revenue, but the end product needs to be profit first, revenue second. To lose sight of this axiom is to put growth ahead of liquidity, which is the primrose path to bankruptcy.

LSS projects will typically follow the Six Sigma sequence of define, measure, analyze, improve, and control. In some cases, we may implement some high-speed techniques, but we feel in these situations, we are simply implementing the five steps at an accelerated pace.

One of the famous techniques for getting to the root cause of problems is the so-called "Five Why" technique, wherein we ask why at least five times in order to drive toward the root cause. On the surface, this technique is naive and, further, it has the liability of assuming one root cause (would that not be nice!). We recommend the eight disciplines approach:

- D0: Planning phase/emergency actions
- D1: Team creation
- D2: Define the problem (who, what, where, when, why, how and how many are useful here as well the "note" versions of each)
- D3: Develop interim containment actions (ICA) to manage the problem until we have a more permanent solution (sometimes containment is the solution!) and validate ICAs
- D4: Identify root causes and escape points
- D5: Select permanent corrective actions (PCA) for root causes and escape points (when possible—PCAs can sometimes be prohibitively expensive)
- D6: Validate PCAs
- D7: Prevent recurrence
- D8: Congratulate the team (do not treat this step as an afterthought)

D. Team Organization and Dynamics

Nearly every activity in lean Six Sigma involves the use of the team and the concept of a project. One of the difficulties we have seen in the business environment is the expectation that by simply designating some individuals as members of the team that we now have a team. In reality, it takes time for a group of people to acquire the amount of trust it takes to have an optimally functioning team.

With lean Six Sigma we can use the same kind of belt system we use in standard Six Sigma. However, the use of the belt system is by no means a requirement for success. As always, we remain pragmatic and therefore any collection of team roles that accomplishes the objectives of bottom-line improvement and value engineering are fine. Sometimes, in the literature, we see a team staging model that has the following components: forming, storming, forming, and performing. Although we have seen these stages in real team, we do not believe it is always necessary to go through the sequence, particularly if the team members have known each other informally for many years.

Even when we have a team where the members have known each other for a substantial length of time, we can expect to see some level of team dynamics. These team dynamics can include such items as power plays, cliques, and nonperformance. Our list of dynamic behaviors is hardly exhaustive; however, a brief overview of any textbook on organizational behavior will reveal a host of other behaviors, many of which are counterproductive. Even when the predominance of behaviors is largely productive, our teams will encounter situations where they need to resolve their conflicts. We recommend training in conflict resolution within days of the creation of any team. Such a course does not have to consume a large amount of time but it does need to provide the team members with tools to settle their differences productively.

We also want our team to understand the use of team tools. Some of the more important team tools are the following: agendas, minutes, status reports, and progress charts. Again, we are not setting an exhaustive list but simply highlighting those items we have seen have the highest effect.

Ultimately, management responsibilities will require some estimate of team performance. We think the best way a team can indicate their performance is by presenting their improvements to the bottom line. At this point, the team is speaking the language of executive leadership. Furthermore, the focus on the bottom line keeps the motivation for the projects at the forefront of everybody's consideration.

E. Defining Opportunities

One of the documents we have found useful for any project-driven initiative is called the project charter. The project charter is usually a relatively brief document that defines the who, why, what, where, how, and how much. Additionally, the project charter will also provide a very high level estimate of cost for the project as well as the anticipated cost-benefit.

One of the tools introduced by the lean approach is the A3 report. A3 refers to the size of a double-wide piece of paper used in many countries. The Toyota automobile company is probably the most famous user of this document. The goal of this form is to document problem-solving activities concisely. We have seen templates in word processing, spreadsheets, and presentation software. While we do not find the A3 report to be a requirement, we do find the concision of this approach to be attractive.

At the beginning of our project, we can use many of the problem definition tools that we encountered in standard Six Sigma; for example, we can collect our thoughts using affinity diagram, we can look for causes to a known problem with Ishikawa diagrams, and we can use Pareto charts to help choose those items that appear to be the most significant. Additionally, we see no reason why customer input should be ignored. While we suggest cautious communication with a customer (sometimes they do not wish to see a perturbation occurring with their supplier), we can always listen to the voice of the customer and use that information as another input for project selection.

Sometimes we may hear the term "lean thinking," referring to the idea of keeping our attention focused on areas where we can reduce waste, illuminate subprocesses, and generally effect value engineering. Often, when we are looking at a process, we measure cycle time with the primary interest being cycle time reduction. Cycle time is not the same as takt time: takt time is what we calculate when we divide the time we have by the number of products we need to build. Such a calculation provides a goal for manufacture—we then need to improve our cycle time to less than the takt time. One of the tools often used when we look at our cycle times is called value stream mapping. With value stream mapping, we show the timing, the quantities, and the amount of money involved in the process; in effect, we have taken process mapping and expanded on the concept. Occasionally, we may perform simple process mapping in order to see if we have produced what is often called a "spaghetti diagram."

F. Measurement Techniques

Process analysis, whether value stream analysis or straight process analysis, is a fundamental component of lean Six Sigma. The factor of primary interest in this kind of analysis is usually the independent variable of time. Occasionally, we will also look at process maps but even those will be related to the time it takes for parts to move across the factory floor.

One place to apply value in sharing lies in the work instructions we supply to our employees. Work instructions need to be reviewed on a frequent basis, say once a month or once a quarter. This frequency may seem extreme but, in fact, work instructions have a tendency to pick up added controls, additional steps, much in the way that ships pick up barnacles. The metaphor is apt because barnacles affect the movement of ships through water; in short, the ship ceases to be streamlined. With careful consideration we are likely to find other mechanisms other than work instructions to improve the process output. We may be able to introduce a new tool or an upstream process change or incoming material change that will negate the need for the work instruction additions. Another reason for this constant review is the possibility that we have learned something more about the process since our last review that will allow us to improve the end result yet further.

We have already mentioned takt time. We use this metric to compare to our actual cycle times to see if we will be able to deliver the product at all. We can also take a closer look at waste.

Seven Classical Wastes

The seven wastes are as follows:

1. *Overproduction*: Manufacturing a product before it is actually required. This activity is wasteful because it inhibits the smooth flow of materials and diminishes quality and productivity (see Figure 9.3 and Figure 9.4). In essence, it violates the famous manufacturing phrase "just in time." The tendency when overproducing is to

Figure 9.3   In the end, we can reduce the waste as much as possible, saving the earth and our company.

stimulate excessive lead times, resulting in high storage costs, as we must increase inventory of both raw material and final product, and it also increases the difficulty of detecting defects. The simple solution to overproduction is turning off the tap; this requires a lot of courage because the problems that overproduction is hiding will be revealed. The concept is to schedule and produce only what can be immediately sold/shipped and improve machine changeover/setup capability.

2. *Waiting:* Whenever we are not producing/processing product, we are waiting. In batch shops, the waiting can be a huge amount of the overall processing time. Linking processes together so that they are synchronized with a signaling system such that one subprocess feeds directly into the next subprocess reduces waiting.

3. *Transporting:* Moving products between processes adds no value to the product. Excessive movement and handling also result in damage and it is an opportunity for degradation of quality. We also have to pay people to move the raw material or subproduct. One of us worked in a plant where we jestingly indicated some of the products would need a passport because of all the travel.

4. *Overprocessing:* Occurs when more work is done on a product than customer requirements dictate. We can also end up in a situation where we are using tools that are more precise, complex, or expensive than absolutely required. One example is the use of selective solder machines (hand soldering with a robot) when we might have designed away the need for this device.

5. *Unnecessary Inventory:* Work in progress (WIP) may be a result of overproduction and waiting (in some cases, it may ease production by reducing the variance in arrival time). Excess inventory tends to obscure manufacturing problems, items we would rather identify and solve so that operating performance improves. Excess inventory

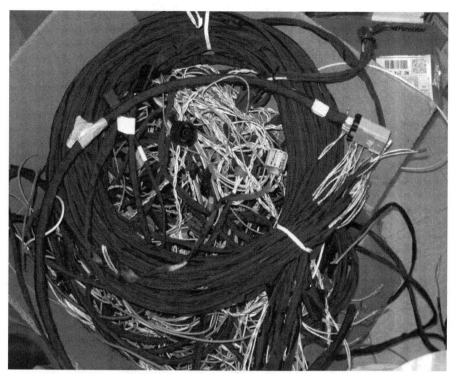

Figure 9.4 Waste wire harnesses can be sent to the local recycler where we can recover some of the money spent to purchase.

increased lead times, floor space consumption, problem identification delays, and poor communications are all tied together in this unholy stew of ineffectiveness and inefficiency.

6. *Unnecessary / Excess Motion*: Usually tied to an ergonomic problem. We want to reduce wasted motion by employees, both to increase efficiency and to benefit the employee.

7. *Defects*: The motto here is quality at the source. In a lean system, the detection of a defect should result in a line shutdown until the problem is resolved. Rework is waste because we are adding no value that should not have already been in the product.

Multivari Analysis
Multivari analysis is sort of a poor man's version of a designed experiment. While this is not quite true, the method allows for a rather speedy and graphical analysis of a set of factors.

With hypothesis testing (see Figure 9.6), we do exactly what the name suggests— we submit an hypothesis and then we test it. A typical example would be the following:

- We have an exact value sample, enough for a t-test (somewhere between two and 30 pieces of each grouping).
- We hypothesize that no difference exists between the groups.

- Our alternate hypothesis is that there is a difference between the groups.
- We perform the appropriate calculations for this test or use software such as the R language.
- An examination of the results will tell us whether the difference is significant or not.
- We will show an example later in this section.

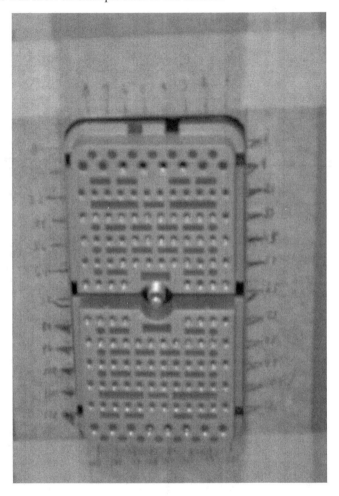

Figure 9.5 We can explore the possibilities of new tools by demonstrating the effectivity prior to building the real thing.

G. Improvement Techniques

Poka-yoke occurs when we mistake-proof our manufacturing devices or apply the same mentality to a service (see Figure 9.5, Figure 9.6, and Figure 9.7). When done correctly, poka-yoke can eliminate quality checking at that workstation, hence this approach is sometimes called "zero quality control." The method was amply documented by the great industrial engineer, Shigeo Shingo (after whom the Shingo prize is named). Quality inspection, especially visual inspection, tends to have "escapes." Furthermore, inspection per se is not a value-added activity. Poka-yoke, on the other hand, eliminates the need for inspection and will not allow an incorrect product to be built. We need to be careful when using the term, however, because we have seen it used to refer to production test equipment, which is *not* poka-yoke, since it is merely an automated form of quality inspection. A good and common example of poka-yoke is the typical keyed connector in automobiles.

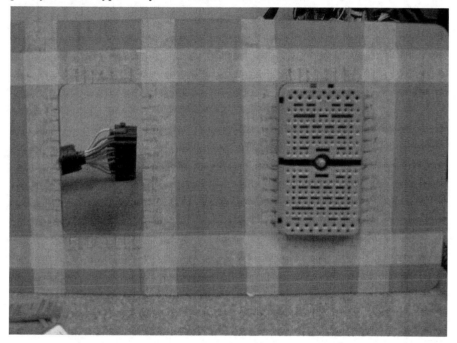

Figure 9.6 We should never be ashamed to model with cardboard.

Flow improvement is usually the by-product of eliminating unnecessary equipment such as conveyors (if they are truly not necessary) and improvements in line layout. The goal is to reduce "spaghetti" layouts, where the product has a great deal of labyrinthine travel around the plant.

Quick response manufacturing is a sophisticated lean approach pioneered and researched by Rajan Suri. Quick response manufacturing (QRM) is an extension of time-based competition, aimed at a prime single target with the goal of reducing lead times. The essential difference between QRM and other time-based programs is that QRM is a tool for the entire organization, from the plant to the office. The method provides guidelines for establishing a QRM enterprise from stem to stern.

The "theory" of constraints approach is a method proposed by Eliyahu Goldratt, most famously in a business novel called *The Goal*. The key concept is that the slowest process (constraint) controls the overall rate of any flow process. He proposed a five-step method for approaching improvement:

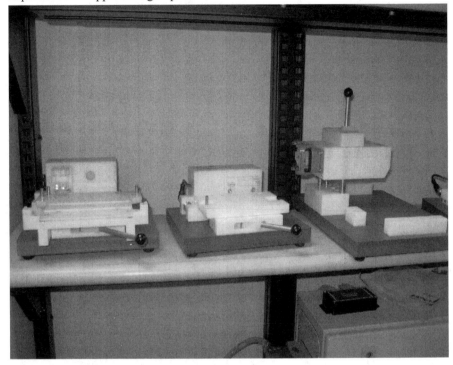

Figure 9.7 Component programming equipment that is poka-yoke means making mistakes in the product programming is reduced.

1. Identify the constraint (the resource or policy that prevents the organization from obtaining more of the goal).
2. Decide how to exploit the constraint (get the most capacity out of the constrained process).
3. Subordinate all other processes to above decision (align the whole system or organization to support the decision made above).
4. Elevate the constraint (make other major changes needed to break the constraint).
5. If, as a result of these steps, the constraint has moved, return to Step 1. Do not let inertia become the constraint.

Control Concepts

The control concept, as with Six Sigma, we use to sustain the improvements we have achieved with our projects. This concept was one of the critical changes as Six

Sigma superseded Total Quality Management as the quality weapon of choice in the enterprise. The same idea applies when applying lean concepts.

The control plan is one of the gifts to quality and cost saving given by the automotive industry (the Automotive Industry Action Group, AIAG, to be precise). A control plan accounts for each stage of the process and includes all relevant metrics, tools, and ancillary information. One of the most important parts of the control plan is the reaction plan, wherein we delineate what occurs when the product falls outside of specification.

The name "control charts" is somewhat of a misnomer since they show when we are out of control but do not always provide the information to get us into control in the first place. They are the brainchild of Walter Shewhart and are a powerful ongoing measurement tool when used correctly. With these charts, we are looking for outlier values from a distribution taken from samples. The initial idea was a stroke of genius because the central limit theorem tells us the distribution of the means of a selection of samples will trend toward a normal distribution regardless of the underlying distribution, which allows us to use all the tools developed for the normal distribution.

Visual systems are used in plants to eliminate textual information and provide easy-to-understand feedback through colors, locations, map lines on the floor, and numerous other cues that trend workers toward the strategic goals of the enterprise. One simple example is the shadow board, where we mark the location of each tool on pegboard, for example, with an outline of the tool, making it obvious what is missing and where the tool should go.

Design Improvement

QFD-Design

QFD refers to Quality Function Deployment, a method started at the Japanese Kobe shipyards in the 1970s. In essence, the practitioner builds a set of matrices that compare parameters of the product; for example, the usual starting point involves the comparison of what the customer wants versus how we propose to meet that need. QFD matrices can vary from extremely qualitative to significantly quantitative. They also become very large quickly and may require dedicated software. Small QFD matrices may be completed using a spreadsheet.

Robust Design

Robust design is the brainchild of Genichi Taguchi, who proposed a sequence of activities that he suggested would lead to more robust products. Robust design does not require that one use the Taguchi Designed Experiment approach, since any designed experiment approach (classical or response surface methodology) can be used. It sequences from concept design to parameter design to tolerance design. The idea is to make the best choices at each of the stages, increase robustness, and reduce cost simultaneously. Parameter design and tolerance design both require designed experiments to support design decisions, so some statistical maturity is expected of the practitioner.

FMECA/FMEA

The failure mode and effects analysis (FMEA) or failure mode, effects, and criticality analysis (FMECA) represent related attempts to forestall design failures. The general idea is that, for design, we break our product into some form of hierarchical structure and proceed to analyze that hierarchy at every point for failure modes. Failure modes occur at designed inputs; failure effects occur at designed outputs. In the midst of all of this analysis, we apply some estimated numerical values to provide a product of severity, occurrence, and detection called the Risk Priority Number (RPN). Clearly, a successful FMEA leads to avoided cost which, in some cases, can be substantial particularly if we can prove we eliminated a potential lawsuit. If we link our FMEA work to our verification and test activities, we can optimize our test plans and test execution around the high value RPNs improving our test focus and cost.

We can also apply FMEA to processes, usually to the manufacturing process although the methodology is not limited to manufacturing. The goal with the process version is to ensure that upstream processes do not contaminate downstream processes; hence, we are looking at input and outputs again. The FMEA is a good place to assess the process for meaningful and efficient installation of production test equipment (detection).

FMEA is only as good as the effort put into the exercise. Furthermore, it is most certainly a team effort, requiring the participation of the best designers and testers in the enterprise. Furthermore, the power of the Design FMEA can be greatly enhanced by using the approach defined by Michael Anleitner in his book *The Power of Deduction*, a well-written exposition of the method that shows how the dedicated reliability practitioner (and cost reductionist) can convert the DFMEA from subjective approaches to largely objective and logical steps. Anleitner's approach involves a great deal of "front-end" work; however, the payoff lies in the completeness of the analysis and the decreased likelihood of failure modes.

DFX

DFX is also a standard Six Sigma tool. However, it is flexible enough to be used with lean manufacturing also. DFX is not an airport acronym but rather a collection of viewpoints regarding design; for example:

- DFQ = design for quality
- DFR = design for reliability
- DFMA = design for manufacturability and assembly
- DFM = design for maintenance (sometimes DFS = design for service)
- DFT = design for testing
- DFC = design for cost!!!!

Design for cost is where we save our money from the very start of the project. DFC does not mean we simply choose cheap components. DFC does mean we consider cost as we make our design choices. In some cases, a requirement may lead to an insurmountable increased cost; for example, we may need to meet regulatory requirements.

TRIZ is a form of systematic innovation that is more sophisticated than the SCAMPER approach, an acronym that expands as follows:

- S = Substitute
- C = Combine
- A = Adapt
- M = Magnify
- P = Put to Other Uses
- E = Eliminate (or Minify)
- R = Rearrange (or Reverse)

When using TRIZ, we have more options than these seven choices. In addition, we have table showing how to overcome known obstacles in designs. The method was created by Soviet thinker Genrich Altshuller. He analyzed hundreds of thousands of inventions, looking for patterns[2].

XII. EXERCISES

- Do we find anything new in the lean and Lean Six Sigma program approaches?

- How do we avoid the new religion of the week syndrome common in enterprises that are forever chasing after the latest management fad?

- Who provides project direction with lean and Lean Six Sigma programs?

- Is Toyota the only real source of authentic lean manufacturing techniques?

- Research training within industry on the World Wide Web. How much of training within industry is contained within the standard lean approaches?

- While Toyota may be considered to be an archetype of a lean manufacturing company, what other companies represent equally aggressive approaches to reducing waste, eliminating inventory, and managing risk?

- Which companies have the highest level of inventory turns in the world? What level of competitive advantage does this achievement provide for them?

- Optimization of freight is generally a complex task. How do we determine the best way—least costly way—to transport material to our facility. Should we use a slow boat from China or should we fly in parts? What well-known company made the decision to fly rather than to float?

- In some cases, we may have to ship with carriers that are called less than loaded carriers, meaning they will fit our materials in with somebody else's parts were somebody else's parts with our materials or, worst case, they will send us a partially loaded container. How do we optimize the situation? What tools are available for us? Who are the biggest suppliers for less than loaded containers?

- Does it make any sense to ever buy their own containers?

- What is the difference between FOB shipping point and FOB destination? As customer, which one do we prefer? Which one will our supplier prefer?

- Is it moral to have our suppliers to keep parts in trailers on our parking lot to avoid delivering the material to our docks? Is this not just game playing or a legitimate way to save money?

- If we are running a very lean manufacturing plant with a set of sole-source suppliers and they are subject to a natural disaster, how much do we lose? How do we manage the risk intrinsic to the situation? (Recall the recent Japanese tsunami.)

- What is the risk if our supplier goes bankrupt? A perfect example of this situation is bankruptcy of Delphi that lasted for several years. Were Delphi customers ever really at risk?

- How much risk do we assume if our supplier is purchased by another corporation? How do we plan for this situation and what would such a plan look like?

- In a more general sense, we might consider mergers and acquisitions of suppliers to be an issue of some concern. How do we manage the situation? Can we manage the situation? At what point, do we become fatalistic and simply accept the facts of life?

- How do we hedge against inflation?

- How do we hedge against the major recession?

- If inflation becomes an issue, then holding cash makes no sense. Does this statement make any sense? We might note, that for years Apple held onto huge amounts of cash thanks to the paranoia of the late Steve Jobs.

ENDNOTES

1. Hagel, John, III, John Seely Brown, and Lang Davison. *The Power of Pull: How Small Moves, Smartly Made, Can Set Big Thing in Motion*. New York City, NY: Basic Books, 2010.

2. King, Bob, Ellen Domb, Karen Tate, and GOAL/QPC Research Committee. *TRIZ: An Approach to Systematic Innovation*. Edited by Michael Clark and Lynne Levesque. Methuen, MA: GOAL/QPC, 1997.

3. Yourdon, Ed, and Larry Constantine. *Structured Design*. Upper Saddle River, NJ: Prentice Hall, 1979.

CHAPTER 10 – Saving Money with Optimization

I. Rubric for Optimization

Criteria	Level 1 (50%–59%)	Level 2 (60%–69%)	Level 3 (70%–79%)	Level 4 (80%–100%)
Analyze research	Analysis of research demonstrates limited use of critical thinking	Analysis of research demonstrates some use of critical thinking	Analysis of research demonstrates considerable use of critical thinking	Analysis of research demonstrates thorough use of critical thinking
Brainstorm design using the design report format	Applies few of the skills involved in the design process	Applies some of the skills involved in the design process	Applies most of the skills involved in the design process	Applies all or almost all of the skills involved in the design process
Communicate the characteristics of a quality product from all aspects	Communicates information regarding design, workmanship and choice of materials with limited clarity	Communicates information regarding design, workmanship and choice of materials with some clarity	Communicates information regarding design, workmanship and choice of materials with considerable clarity	Communicates information regarding design, workmanship and choice of materials with a high degree of clarity and with confidence
Establish work schedules for a cost reduction project	Establishes work schedules for a cost reduction project demonstrating limited thought	Establishes work schedules for a cost reduction project demonstrating some thought	Establishes work schedules for a cost reduction project demonstrating considerable thought	Establishes work schedules for a cost reduction project demonstrating a high degree of thought
Evaluate information using a logical process	Demonstrates limited ability to evaluate information using a logical process	Demonstrates some ability to evaluate information using a logical process	Demonstrates considerable ability to evaluate information using a logical process	Demonstrates a high degree of ability to evaluate information using a logical process
Evaluate information using criteria	Evaluates information with limited use of criteria	Evaluates information with some use of criteria	Evaluates information with considerable use of criteria	Evaluates information with thorough use of criteria
Identify materials for components of cost reduction projects	Demonstrates limited knowledge of various materials that may be used for a variety of components of a cost reduction project	Demonstrates some knowledge of various materials that may be used for a variety of components of a cost reduction project	Demonstrates considerable knowledge of various materials that may be used for a variety of components of a cost reduction project	Demonstrates thorough knowledge of various materials that may be used for a variety of components of a cost reduction project
Identify the roles of various personnel involved in the cost reduction team	Identifies few personnel involved in the cost reduction team	Identifies some personnel involved in the cost reduction team	Identifies many personnel involved in the cost reduction team	Identifies a wide variety of personnel involved in the cost reduction team

Criteria	Level 1 (50%–59%)	Level 2 (60%–69%)	Level 3 (70%–79%)	Level 4 (80%–100%)
Interpret electrical and mechanical drawings	Interprets language symbols and visuals with limited accuracy and effectiveness	Interprets language symbols and visuals with some accuracy and effectiveness	Interprets language symbols and visuals with considerable accuracy and effectiveness	Interprets language symbols and visuals with a high degree of accuracy and effectiveness
List the benefits and drawbacks of a variety of different energy sources	Demonstrates limited knowledge of facts and terminology when listing benefits and drawbacks of different energy sources	Demonstrates some knowledge of facts and terminology when listing benefits and drawbacks of different energy sources	Demonstrates considerable knowledge of facts and terminology when listing benefits and drawbacks of different energy sources	Demonstrates thorough knowledge of facts and terminology when listing benefits and drawbacks of different energy sources
Look at a variety of cost reduction projects in terms of their impact on standard gross margin	Demonstrates limited understanding of the impact cost reduction projects may have on standard gross margin	Demonstrates some understanding of the impact cost reduction projects may have on standard gross margin	Demonstrates considerable understanding of the impact cost reduction projects may have on standard gross margin	Demonstrates thorough understanding of the impact cost reduction projects may have on standard gross margin
Prepare a business case	Prepares a limited business case	Prepares an adequate business case	Prepares a good business case	Prepares a thorough business case
Produce a work portfolio	Produces a limited work portfolio	Produces an adequate work portfolio	Produces a good work portfolio	Produces a thorough work portfolio
Use criteria to make a cost comparison	Rarely uses criteria to make a cost comparison	Sometimes uses criteria to make a cost comparison	Often uses criteria to make a cost comparison	Routinely uses criteria to make a cost comparison
Use problem-solving methods when constructing mock-ups or models	Uses problem-solving methods when constructing mock-ups or models with limited success	Uses problem-solving methods when constructing mock-ups or models with some success	Uses problem-solving methods when constructing mock-ups or models with good success	Uses problem-solving methods when constructing mock-ups or models with excellent success

II. Questions to Ponder

- How can simulation help us in our cost improvement activities?
- How does simulation in product or process development improve our cost and reduce risk?
- What are the costly prerequisites for simulation?
- How would you make the most of simulation efforts?
- What are the steps to develop accurate models?
- What actions do you take to ensure the validity of the models for simulation?

III. Cost Improvement Scenario

A. Situation

A new feature is defined to go into a heavy-duty vehicle. The feature consisted of a number of electronic control units that already exist on the vehicle. The need for the implementation is urgent to take advantage of market opportunities.

B. Objective

Generate a number of ideas and qualify those ideas as quickly as possible to expedite the requirements phase of the project. Select a concept that meets the customer requirements. Secure the detailed requirements in such a way to minimize the design risks from the supplier of the software on the system.

C. Action

The feature consisted of a number of electronic control units that already exist on the vehicle. The change is within the software of these existing embedded modules.

The systems group had generated a number of ideas that could work to meet the customer demands. When these were documented sufficiently, the concepts were put on the hardware in the loop simulator for the vehicle. This provided a review of the systems level design incarnation including the performance before securing tooling money for the software.

D. Results

Two concepts were investigated using the hardware in the loop simulators. The simulators were set up with existing vehicle models and the use of the core electronic control units. The exploration proved one concept superior but not without some performance issues. The concept was adjusted and another simulation was performed in which the performance was as desired.

E. Aftermath

The learning from the simulation reduced risk on the documentation of the system as the performance as witnessed. The simulation proved a design concept and allowed for detailed explanation via specification. The risk was reduced as the system performance was witnessed and limitation adjusted before receiving the first piece of software.

IV. Operations Research Approaches

Today, businesses should meet the challenges of the global market by offering value to customers with products and services. These customers expect a combination of low cost, high quality, and real-time information. With the global market growing and increasing competition, operational research (OR) is a basic method that helps.

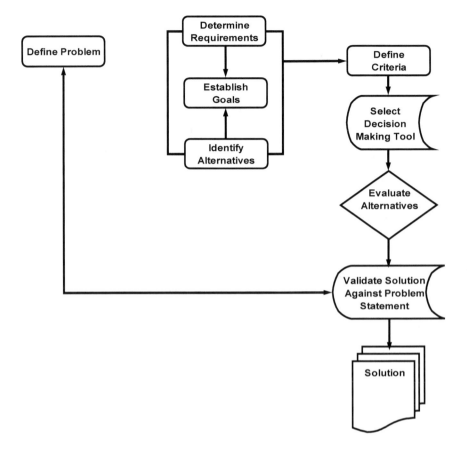

Figure 10.1 We need to ensure that any decision-making process is logical and omits nothing.

Operations research is a discipline on applied mathematics for quantitative system analysis, optimization, and decision making (see Figure 10.1). It is one of the well-accepted managerial decision science tools used by organizations and significantly in applications like manufacturing systems (world class manufacturing), lean production, Six Sigma quality management, benchmarking, and just-in-time (JIT) inventory methods. In general, this method is applied in the manufacturing and service industries, government, and the military. The manufacturing examples include the improvement of car body production, optimal planning of maintenance operations, and the development of policies for supply chain coordination.

A. Evolution of Operations Research in Academics

Previously, government departments recognized operations research as a legitimate management tool for resource planning in defense research establishments. This was later supported by businesses through funding of real and potential applications. Over a period, relationship between governments, businesses, and academia became strong for their mutual benefit. The operations research discipline has evolved as a multidisciplinary function involving mathematics, economics, statistics, management, and industrial engineering, which are tools, models, and methodology. The categories include:

- Tools——ABC analysis, 80:20 rule and break even analysis

- Models——Blending models, portfolio optimization of assets, and optimized distribution system

- Methods——Project management systems, simulation methodology, multi-criteria optimization, game theory, enterprise resource planning systems, data envelopment analysis, and conflict resolution methods

Several academicians have been continuously contributing to the development of this discipline. Some of the most commonly used techniques and methods are linear programming, inventory control models, decision models, queuing theory simulation, network theory, sequencing, game theory, replacement theory, reliability, and the markovian models remain the same.

B. Origin, History, and Developments

In the late 1930s, a new field of applied science known as operations research started growing and has expanded remarkably in last 30 years. The British Army carries out exercises for detecting aircraft on the radar system. In July 1938, at the Bawdsey Research Station, the superintendent announced that the operational achievements did not meet requirements despite the fact that these exercises demonstrated technical feasibility for detecting aircraft on the radar system. Therefore, a research program on operations was initiated despite the technical difficulties.

Similarly, on May 15, 1940, Stanmore Research Section France evaluated 10 additional fighter squadrons in need to deal with German forces advancing rapidly. Reports were made based on study of current losses and replacement rates to identify fighter strength, and forces were recalled. That is how Coastal Command carried out well-known operational research work during World War II and the Operational Research Section was established as a separate specialization.

Later in the 1950s, there was significant progress in the operations research techniques amongst civilians as well. Colleges and universities introduced operations research in their curriculum and showed increasing interest in professional development and education. Moreover, in 1958, project scheduling techniques such as PERT (program evaluation and review technique) and CPM (critical path method) that were meant for scheduling and monitoring complex projects were developed as efficient tools. In India, the development occurred in 1953 to help resolve problems relating to national planning and survey. It helped in areas such as waiting or queuing of passengers for tickets at booking windows or trains queuing up in yards.

The growth of operations research can be largely attributed to the extensive use of computers as it involves large number of numeric calculations, which was impossible without computers. Meanwhile, operations managers of functional entities such as industrial or systems engineering began using tactics to provide possible alternatives in decision making. It helped decision makers, engineers, and analysts to verify and validate alternatives beforehand.

C. Operational Research Activities

Operational research deals with wide variety of problems in transportation, computer and communication operations, production and inventory planning, risk and revenue management, financial assets, and other fields where increasing business productivity is a dominant factor. In the case of public sector, operational research studies focus on energy, healthcare, water resource planning, defense, criminal justice or urban emergency systems. In simple words, operations research is an analytical method of problem solving and decision making that is useful in organizational management. Problems are first dissolved into basic components and then solved through mathematical analysis. The three steps involved in this process are:

1. Identification and development of a set of potential solutions to a problem

2. Analyzing alternatives and reducing them to a smaller set of solutions

3. Alternatives from subsets are subjected to implementations that can be used as an actual analyses/solutions

Operations research benefits organizations by helping improve their efficiency and effectiveness:

- Decreasing cost or investment
- Increasing revenue or return on investment
- Increasing market share
- Managing and reducing risk
- Improving quality
- Increasing throughput while decreasing delays
- Achieving improved utilization from limited resources
- Demonstrating feasibility and workability

Operations Research Functions and Methods

Operations research helps decision makers deal with all types of management functions such as resolving critical problems, designing multistep processes for improvement, setting up guidelines, planning and forecasting, and measuring outcomes. Despite a number of labels available in operations research, projects can be segregated into three broad categories. In addition, these three groups provide many methods to assess risks and uncertainty factors which are as follows:

- Simulation method——This method aims to develop simulators that would aid the decision maker in conducting sensitivity studies seeking for improvements and in assessing and benchmarking these improvement ideas.

- Optimization method——This method helps the decision maker to efficiently look for possible choices in environments where millions of choices could prove to be feasible, or in situations where choice comparisons are rather complex. The ultimate goal is to identify and locate the best choice based on certain criteria.

- Data-analysis method——This method helps the decision maker in identifying actual patterns and links in a data set. It is very helpful in many applications such as forecasting and data mining.

Techniques Used in Operations Research

Decision analysis techniques form a group of quantitative methods that make use of "expected utility" as a criterion for identifying the preferred alternative. It also provides tools that analyze uncertain and multiple conflicting decisions. These tools are especially useful when limited relevant data is available in the decision-making process. A decision-making process can be divided into several easy steps as illustrated in the flow chart below:

1. Define the problem

2. Determine the requirements

3. Establish goals

4. Identify alternatives

5. Define criteria

6. Select a decision-making tool

7. Evaluate alternatives against criteria

8. Validate solutions against problem statement

During World War II, linear programming was developed as a mathematical model to help plan expenditures and returns while reducing costs for the army and increasing losses for the enemy. In operations research, optimization refers to finding out the maximum profit and minimum loss in any deal. This can be done using quantitative techniques and thereby narrow our choices to obtain the best out of innumerable feasible options. This is a constrained optimization technique, where certain criteria are optimized within some constraints. In linear programming, the objective function (profit, loss, or return on investment) and constraints are linear.

The standard form of describing a linear programming problem includes the following three parts:

A linear function to be maximized:
e.g.: maximize $c1x1 + c2x2$

Problem constraints of the following form:
e.g.: $a11x1 + a12x2 <\backslash b1$

$$a21x1 + a22x2 <\backslash b2$$
$$a31x1 + a32x2 <\backslash b3$$

Nonnegative variables:
e.g.: $x1 >/ 0$
       $x2 >/ 0$

Simulation

A model can be prepared on a real situation and various experiments can be performed so as to know more about different situations so that the model may be further used in an artificial model. When a simulation model is built, it helps reveal the imperceptible relationships to help analyze the situation. For example, the Marine fisheries industry is highly complex and stochastic. Therefore, in order to obtain the objective function values of a specific fishing schedule, simulation-based optimization uses the simulation model. The decision support system for fishery management will assist government agencies and the fishing industry in using sound data and management science techniques for arriving at policy decisions in fishing activities. Transferable rights to fish have proven to be a reliable and effective means of creating incentives to conserve marine resources. By strengthening individual fishing rights, the flexible quota management systems make a significant contribution in terms of conserving fish stocks, reducing excess capacity, and raising the profitability of the fisheries industry.

Queuing Theory

Queuing systems in operations research refers to the analysis of queues that are formed in different situations. Some real-time examples include customers waiting in the queue in banks, customers waiting for service, customers buying groceries in departmental stores, aircraft waiting for landing, jobs waiting to be processed in the computer system. The computer maintains the queue according to the arrival time of the event (customers) and processes each event one after the other according to their arrival time. The objective of this system is to minimize the cost of waiting without increasing the cost of servicing as well as to derive an explicit expression for the queue-length or waiting-time distribution (or its transform), usually in steady state.

Simulation represents the full extent of the models covering all perceivable systems which incorporate characteristics of a queue. As customers, we identify as the unit demanding service, whether it is human or otherwise, meanwhile, the unit providing service is known as the server. Regardless of the nature of the physical context, the terminology of customers and servers is used in a generic sense. Some examples are provided below:

- In communication systems, voice or data traffic queue up in lines for transmission, for example, a telephone exchange.

- In a manufacturing system where there are several workstations, units that complete work in one station wait for access to the next.

- Vehicles requiring service waiting for their turn in a garage.
- Patients waiting at a doctor's clinic for treatment.

Transportation Technique

F.L. Hitchcock presented the origin of transportation in 1941; in addition, he also presented a study, "The Distribution of a Product from Several Sources to Numerous Localities." This presentation is considered to be the first important contribution to the solution of transportation problems. In 1947, T.C. Koopmans presented an independent study, "Optimum Utilization of the Transportation System," which was not related to Hitchcock's study. Both these contributions significantly helped in developing transportation methods that involved large numbers of shipping sources and destinations. The transportation problem is a special class of linear programming problem. Under this problem, the objective is to minimize the cost of distributing a product from a number of sources (e.g., factories) to a number of destinations (e.g., warehouses) while satisfying both the supply limits and the demand requirement. The simplex method of problem solving is not suitable for the transportation problem due to the problem's special structure. The model assumes that the distributing cost on a given route is directly proportional to the number of units distributed on that route. Moreover, the transportation model can be extended to areas other than direct transportation of a commodity, including among others, inventory control, employment scheduling, and personnel assignment. The objective of the transportation problem is to satisfy by providing the required quantity of goods or services at each demand destination and within the limited quantity of goods or services available at each supply origin, as well as at the minimum transportation cost or time.

Project Management with PERT and CPM

Both techniques, CPM (critical path method) and PERT (project evaluation and review technique) are based on the idea that a small set of activities, which make up the longest path through the activity network, control the entire project. If these "critical" activities could be identified and assigned to responsible persons, management resources could be utilized optimally by concentrating on the few activities which determine the fate of the entire project. Noncritical activities can be rescheduled and resources for them can be reallocated flexibly, without affecting the whole project. Both are project management techniques, which have been created out of the need of western industrial and military establishments in order to help plan, schedule, and control complex projects.

Usefulness

CPM/PERT have been useful in planning costs and in scheduling manpower and machine time. CPM/PERT can provide answers to the following important aspects:

- Project duration and risks involved/dependencies/assumptions involved
- Critical activities, which delay the project if they were not completed on time

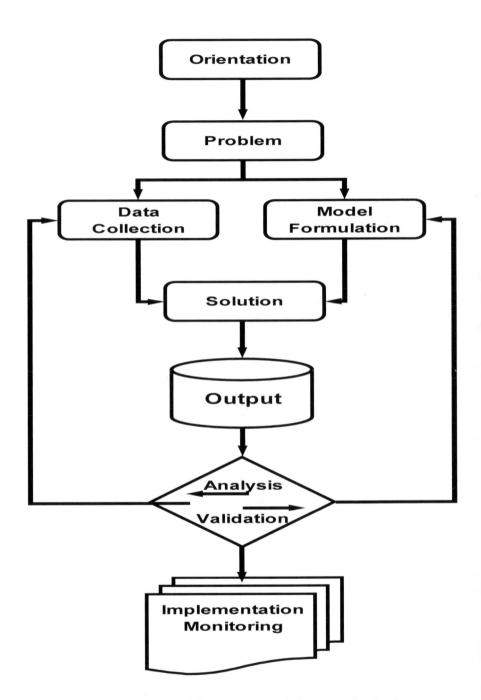

Figure 10.2 Operations research is one way to optimize certain kinds of systems.

- Current status of the project, i.e., whether the project is on schedule, behind schedule, or ahead of schedule

- Whether the project has to be finished earlier than planned and the best way to do this at the least cost

The procedure of drawing a network is as follows:

1. Specify the individual activities: a list of all the activities in the project can be made from the work breakdown structure. This list can be used as the basis for adding sequence and duration information in the later steps.

2. Determine the sequence of the activities: some activities are dependent on the completion of certain other activities. A list of the immediate predecessors of each activity is useful for constructing the CPM network diagram.

3. Draw the network diagram: The CPM diagram can be drawn once the activities and their sequencing have been defined. CPM originally was developed as an activity on node (AON) network, but some project planners prefer to specify the activities on the arcs.

4. Estimate Activity Completion Time: The time required to complete each activity can be estimated using past experience or the estimates of knowledgeable persons. CPM is a deterministic model that does not take into account variation in the completion time; so, only one number is used for an activity's time estimate.

5. Identify the critical path: The critical path is the longest-duration path through the network.

The significance of the critical path is that the activities involved cannot be delayed without delaying the project. Therefore, critical path analysis plays an important role in project planning. Determining the four parameters for each activity can identify the critical path. These four parameters are "earliest start," "earliest finish," "latest finish," and "latest start."

Models and Modeling in Operations Research

A model is defined as the approximation or abstraction, maintaining only the essential elements of the system, which may be constructed in various forms by establishing relationships among specified variables and parameters of the system (see Figure 10.2). A model does not and cannot represent every aspect of reality because of the innumerable and changing characteristics of the real life problems to be represented. Modeling is the essence of an operations research approach. By building a model, the complexities and uncertainties of a decision-making problem can be changed to logical structure that is amendable to formal analysis. In short, a model provides a clear structural framework to the problem in order to understand and deal with reality.

D. The Operations Research Approach

Based on the fact that operations research (OR) represents an integrated framework to help make decisions, it is important to have a clear understanding of this framework in order to be able to apply it to a generic problem. This approach comprises the following seven sequential steps:

1. Orientation
2. Problem definition
3. Data collection
4. Model formulation
5. Solution
6. Model validation and output analysis
7. Implementation and monitoring

In order to illustrate how the steps might be applied, consider a typical scenario where a manufacturing company is planning production for the upcoming month. The company uses numerous resources (such as labor, production machinery, raw materials, capital, data processing, storage space, and material handling equipment) to manufacture a number of different products, which compete for these resources. The products have differing profit margins and require different amounts of each resource. Many of the resources are limited in their availability. Additionally, there are other complicating factors such as uncertainty in the demand for the products, random machine breakdowns, and union agreements that restrict how the labor force can be used. An illustration of how one might conduct an operations research study to address this situation would be as follows: consider a highly simplified instance of a production planning problem where there are two main product lines (widgets and gizmos) and three major limiting resources (A, B, and C) for which each of the products compete. Each product requires varying amounts of each of the resources and the company incurs different costs (labor, raw materials, etc.) in making the products and realizes different revenues when they are sold. The objective of the (operations research) project is to allocate the resources to the two products in an optimal fashion.

E. Significance of Operations Research

The operations research approach is particularly useful in balancing conflicting objectives (goals or interests) where there are many alternative courses of action available to decision makers. In a theoretical sense, the optimum decision must be one that is best for the organization and as a whole it is often called the global optimum. A decision that is best for one or more sections of the organization is usually called a suboptimal decision. Operations research attempts to resolve the conflicts of interest among various sections of the organization and seeks the optimal solution, which may not be acceptable to one department, but is in the interest of the organization as a whole. Operations research is concerned with providing the decision maker with decision aids (or rules) that are derived from the following:

- A total system orientation
- Scientific methods of investigation
- Models of reality, generally based on quantitative measurement and techniques

Besides being used in the industry, this new technique was also utilized in a number of socioeconomic problems which came up after the war. Operations research is used in a large number of areas such as traffic problems, question of deciding a suitable fare structure for public transport, or an industrial process like ore-handling. Its use has now extended to academic spheres, such as the problems of communication of information, socioeconomic fields, and national planning.

F. Operations Research in Manufacturing

As operations research has made significant contributions over the years in virtually all industries, in almost all managerial and decision-making functions, and at most organizational levels, the list of OR applications is prodigious. Hence, this report focuses on the manufacturing industry, and introduces some of the application where OR is being used (see Figure 10.3).

The term operations in OR may suggest that the manufacturing application category represents the original home of OR. However, this is not quite accurate, because the name originated from military operations and not from business operations. Nevertheless, it

Figure 10.3 The basic operations research model.

is true that the success of OR in contemporary business pervades manufacturing and service operations, transportation, distribution, logistics, and telecommunication. The myriad applications include scheduling, routing, elimination of bottlenecks, workflow improvements, inventory control, business process reengineering, site selection, or facility and general operational planning. Revenue and supply chain management reflect two growing applications that are distinguished by their use of several OR methods to cover several functions. Revenue management entails first to accurately forecast the demand, and second to adjust the price structure over time in order to more profitably allocate the fixed capacity. Supply chain decisions describe the who, what, when, and where abstractions from purchasing and transporting raw materials and parts, through manufacturing actual products and goods, and finally distributing and delivering the items to the customers. The prime management goal here may be to reduce overall cost while processing customer orders more efficiently than before. The power of utilizing OR methods allows examining this rather complex and convoluted chain in a comprehensive manner, and to search among a vast number of combinations for the resource optimization and allocation strategy that seem most effective, and hence beneficial to the operation.

Helping the Modern Manufacturing Engineer

Operations research can be applied at the nonmanager levels as well, as engineers or consumers alike can benefit from the improved and streamlined decision-making process.

The modern manufacturing professional who is familiar with OR tools gains significant advantages by making data-driven decisions and having a deeper understanding of the problem at hand. Often operations research models lead to the formalization of intuition and expert knowledge—explaining why it may not be a good idea to give priority to producing the highest profit product on a bottleneck station, or producing the most urgent job first is not necessarily the best option. Operations research helps the decision maker to not only find a solution that works, but to find the one that works best. For instance, it guides the decision maker to form flexible cells and corresponding part families to minimize material handling and setup costs. With OR tools one can also assess the past and expected performance of a system. Finally, a family of operations research tools is specifically designed to formulate decision problems in a variety of scenarios.

In summary, operations research tools can help the manufacturing engineering professional to

- Better understand system properties and behavior
- Quantify expected system performance
- Prescribe optimal systems
- Make rational, data-driven decisions

G. The Operations Research Experience in the U.S.

In the United States, there was certainly some sympathy for particular elements of Ackoff's criticism of the state of OR in the 1970s and 1980s—notably the trend towards "mathematization," and hence, OR's increasing irrelevance to the needs of managerial decision makers. For example, Corbett and Van Wassenhove (1993) identified the phenomenon of "natural drift," as did Reisman and Kirschnick (1994), thereby lending support to Ackoff's argument that OR was being "devolved" and downgraded in managerial structures. Thus far, as these authors were, like Ackoff, concerned with challenging the ongoing trend towards "mathematization" in OR, their worries conformed to critical elements in Abbott's (1988) thesis of "professional regression."

In a wide-ranging analysis of "the expert division of labor" with reference to the modern professions, Abbott argued that the preeminence of the mathematical paradigm was both inevitable and irreversible in view of the existence of "a small but very elite core" enjoying "intellectual control over a much wider jurisdiction" (Abbott 1988). This was of direct relevance to the operations research community because "the elite core" responsible for "mathematization" was concentrated in the American university sector. However, it is significant that even amongst those who empathized with Ackoff's critique and ultimate apostasy, few American academics, and still fewer practitioners, agreed with his remedies in the form of either participatory or interactive planning (Kirby and Rosenhead 2005). In this respect, it should be pointed out that in the Anglo-American context the development of the alternative "soft" paradigm by reformers and revolutionaries was not an American phenomenon. In the first instance, we can refer back to Brockelsby's emphasis on the cultural obstacles to paradigm change. If anything, these obstacles were even more pronounced in the United States because it was the American community of operations researchers that had driven forward the methodological basis of the traditional paradigm. In these respects, the rapidly advancing frontier of computer technology was of decisive importance (Abdel-Malek et al. 1999). The record in the Edelman finalist papers published under the auspices of *Interfaces* serves as proof to the extent of computer-assisted methodological innovation, as it is a journal which, over the years, developed an increasing editorial preference in favor of the publication of articles with a practitioner, rather than an academic orientation. The purpose of the Edelman papers was to encourage the diffusion of best OR practice throughout the practitioner community. Secondly, the "revolutionary," the classical paradigm was notable for its complete absence in America. As suggested already, Rosenhead and Thunhurst's (1982) "materialist analysis" would, in all likelihood, have failed the editorial test if it had been submitted to the *Journal of the Operational Research Society* from the mid-1980s onwards. It is virtually certain that if their article had been submitted to an established American OR journal at any time, it would have received very short shrift. Thirdly, the general consensus is that the country remained relatively insulated from the macro and microeconomic turbulence of the 1970s. Deindustrialization was certainly underway as a consequence of enhanced foreign competition in manufacturing both at home and abroad, but at a much slower rate. In simple terms, the destabilizing forces that encouraged the emergence of the alternative paradigm were less forceful and compelling in the United States.

To the extent that the development of operations research in practice had been propelled by this particular organizational form—in effect, internal consultancies—its contraction was bound to fuel concerns about the future of operations research in both countries.

1. Deindustrialization as a long-term trend was bound to have an adverse impact on the number of OR groups in corporate manufacturing.

2. The increasing standardization of modeling languages and the development of standard PC packages undermined the role of OR groups as "gatekeepers to solving problems dependent on the IT function."

3. Post-1970, the managerial style and culture became increasingly antipathetic to "rational analysis," favoring a postmodern holistic response to a problem rather than one based on decomposition and the explicit analysis of alternative options.

4. The abandonment of "normative models of rationality" could well be "a reflection of an increasingly widespread belief that a coherent corporate ideology focused on the organization's mission is more valuable than the questioning methods of decision rationality."

5. The failure of OR groups to respond positively to changes in management culture—as represented by the "Quality Movement" and "Business-Process Reengineering"—led to the penetration of "alternative consultants, internal or external."

6. One of the key functions of a central OR group is to reconcile "conflicting objectives across different businesses and functional areas." To the extent that this was consistent with "top-down management of a portfolio of businesses," the mounting skepticism of the value added by centrally provided services resulted in the dispersal of OR leading to the loss of "professional identity" and "critical mass."

There is some, albeit limited, evidence that a number of these influences were at work in the United States after 1970. For example, Geoffrion noted in the early 1990s that the obvious term to describe the process of operations research in industry was "dispersed" in the sense that the "long-term net decentralization and disbanding of operations research groups" from the late 1960s onwards meant that operations research in practice was conducted mainly "by individuals in myriad types of staff groups and functional areas." In explaining the demise of internal operations research groups, Geoffrion identified the following interrelated factors:

1. Operations research groups are susceptible to cost cutting in response to "lack of functional responsibility," especially if senior management champions move on.

2. The move towards "leaner staffs in headquarters, flatter organizational structures and greater decentralization" had resulted in the dispersion of central or/ms

groups.

3. Standard operations research techniques had diffused into other disciplines and professions, notably "actuarial science, applied mathematics, computer science, finance, industrial and other kinds of engineering, logistics, marketing and operations management." This had undermined the uniqueness of central groups, thereby encouraging the use of operations research ideas by other professionals.

4. The diffusion of operations research computer software had augmented the above process.

5. In its early days, operations research had enjoyed a "bandwagon effect," which had dissipated. This meant that it was increasingly unlikely that operations research was going to attract the attention of senior managers.

6. Although R/MS groups had enjoyed "strategic impact," too much of their work was conducted at the tactical level, leading to a decline in managerial interest.

7. Some operations research practitioners had harmed their cause as a result of arrogance, poor communication skills, and ineffective marketing of their skills.

There is clearly an interface between Geoffrion's observations and the findings of the Operations Research Society's project. However, in both the cases, the current state and future of operations research was defined exclusively in relation to the ongoing demise of central operations research groups in the corporate industry. As indicated above, this was guaranteed to raise concerns about the future state of operations research in the world of practice. However, it can be argued with equal veracity that focus on the fate of internal operations research groups did not present an accurate portrait of the contemporary state of the practitioner community in america. In this respect, there are two critical points. In the first instance, both Geoffrion and the authors of the SSOR project pointed to the "democratization" of operations research as a result of the widespread diffusion of operations research based computer software, leading to the loss of "uniqueness" of central operations research groups. It is a point well taken that this process served to exacerbate "the lack of branding" of the operations research profession. As Randy Robinson pointed out at the beginning of the 21st century, operations research is in fact undertaken under a variety of different names. They include synonyms and near-synonyms (e.g., management science, decision technology, operations analysis, analytics, etc.), Names of operations research specialties in particular applications (e.g., financial engineering, marketing engineering, and operations management). While the medical profession guarantees that all their practitioners regardless of specialty are recognized to be doctors, within the umbrella medical profession, operations research lacks assured identification of practitioners with its umbrella profession. In this light, investigation of the state of operations research in practice is bound to be compromised by the "embarrassment of riches in names" leading to substantial underestimates of the true number of practitioners. The second point, strongly articulated by Ormerod, and applicable American experience, is that the movement away from internal groups in favor of external consultancy and dispersed practitioners has been the product of changes in the pattern of work. This can be explained by the application of transactions cost economics and agency theory. In borrowing from the literature of applied economics, Ormerod has commented as follows:

> In choosing whether to maintain an internal operations research group or whether to use external agencies, an organization has to determine whether the purchase and transaction costs of using external services (for instance, the costs of buying, selling and managing the contract) outweigh the production and agency costs of maintaining an internal group of relevant expertise. At the same time they have to take into account the quality of the internal and external services as they see them. They also have to weigh up the merits of using internal advisors with employment contracts, with the loyalty and goal alignment that it is assumed this ensures, against the merits of using external providers controlled through explicit principal agent relationships and contracts. As these factors are not easily quantified, the choices have to be made on the basis of subjective views.

As Ormerod has stated in his most recent contribution on this theme, these developments in favor of "the more commercially oriented service providers and consultants is an uncomfortable one for many members of the operations research profession," bearing in mind that "some, mainly academics, want operations research to hold true to higher, noncommercial ideals" whereby the vagaries of the market are tempered by "rational policy analysis." This does, serve as a reminder of the Rosenhead-inspired "revolutionary" agenda of the 1970s, but as Ormerod concludes, the continuing and primary function of operations research "is to support and enable change agendas set by others, usually the powerful elite within organizations."

Role of Computers in Solving Operation Research Problems

The Operation Research problems are time consuming and involve tedious computations. Even a simple problem with few variables takes a long time to solve manually and by a hand calculator. The advent of computers accelerated the wide use of operation research techniques for solving complex business problems faced by managers and administrators in business and government. The automation of computational algorithm allows decision makers to concentrate on problems formulation and the interpretation of the solutions. Major computer manufacturers and vendors have developed software packages for the various computer systems providing computational support for problems to be solved by the application of operation research techniques. Some academic departments in different universities have also produced software packages for solving various operation research problems. Over the year, computer manufacturers like IBM, CDC, Honeywell, UNIVAC, ICL, and so forth, have invested substantial amounts in developing software programs for solving problems such as optimizing, scheduling, inventory, simulation, and other operation research problems. In addition, large-scale simulations are possible only through computers using GPSS software packages.

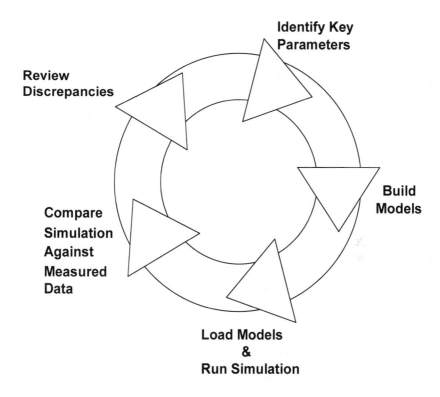

Figure 10.4 Gathering enough data we can perform complex simulations using computers to help assess the best solution.

H. Growth of Operations Research in Different Sectors

Initially, industries like Hindustan Lever Ltd., the Metal Box Company Ltd., Union Carbide (India) Ltd., Larson and Toubro Ltd., Indian Chemical Industries Ltd., and DCM Ltd. set up operation research groups to work on problems of optimization and forecasting of market requirements relevant to their companies.

The type of industries in which these techniques were applied includes steel, textiles, heavy engineering, transportation and distribution, chemical and fertilizers, and electronics. The terminology "operations research" is somewhat misleading, since it is not only concerned with operations, but has applications involving research in different areas and fields. Operations research is the discipline of applying advanced analytical methods to help make better decisions. By using techniques such as mathematical modeling to analyze complex situations, operations research gives executives the power to make more effective decisions and build more productive systems. The role of operations research in the indian context is clear. It is not only important, it is even critical, given the size and magnitude of the tasks ahead to transform India as a developed nation. In order to achieve these goals, we need a responsive and accountable government to promote a positive environment of OR applications. It is hoped that the Indian democracy would lead to this. It is believed that globalization would further accelerate this transition.

Typical applications of operations research include the following:

- Capital budgeting

- Asset allocation

- Portfolio selection

- Fraud prevention, antimoney laundering

- Benchmarking

- Marketing channel optimization, customer segmentation

- Direct marketing campaigns, predicting customer response, and campaign optimization

- Supply chain planning

- Distribution, routing, scheduling, traffic flow optimization

- Resource allocation, staff allocation

- Inventory planning

- Retail planning, merchandize optimization

- Product mix and blending, industrial waste reduction

I. Challenges in Operations Research

As vast quantities of data and calculations are involved, solving optimization problems is challenging and time consuming. Thus, such approach towards performance improvement may or may not be economically feasible for some organizations. Numerous studies are conducted on development of more effective and efficient heuristic and exact algorithms that can solve large scale optimization problems. OR is a quantitative problem solving technique; hence, data plays an important, if not the most important, role in producing high quality and executable solutions. An organization that has data readily available, using information system such as MRP and ERP should be able to use data with certain level of integrity. However, for a system that is highly manual, data-driven decision science techniques presented here may or may not be the appropriate approach. With companies moving towards managing businesses with some form of company-wide information system, linear programming, discrete event simulation, and queueing theory will be most suitable and appropriate decision tools. Data integrity depends on many factors. Some of the factors are an information system that requires manual input of data, unstable network systems, unstable programs, and defective hardware. The most important factor that determines high data integrity is human error when inputting data. Human errors can be minimized through education combined with hands-on training such as on-the-job training. Unfortunately, many organizations tend to focus heavily on physical system implementation and give little or no attention on education and training. Regardless, employees are often reprimanded for not entering the data correctly and the quality of hardware and/or software is questioned for poor data integrity. Sustainment is as important as implementation. An organization can implement the world's greatest database, but if the personnel responsible for operating and sustaining the system lacks knowledge of performing his or her job, attaining and implementing the world's greatest system is meaningless.

J. Future Trends

Advances in information and computer technologies are the reasons for explosive change in operations research. The application of OR is undergoing an explosive period due to advances in information and computer technologies. The Internet, fast inexpensive computers, and user-friendly software allow decision makers with different specialties to use OR techniques that could be applied only by specialists in the recent past. Even the immense computer power available today is not sufficient to solve some difficult decision and optimization problems in a reasonable time. Recent advances in mathematical programming theory are allowing practitioners to tackle these difficult problems. The widespread use of Web-based applications and enormous amount of data that can be accessed ubiquitously, together with emerging data mining techniques, allow the extraction of useful information and new knowledge for competitive advantage. Finally, the connectivity among geographically and organizationally dispersed systems and decision makers will benefit from recent developments in distributed decision making and collaboration methodologies. Future trends indicate that OR will be at the heart of decision-making software applications.

K. Conclusion

To survive and lead today's highly competitive and demand driven market, there is pressure on managements to make economical decisions. One of the essential managerial skills is the ability to allocate and utilize resources appropriately in the efforts of achieving the optimal performance efficiently. In some cases such as small-scale low complexity environment, decisions based on intuition with minimal quantitative basis may be reasonably acceptable and practical in achieving organization's goal. However, for a large-scale system, both quantitative and qualitative (i.e., intuition, experience, common sense) analyses are required to make the most economical decisions. Using operations research techniques including linear programming and discrete event simulation and queuing theory, organization leaders can make high quality decisions. Operations managers are not expected to be experts in any decision science tools; however, they must have fundamental knowledge of such tools to acquire the right resources and to make the most economically sound decisions for the company as a whole.

V. Genetic Algorithms

Genetic algorithms are often used to find solutions in what we call fitness space. Any results we may calculate are assessed with a fitness function. Optimal solutions are either maxima minima in our fitness space. The algorithms are called genetic because they emulate some of the attributes of biological genetic programming; for example:

- They provide for mutation
- They provide for crossover of genes
- They can modify themselves over time
- Those that are fittest adapt the best

VI. Particle Swarm Optimization (PSO)

Particle swarm optimization (PSO) is a computational method that optimizes a problem by repeatedly endeavoring to improve a potential solution with regard to a given measure of quality; that is, we are trying to mind a global optimum using a fitness function on a fitness "landscape." PSO optimizes a problem using a "swarm" of population solutions, usually called "particles," and moving these particles about in the search-space (fitness landscape) according to relatively elementary mathematical formulas, changing the particle's position and velocity at each iteration. The movement of each swarm member (particle) is affected by its *local* optimum and is also maneuvered in the direction of less local optima in the fitness landscape, receiving updates as better locations are found by other particles. Hence, we should see a trend toward improving optima as the algorithm progresses.

PSO optimizes a problem by iteratively trying to enhance candidate solutions with regard to a fitness function—it makes few or no assumptions about the problem under analysis and it can search immense spaces with candidate solutions (hence, "swarm"). We have no guarantee that a PSO will converge to an optimal solution, which may not be necessary, since a good solution will often provide sufficient satisficing. PSO can be used on seemingly intractable optimization problems that are partially irregular, noisy, variable over time, and other "nasty" factors.

VII. Ant Path Optimization

Ant colony optimization (ACO) is a *probabilistic* technique for solving computational problems, which can be reduced to finding good paths through graphs (graphs are a mathematical entity—an abstract representation of a set of objects where some pairs of the objects are connected by links). ACO is another metaheuristic technique with no guarantee of optimal convergence (much like PSO).

Real ants will commence their food search by wandering randomly. After finding food, they return to their colony while depositing pheromones to create a trail. If other ants detect this pheromone path, they are more likely to follow the trail than not, returning and reinforcing it by depositing their own pheromones if they eventually find food.

After a while, the pheromones start dissipating, reducing the reinforcing effect of the trail. The more time an ant takes to journey down the path and return, the more time the pheromones have to dissipate. A short path will get traveled over more frequently, and the pheromone density increases on shorter paths more than on longer ones. Pheromone dissipation has the benefit of *eluding the convergence* to a locally optimal solution. If no dissipation occurs, the paths chosen by the initial ants would be too attractive to the following ones. Then, the exploration of the fitness landscape would be sufficiently constrained and the efficiency of the algorithm would suffer.

When any ant finds a good path from the colony to a food source, other ants are more likely to follow that path, and the positive feedback effect eventually impels all the ants to follow a single path. The ant colony algorithm mimics real ants with "simulated ants" walking around the graph that represents the problem to be solved.

One of the most famous uses of the ACO approach has been to produce near-optimal solutions to the traveling salesman problem, a problem considered nearly intractable to standard analytical optimization methods. We can also use ACO to help find solutions to:

- Production or service scheduling problems

- Job-shop scheduling

- Resource-constrained project scheduling

- Vehicle routing

- Multidepot vehicle routing (think distribution facilities)

- Vehicle routing problem with pick-up and delivery

In short, we have an iterative method that supplies good solutions that can satisfice our optimization requirements.

VIII. Simulations

Simulations allow us to create virtual worlds for manipulation. Three kinds of simulations are:

- Real-time (aircraft simulation for pilot training)

- Discrete event

- Agent-based

Real-time simulations are perhaps the least useful for finding savings. However, they do save money in the sense, for example, we do not have to necessarily train pilots by having them always fly an actual aircraft. Additionally, mistakes do not cost us money, unlike airplane crashes, lost sales, and other anomalies. Another example would be a hardware-in-the-loop simulation for a system.

Discrete event simulators are, as their name suggests, a means by which we can create a sequence of events that include some decisions and see how the situation plays out. One of the benefits of DES is that we can accelerate the sequence (decreasing the elapsed time) and achieve results in a much shorter period of time. In general, this acceleration will not have a negative effect on the results of the simulation.

Agent-based simulation uses autonomous "agents" who act based on collections of rules. In a sense, we start our simulation and then allow the agents to perform. The simulations of bird flocks are agent-based simulations, with each bird following less than a handful of rules, yet yielding a surprisingly complex body of behavior.

IX. EXERCISES

- What is the cost of using exotic algorithms such as particle swarm optimization?

- What is the cost of using older residents such as those that have been developed in operations research for the last 60 years?

- How easy is it to modify the inputs and constraints of an operations research algorithm when conditions change?

- How do we discern whether we are looking at a meaningless mathematical abstraction or useful tool for optimization and margin improvement?

- How much education and training this employee have to possess in order to be able to implement these algorithmic approaches? Do we factor this into the cost of our cost reduction?

- Do some research on the World Wide Web to see if we can find software support for the kind of algorithms we have discussed in this chapter. Be prepared to present a report to your peers. Such a report should also include the drawbacks associated with using the software.

- What kinds of organizations can benefit from these algorithmic, mathematical approaches?

- Would we be better served hiring consultants to help us use these algorithms?

- How do we deal with the situation where consultant provides substantial optimization but holds the patent or copyright for the algorithm? How do we modify the tool if we do not own it?

CHAPTER 11 – Regaining Money with Cost Recovery

I. Rubric

Criteria	Level 1 (50–59%)	Level 2 (60–69%)	Level 3 (70–79%)	Level 4 (80–100%)
Analyze control measures used in business	Analyzes control measures used in business with limited understanding	Analyzes control measures used in business with some understanding	Analyzes control measures used in business with considerable understanding	Analyzes control measures used in business with thorough understanding
Analyze the financial status of a business by reviewing financial statements	Analysis of the financial status of a business by reviewing financial statements provides limited conclusions	Analysis of the financial status of a business by reviewing financial statements provides some conclusions	Analysis of the financial status of a business by reviewing financial statements provides good conclusions	Analysis of the financial status of a business by reviewing financial statements provides thorough conclusions
Analyze the financial status of a company by using comparative information	Analysis of the financial status of a company by using comparative information demonstrates limited comprehension	Analysis of the financial status of a company by using comparative information demonstrates some comprehension	Analysis of the financial status of a company by using comparative information demonstrates considerable comprehension	Analysis of the financial status of a company by using comparative information demonstrates thorough comprehension
Analyze the financial status of a company using ratios	Analysis of the financial status of a company using ratios demonstrates limited comprehension	Analysis of the financial status of a company using ratios demonstrates some comprehension	Analysis of the financial status of a company using ratios demonstrates considerable comprehension	Analysis of the financial status of a company using ratios demonstrates thorough comprehension
Analyze the financial status of a company using trend analysis	Analysis of the financial status of a company using trend analysis demonstrates limited comprehension	Analysis of the financial status of a company using trend analysis demonstrates some comprehension	Analysis of the financial status of a company using trend analysis demonstrates considerable comprehension	Analysis of the financial status of a company using trend analysis demonstrates thorough comprehension
Assess how transactions affect the accounts of a merchandising business	Assesses how transactions affect the accounts of a merchandising business with limited accuracy	Assesses how transactions affect the accounts of a merchandising business with some accuracy	Assesses how transactions affect the accounts of a merchandising business with considerable accuracy	Assesses how transactions affect the accounts of a merchandising business with excellent accuracy

Criteria	Level 1 (50–59%)	Level 2 (60–69%)	Level 3 (70–79%)	Level 4 (80–100%)
Assess methods of accounting for capital assets	Assessment of methods of accounting for capital assets demonstrates limited understanding	Assessment of methods of accounting for capital assets demonstrates some understanding	Assessment of methods of accounting for capital assets demonstrates considerable understanding	Assessment of methods of accounting for capital assets demonstrates thorough understanding
Calculate necessary ratios	Calculates necessary ratios with limited success	Calculates necessary ratios with some success	Calculates necessary ratios with considerable success	Calculates necessary ratios with a high degree of success
Compare alternative forms of financing	Comparison of alternative forms of financing demonstrates limited use of criteria	Comparison of alternative forms of financing demonstrates some use of criteria	Comparison of alternative forms of financing demonstrates considerable use of criteria	Comparison of alternative forms of financing demonstrates thorough use of criteria
Demonstrate how profits or losses are shared between partners	Demonstrates how profits or losses are shared between partners with limited understanding	Demonstrates how profits or losses are shared between partners with some understanding	Demonstrates how profits or losses are shared between partners with considerable understanding	Demonstrates how profits or losses are shared between partners with thorough understanding
Demonstrate skills required to interpret financial information	Demonstrates limited skills required to interpret financial information	Demonstrates some skills required to interpret financial information	Demonstrates considerable skills required to interpret financial information	Demonstrates a high degree of skills required to interpret financial information
Demonstrate understanding of the regulatory and ethical framework	Demonstrates limited understanding of the regulatory and ethical framework	Demonstrates some understanding of the regulatory and ethical framework	Demonstrates considerable understanding of the regulatory and ethical framework	Demonstrates a thorough understanding of the regulatory and ethical framework
Demonstrate understanding of cost recovery	Demonstrates limited understanding of cost recovery	Demonstrates some understanding of cost recovery	Demonstrates considerable understanding of cost recovery	Demonstrates thorough understanding of cost recovery
Describe costing procedures for intangible assets	Description of costing procedures for intangible assets demonstrates limited knowledge	Description of costing procedures for intangible assets demonstrates some knowledge	Description of costing procedures for intangible assets demonstrates considerable knowledge	Description of costing procedures for intangible assets demonstrates thorough knowledge

Criteria	Level 1 (50–59%)	Level 2 (60–69%)	Level 3 (70–79%)	Level 4 (80–100%)
Describe costing procedures for natural resources	Description of costing procedures for natural resources demonstrates limited knowledge	Description of costing procedures for natural resources demonstrates some knowledge	Description of costing procedures for natural resources demonstrates considerable knowledge	Description of costing procedures for natural resources demonstrates thorough knowledge
Describe costing procedures for plant and equipment	Description of costing procedures for plant and equipment demonstrates limited knowledge	Description of costing procedures for plant and equipment demonstrates some knowledge	Description of costing procedures for plant and equipment demonstrates considerable knowledge	Description of costing procedures for plant and equipment demonstrates thorough knowledge
Describe how GAAPs and practices apply to a merchandising business	Description of how GAAPs and practices apply to a merchandising business demonstrates limited knowledge	Description of how GAAPs and practices apply to a merchandising business demonstrates some knowledge	Description of how GAAPs and practices apply to a merchandising business demonstrates considerable knowledge	Description of how GAAPs and practices apply to a merchandising business demonstrates thorough knowledge
Describe how GAAPs and practices apply to a service business	Description of how GAAPs and practices apply to a service business demonstrates limited knowledge	Description of how GAAPs and practices apply to a service business demonstrates some knowledge	Description of how GAAPs and practices apply to a service business demonstrates considerable knowledge	Description of how GAAPs and practices apply to a service business demonstrates thorough knowledge
Explain the methods used to safeguard the assets of a business	Explanation of the methods used to safeguard the assets of a business demonstrates limited knowledge	Explanation of the methods used to safeguard the assets of a business demonstrates some knowledge	Explanation of the methods used to safeguard the assets of a business demonstrates considerable knowledge	Explanation of the methods used to safeguard the assets of a business demonstrates thorough knowledge
Summarize the nature of a partnership	Summarizes the nature of a partnership with limited reference to partner obligations	Summarizes the nature of a partnership with some reference to partner obligations	Summarizes the nature of a partnership with considerable reference to partner obligations	Summarizes the nature of a partnership with thorough reference to partner obligations

Criteria	Level 1 (50–59%)	Level 2 (60–69%)	Level 3 (70–79%)	Level 4 (80–100%)
Summarize the risks of credit sales	Summarizes the risks of credit sales with limited reference to risk management	Summarizes the risks of credit sales with adequate reference to risk management	Summarizes the risks of credit sales with considerable reference to risk management	Summarizes the risks of credit sales with thorough reference to risk management

II. Questions to Ponder

- How do our suppliers' activities (or inactivity) affect our cost improvement work?

- What tools can reduce the probability of having to go through a cost recovery effort?

- Does cost recovery get any easier if we have a long-term relationship with our supplier?

- Does your company or service have a cost recovery strategy or formal methodology?

- How do you know when to consider cost recovery efforts?

- What is the cost to your company for losing one customer? How much money/ time does it take to replace an existing customer?

- How do contracts help us with cost recovery? Do contracts really matter?

III. Cost Improvement Scenario

A. Situation

As a new vehicle emission project gets underway, we start building some vehicles made of these prototype parts. The new emissions project requires addition of multiple new pressure sensors to various components in the engine assembly. These sensors provide vital information for the rest of the system. These signals go into respective electronic control units, are processed and will be broadcast over the data link. The pressure sensors have the same type of connectors right down to the color and envelope. In the course of reviewing the first prototype built vehicle, we find that we are unable to get the vehicle to run. As we troubleshoot the vehicle we find out that the sensors are connected to the incorrect wire harness and therefore the signals are interpreted incorrectly.

B. Objective

If the vehicles can be built incorrectly by engineers and mechanics that do not have the time pressure of production line, we can be sure that we will have this problem in our manufacturing unless we keep this crossing of the sensors. Towing vehicles off the production line does not improve throughput of the manufacturing system and wastes valuable time. Solve the problem of missed connections between the sensors and the respective function monitored and electronic control unit.

C. Action

The sensors required are identical, including the connectors. However, we do have the option of altering the sensors' connections in some way to alleviate this mix up. We discuss with the supplier the possibility of altering the colors of one of the connectors. This is the quickest and easiest solution.

D. Results

Color-coding the connectors to the pressure sensors eliminates the possibility of crossing the sensors including at the production level. Subsequent prototype vehicle builds confirm this hypothesis, since we no longer see the problem on our fault lists.

E. Aftermath

Alteration of the connector colors making the connector on the sensor match the color of the wire harness end eliminated the problem of having two of the same type connectors that connect to two different sensors of different signals. The subsequent production launch of the product had none of the problems witnessed when the sensors were cross-connected.

IV. What Is Cost Recovery?

Cost recovery often occurs when we have had a product fiasco and our customer is complaining bitterly about the quality of our product. They will attempt some level of cost recovery with us and we, in turn, will attempt cost recovery with our supplier if we can show the supplier is culpable. We are not saying, "beat up the supplier" every time an untoward event occurs but, rather, suggesting that some recompense is proper when the supplier has *demonstrated* culpability. We know of cases where some of the staff was ready to blame the supplier without testing the parts to ensure that, in fact, the supplier was responsible for the issue. It is in our best interest to confirm our hunches rather than blame the supplier across-the-board. Assuming the cause and responsibility is never a solution and we can see the problem resurface if we have not in fact explored to find the truth.

V. When to Use Cost Recovery

We can pose a hypothetical situation: we have just been informed by our customer that our product will be part of a campaign and we will be replacing everything we sold them—replacing, not repairing. That means we will assume not only the cost of developing a new product that functions properly but we will also have to participate in the replacement of the parts. If this were an automotive example, we would be participating at dealerships. Needless to say, these kinds of campaigns (pseudo-recalls) can get expensive quickly. If we can prove that one of our suppliers provided a defective part to us, then we are only partly guilty—of inadequate testing. Nevertheless, the supplier shares a portion of the burden and we should use the procurement arm of our enterprise to recover some of the cost of the campaign. The primary catch to this cost recovery occurs when our supplier is significantly larger than we are or when they are a sole source and we have no other recourse (bad design practice, by the way!). Then, we would have to proceed to legal action to recover our money.

VI. Benefits of Cost Recovery

It should be fairly obvious that cost recovery is usually a form of cost avoidance. As we have indicated in other areas, verifiable and meaningful cost avoidances are not a bad thing. Also notice that cost recovery will allow us to offset a negative to the bottom line, so we do have an influence on the profitability of the enterprise when we proceed to cost recovery mode.

Cost recovery can also provide some punitive benefit with a supplier who has less than acceptable quality practices. For example, in the U.S. automotive industry we expect to Advanced Product Quality Planning, which includes:

- Failure Mode and Effects Analyses (FMEA) for product and process
- Production part approval process
- Product and process verification and validation
- Corrective action system
- Process control plan
- Statistical quality studies
- Reliability assessments

We can add whatever else fits into the AIAG automotive quality system as well as any requirements pertaining to ISO-9000, ISO/TS 16949, and other standards. If our suppliers are not implementing reasonable quality practices, then we can "crack the whip" with some cost recovery. This approach may sound heartless, but for some suppliers it functions as a wake-up call. We also need to be careful that our procurement group practiced appropriate diligence when vetting the supplier at the beginning of the relationship.

Suppliers should also understand that they have a responsibility to alert their customers to product and process changes, often through a formal system. Sometimes, suppliers go around these systems because they delay the change; however, all a supplier needs is one major catastrophe and all savings from rushing through the change process will have been lost and more.

VII. Steps to Cost Recovery

We need to take care when participating in a cost recovery initiative in order to avoid offending suppliers and customers alike. We have used the following steps to pursue a rational course of action:

1. Take emergency action if necessary

2. Define the problem explicitly

3. Define what is not the problem

4. Establish containment of the product if necessary

5. Establish the dates when we produced the product

6. Look for documented process changes

7. Contact supplier and request information about process changes, material changes, any changes

8. Contact customer and request information about usage changes, physical locations of the parts, geographical locations, and end users (some corporate end users are harder on products than others)

9. Look for undocumented process changes (much more difficult)

10. Sequester samples of anomalous material

11. Submit material to surface-level inspection for obvious flaws

12. If we have enough returned parts, pull some aside for internal examination

13. Again, if we have enough returned parts, submit them to a select set of useful tests under controlled conditions

14. Meet with supplier and discuss results of inspections and tests

15. Meet with customer and discuss results of inspections and tests

16. Make a recommendation

17. Make an irreversible corrective action if possible

The cost recovery occurs in the situations where we can prove either the supplier or the customer produced the issue. Recovering money from customers can become a *cause célèbre* unless the customer agrees they were at fault. Recovering money from suppliers is less difficult if we have leverage with the supplier. As we have mentioned, we have seen cases where the supplier was much larger than our company, making it difficult to leverage a payback.

We should note that we always follow an ethical course of action during these investigations. Prematurely pointing fingers at suppliers is a counterproductive behavior and unlikely to lead to the open-book behavior we want with our suppliers. The case for ethical behavior is even stronger when dealing with a customer.

VIII. Two-Way Cost Recovery

In some cases, we will have a customer attempting to achieve cost recovery from us as the supplier and we, in turn, will go after a supplier if they are indeed guilty of an unauthorized process or product change. In the cases we have experienced, the customer was not going to wait for the supplier to come up with the cash because that was our problem not their problem. We cannot overemphasize the importance of relationships when dealing in both directions.

When we choose to go after a supplier, we need to ensure that our investigation does not have a "shadow of a doubt" as to whom is really the guilty party. We have seen cases where knee-jerk reactions produced accusations about a supplier that were found later to be unjustified. In one case, the supplier's process was, in fact, poorly controlled and gave the appearance of being a potential cause of a plastic breakage problem with a housing. We later discovered that a production engineer had made an undocumented change to the process that was the real root cause of the issues we saw. We recovered nothing from the supplier because he was not guilty and we had to eat the cost of excessive line testing performed to eliminate the possibility that bad parts would be shipped to the customer. We received no cost recovery from the customer because we were at fault.

We have heard complaints about the level of documentation required for the ISO quality certifications, but we think they are a huge component of the configuration management process. We need to remember that configuration control applies to process controls just as much as it does to products. Interestingly, we never accounted for the cost of the investigation of the product we have been discussing, a form of expense or "anti-cost reduction."

One-way or two-way cost recovery requires rigorous documentation at the best of times. Even when we have a strong case, we may never see any recompense if we are dealing with a supplier or customer who is many times the size of our own firm. They can stonewall our queries, ignore meetings, and simply avoid ever paying us what they owe us. If the supplier/customer is bankrupt but still doing business, we probably never see the cost recovery. We have seen this occur with a giant supplier's connector; the supplier was clearly at fault, we had the data, we had the hard evidence—we never received a nickel for our troubles, finally writing off the expense as a loss. We ultimately decided we had no reason to continue to pour money into the investigation and negotiations because this particular supplier was bankrupt and had no intention of ever paying off their debt.

The previous situation suggests we have some responsibility when we choose a supplier because we may not be able to pursue cost recovery when we have a quality issue. We are in an unenviable situation when our customer requires us to sole source to a giant supplier who owns a patent on a unique part.

IX. EXERCISES

- How do we achieve cost recovery when our supplier is larger than we are?

- On the other hand, how do we achieve cost recovery when our supplier is much smaller than we are and the cost recovery activity may in fact bring them to bankruptcy?

- Under what conditions do we share responsibility for the supplier based fiasco? How do we determine who will bear the burden of the cost without getting ourselves involved in extended litigation?

- How can we reduce risk with our suppliers? Do we try to get same or similar parts from different suppliers?

- How do we manage the situation when our supplier is the only enterprise in the universe that holds a patent to a customer required part and is, in fact, a sole source for that part?

- What is the best way to establish a long-term relationship with our suppliers? Is this approach more advantageous than that of beating our suppliers until they give us price downs?

- What is the price of ruthlessness? Do we pay a moral price internally? What about the damage done to our suppliers?

- How do we determine if the supplier failure is the result of an act of God? Do we blame the supplier for not having appropriate contingency plans?

- We have been in the situation where we had to rewrite a portion of a cross compiler in order to have basic mathematical capability in our own code; should we have pursued cost recovery with this supplier?

- How do we flow down our policies and procedures to our suppliers in such a way that we do not need to practice cost recovery very often?

- So far, we have primarily discussed suppliers in these questions. How about the potentially more difficult situation where we need to seek cost recovery from a customer? Under what conditions would we need to do this act? What level of our enterprise needs to negotiate with what level of their enterprise in order to make this happen?

- Is it legitimate to blame incompetent statements and a customer specification? How much ownership do we have if they refuse to listen to our recommendation?

- Research the cost of a typical cost recovery activity in your own enterprise. If you cannot do this, check the World Wide Web for whatever you can find on cost recovery. Report on what you find.

- Create a process for cost recovery with a supplier. You may represent your process graphically.

- Create a process for cost recovery with the customer. You may represent your process graphically.

CHAPTER 12 – Other Methods

I. Rubric for Other Methods

Criteria	Level 1 (50–59%)	Level 2 (60–69%)	Level 3 (70–79%)	Level 4 (80–100%)
Create design briefs	Creates design briefs with limited effectiveness	Creates design briefs with some effectiveness	Creates design briefs with considerable effectiveness	Creates design briefs with excellent effectiveness
Assess problems associated with improper or inadequate design	Assesses problems associated with improper or inadequate design using limited critical thinking	Assesses problems associated with improper or inadequate design using some critical thinking	Assesses problems associated with improper or inadequate design using good critical thinking	Assesses problems associated with improper or inadequate design using excellent critical thinking
Apply the design process to the design and manufacture of products	Applies the design process with limited success to the design and manufacture of products	Applies the design process with some success to the design and manufacture of products	Applies the design process with considerable success to the design and manufacture of products	Applies the design process with a high degree of success to the design and manufacture of products
Assess projects and recommend changes for improvement	Demonstrates an ability to assess projects and recommends changes for improvement with supervision	Demonstrates an ability to assess simple projects and recommends minor changes for improvement	Demonstrates an ability to assess projects and recommends changes for improvement	Demonstrates an ability to assess complex projects and is able to assist others with their assessment as well as recommend many changes for improvement
Communicate design ideas	Communicates design ideas with limited clarity	Communicates design ideas with some clarity	Communicates design ideas with considerable clarity	Communicates design ideas with a high degree of clarity
Compare given aspects for validity	Comparison of given aspects demonstrates limited understanding of validity	Comparison of given aspects demonstrates some understanding of validity	Comparison of given aspects demonstrates considerable understanding of validity	Comparison of given aspects demonstrates thorough understanding of validity
Create a design plan	Creates a design plan with limited organization	Creates a design plan with some organization	Creates a design plan with considerable organization	Creates a design plan with excellent organization
Create a design solution to user needs	Creates a design solution with limited understanding of user needs	Creates a design solution with some understanding of user needs	Creates a design solution with considerable understanding of user needs	Creates a design solution with excellent understanding of user needs
Create design drawings	Creates design drawings with limited awareness of accuracy	Creates design drawings with some awareness of accuracy	Creates design drawings with competent awareness of accuracy	Creates design drawings with thorough awareness of accuracy
Demonstrate product testing with established criteria	Demonstrates limited understanding of product testing	Demonstrates some understanding of product testing	Demonstrates considerable understanding of product testing	Demonstrates thorough understanding of product testing

Criteria	Level 1 (50–59%)	Level 2 (60–69%)	Level 3 (70–79%)	Level 4 (80–100%)
Demonstrate skill in fabricating mock-ups, models, or prototypes	Demonstrates limited skill in fabricating mock-ups, models, or prototypes	Demonstrates some skill in fabricating mock-ups, models, or prototypes	Demonstrates considerable skill in fabricating mock-ups, models, or prototypes	Demonstrates excellent skill in fabricating mock-ups, models, or prototypes
Demonstrate the use of a product in a new way	Demonstrates the use of a product in a new way with limited effectiveness	Demonstrates the use of a product in a new way with some effectiveness	Demonstrates the use of a product in a new way with considerable effectiveness	Demonstrates the use of a product in a new way with outstanding effectiveness
Describe engineering principles	Describes engineering principles with limited understanding	Describes engineering principles with some understanding	Describes engineering principles with good understanding	Describes engineering principles with thorough understanding
Describe solutions to a design problem using a design report format	Is able to describe solutions to design problems using limited knowledge and creativity	Is able to describe solutions to design problems using some knowledge and creativity	Is able to describe solutions to design problems using considerable knowledge and creativity	Is able to describe solutions to design problems using excellent knowledge and creativity
Describe the ISO 9002 quality control systems	Is able to describe the ISO 9002 quality control systems with limited comprehension and clarity	Is able to describe the ISO 9002 quality control systems with some comprehension and clarity	Is able to describe the ISO 9002 quality control systems with good comprehension and clarity	Is able to describe the ISO 9002 quality control systems with excellent comprehension and clarity
Estimate costs for a project	Estimates costs for a project with limited accuracy	Estimates costs for a project with some accuracy	Estimates costs for a project with considerable accuracy	Estimates costs for a project with a high degree of accuracy
Evaluate consumer needs	Evaluates consumer needs with limited reference to criteria	Evaluates consumer needs with some reference to criteria	Evaluates consumer needs with considerable reference to criteria	Evaluates consumer needs with thorough reference to criteria
Fabricate models and prototypes	Fabricates models and prototypes with limited skill	Fabricates models and prototypes with some skill	Fabricates models and prototypes with good skill	Fabricates models and prototypes with a high degree of skill
Include roles played by team members in a group project	Includes their own role played in a group project	Includes two roles played by team members in a group project	Includes all roles played by team members in a group project	Includes all roles played by team members in a group project with a rating scale
Produce technical reports	Produces technical reports that begin to follow a prescribed format	Produces technical reports that somewhat follow a prescribed format	Produces technical reports that largely follow a prescribed format	Produces technical reports that expertly follow a prescribed format
Use criteria to analyze information	Rarely uses criteria to analyze information	Sometimes uses criteria to analyze information	Often uses criteria to analyze information	Routinely uses criteria to analyze information
Use criteria to evaluate information	Makes limited use of criteria to evaluate information	Makes some use of criteria to evaluate information	Makes considerable use of criteria to evaluate information	Makes thorough use of criteria to evaluate information

Criteria	Level 1 (50–59%)	Level 2 (60–69%)	Level 3 (70–79%)	Level 4 (80–100%)
Use criteria to make a comparison	Rarely uses criteria to make a comparison	Sometimes uses criteria to make a comparison	Often uses criteria to make a comparison	Routinely uses criteria to make a comparison
Use engineering principles	Uses engineering principles with limited success	Uses engineering principles with some success	Uses engineering principles with good success	Uses engineering principles with a high degree of success
Work cooperatively in groups	Rarely works cooperatively in groups	Sometimes works cooperatively in groups	Often works cooperatively in groups	Always works cooperatively in groups

II. Questions to Ponder

- What other possibilities do we have to improve our organization's value proposition?

- What methods to improve the value proposition have you employed?

- How can we improve our organization's efficiency? How is this a value improvement?

- What role does quality play in profitability?

- What actions does your organization take to improve efficiency?

- How does your company control the costs?

- How does project management maturity improve our organization's profitability?

- What happens when we do not anticipate the risks associated with our cost improvement activities?

III. Cost Improvement Scenario

A. Situation

This is not a cost reduction project or case study. However, this case will illustrate the impact of an ineffectual project management on the efficiency of the delivery. A Chief Project Manager (CPM) is approaching the delivery of the product for testing. The CPM goes to the verification group manager to get the verification activities underway. The schedule is shown to the verification manager. The group manager then proceeds to point out the missing points in the schedule.

The first error was the scheduled start date for the testing does not coincide with the delivery of the entire system. The first component of the system, for example, arrives on week five. However, the remaining portions of the system are not available until a few weeks later. The start date of week five neglected these other parts of the system, which are absolutely necessary for the verification work.

The second error came in the form of the vehicle for the systems testing. The assumption that any vehicle would meet the need for systems verification was incorrect. There are attributes that must be considered when selecting a test subject. For example, a vehicle equipped with electrical / electronic systems that are a number iterations back would not be a good candidate. Neither would a vehicle that has been thoroughly abused in endurance testing as a product close to wear out will require discerning what failed due to software errors and what failed due to other hardware life issues, thus slowing test progress. The experience of the verification manager suggests that to prepare and qualify a vehicle for this level of testing requires anywhere from one to three weeks of effort from a variety of departments. This leads to the third error, the assumption that the testing can start the second day the vehicle arrives at the test facility.

Lastly, there was an assumption that the product would pass verification testing, an ungrounded optimism, since there was no plan for a corrective action loop. This loop is where the problems or failures that are found in testing are then reported back to the development engineers and the appropriate corrections are made in the product/ system.

B. Objective

The project and the test department must address the testing needs for this project.

Figure 12.1 We can even prototype and model complex devices such as instrument clusters.

Figure 12.2 Example of a product under development.

Figure 12.3 We could model a cluster with a wooden board, CNC cut plastics, and other parts.

The additional features, the hardware and software associated with this update must be verified before sending the product to the customer.

C. Action

The present schedule will not work since the verification tasks were not identified and included in the Work Breakdown Structure for the project. The project now has the verification as the critical path. The verification and project personnel identify the steps and specific tasks needed to accomplish this system verification. In the event the verification activities find faults that must be corrected, the plan includes a second loop of development to correct those problems found in verification.

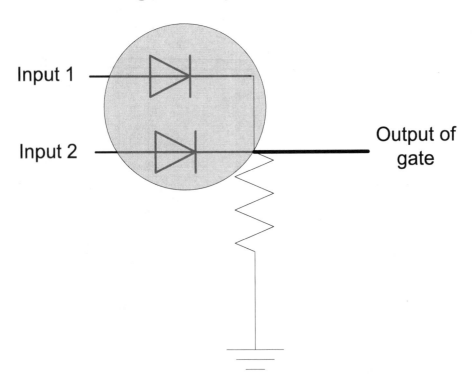

Figure 12.4 This discrete component is an "OR" gate.

D. Results

The proposed test vehicle was reviewed and corrected to make the vehicle suitable for integration testing. This consumed a number of weeks as the vehicle was dismantled and parts replaced that represented the system version for production. The first round of testing provided a list of failures for correction. A second loop of testing occurred—the product was about six months later than the desired production start date.

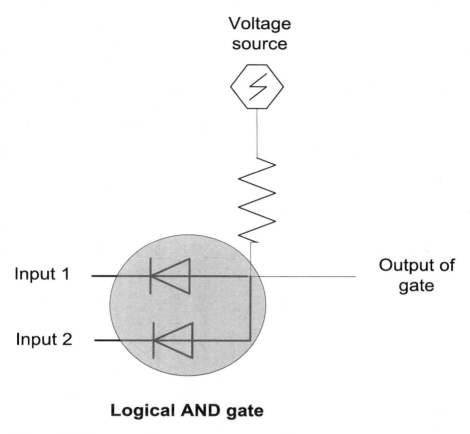

Voltage source

Input 1

Input 2

Output of gate

Logical AND gate

Figure 12.5 We can use discrete components to model a system.

E. Aftermath

While the project was off target considerably in the original WBS and the project was indeed late, there was opportunity for growth. The CPM and others in the project organization was introduced to software testing and the consequences of not considering these activities required when delivering a quality product. In the end, the lesson spread through the entire project organization. Testing must be considered early in the project. There were presentations on software handling and testing processes to the project organization.

IV. Other Tools

A. Project Management

Project management for many organizations is the set of activities that reduce the risk to the organization in achieving its goals while improving efficiency. We can see that an organization can incur costs when unaccounted for risks result; we also know inefficiency is not helpful when it comes to improving our cost structure and bottom

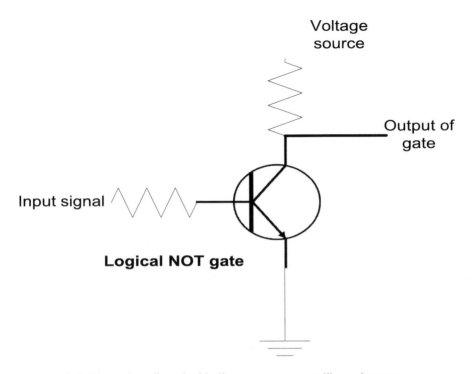

Figure 12.6 We can breadboard with discrete components like an inverter.

line. Therefore, a well functioning project management organization can help reduce the costs associated with developmental brain lapses.

Risk

One of the principal objectives of project management is to minimize risk to the organization and specifically to the project's objectives. Risk mitigation may cost but the avoidance of risk saves the company money and more—reputation and customer satisfaction for example.

B. What Is DFA?

We use the tool design for assembly (DFA) during the development process to make sure the design engineers have included the manufacturing perspective. Designing an award-winning product that cannot be produced—or the costs are too high to produce it—which erodes the product margins, and alters your value proposition in a negative way. The cost outpaces the value received by the customer. Use of this methodology generally produces a higher quality and more reliable product. However, the real benefit is the streamlining of the production process.

Design for Assembly in Product Development

One tool to use during product development is design for assembly:

- Select an assembly method—often the existing assembly methods and standards
- Compare the proposed designs against the ability of the assembly methods
- Provide feedback to the development personnel to alter the design
- Repeat the exchange between the development and manufacturing groups

Design for Assembly as Part of Teardown

We can use the DFA tools and the product teardown to understand how the assembly of the product is achieved. We can identify those parts, which appear to be a manual assembly. These are the parts which labor is the principle to achieve the assembly. There will be tools and maybe some specialty hand tools to put the parts together to make the assembly. Where we need to be adaptable to put the parts together we will use the manual method. We can glean the amount of manual assembly required by the complexity of the assemblies.

We may also be able to ascertain the amount of automation of the subassembly as well. We are still working with mass produced products when we have fixed or hard automation. The machine is tooled or developed to address a specific set of tasks within the assembly process. There can be multiple machines each with areas of the build, that will do very specific tasks required for the assembly. This automation will be intermixed with the manual work.

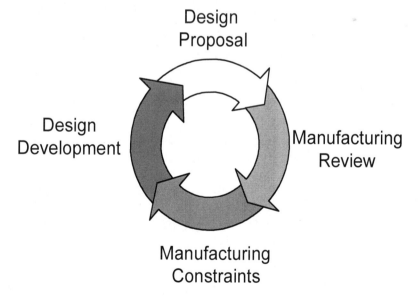

Figure 12.7 Design for manufacture can improve the throughput in manufacturing.

Lastly, we may discover evidence that robotics was used to build the assemblies. For example, we may spot welds in the assembly that provide clues that suggest the assembly was operated on by a robot. We may see indexing points on the part for the handling of the material by the robot.

C. Design for Manufacturing

Design for manufacturing provides us with the ability to critique the design as it applies or impacts the manufacturing line. Do we ever wonder why the phrase "hits production" exists? It is because insufficient attention to the integration of the design and the manufacturing often result in trauma at the manufacturing site. Design for manufacturing is one tool for improving this situation. our objective is to design the product in such a way that we minimize the impact on manufacturing. We essentially want the design to play to the existing manufacturing strengths and capabilities. We know that the design dictates to a large degree the cost to manufacture the product. Some estimates indicate that 70% of the manufacturing costs originate in design decisions, and only 20% originating in production or manufacturing decisions. This makes this area rife for value optimization.

Like the design for assembly, we integrate the design and development work with the manufacturing endeavors of the project. In this case, our focus is not the assembly process, but all the manufacturing aspects of the product. To have the greatest impact, we perform this work while the product is under development (thus the idea of integrated design and manufacture).

While the best situation is this exchange between design and manufacturing, value can be obtained even after the product design has been completed and the manufacturing line has been running for some period. However we sacrifice the ability to modify the design while the design is evolving. This means we may have to rework the original design or accept the implications of the design on the manufacturing process, minimizing the area of consideration for value improvement.

Modular Design

We can look at things like a modular design. The modular design concept means we have a number of parts that we use in a variety of ways and on a variety of products. Use of existing parts has a litany of implications including the quality of the product.

Modular design elements are a prerequisite for mass customization. With our modular systems in place we can consider a philosophy of mass customization, in which we can present a number of possible value propositions toward our customers. The building blocks of this mass customization are the various modular approaches below:

1. Component sharing

2. Component swapping modularity

3. Cut to fit modularity

4. Mix modularity

5. Bus modularity

6. Sectional modularity

Consider a vehicle manufacturer that offers a variety of product solutions in the heavy vehicle industry. This vehicle variety requires a range of display products to meet the various needs. The manufacturer decides they need to improve the material costs for the product across this variety of vehicle applications and geographic regions. A project is undertaken to deliver this product line. We see in the next set of images, the variety of products that are built from the core developed parts.

Reduction in Total Number of Parts

Our modular designs can help with our part count reduction. However, there are yet other possibilities. Our design for manufacturing exercise includes a review of the parts list and exchanges for existing parts already being used. We have less inventory variety, and the purchasing of those parts. Our design for manufacturing work will ferret out our inefficiencies in our material handling.

Successful modular designs moves our organization a step closer to mass customization. That is we make products that can be easily adapted to meet a variety of customer demands. Mass customization may appear to be a relatively recent manufacturing technique. This is not necessarily true. Ying Zheng, also known as China Qin Shi Huang Di or the first emperor of Qin took the throne in 246 B.C. He is credited with a number of successes, the most notable was the unification of the kingdoms. However, according to a recent article in the June 2012 (page 86) issue of *National Geographic*:

> Aside from building the first lengths of the Great Wall, the tyrannical reformer standardized the nation's writing system, currency and measurements and provided the source for the English word we now use for China (Qin is pronounced Chin).

However, these great accomplishments pale by comparison to the thousands of terra cotta soldiers that were interred as guards for the emperor in his afterlife. The *Smithsonian Magazine* (June 2012, page 77) further elaborates:

> Qin Shi Huangdi decreed a mass-production approach; artisans turned out figures almost like cars on an assembly line. Clay, unlike bronze, lends itself to quick and cheap fabrication. Workers built bodies, then customized them with heads, hats, shoes, mustaches, ears and so on, made in small molds. Some of the figures appear so strikingly individual they seem modeled on real people, though that is unlikely. "These probably weren't portraits in the Western sense," says Hiromi Kinoshita, who helped curate the exhibition at the British Museum. Instead, they may have been aggregate portraits: the ceramicists, says Kinoshita, "could have been told that you need to represent all the different types of people who come from different regions of China[1].

The body was created separately and displayed a similar combination of standard elements. All together, the completed figures gave an impression of infinite variety, as in a real army.

We can see that visionaries have known the benefits of mass customization. This is no less true today. Mass customization can shorten the time to deliver the product to market. Additionally, we have the possibility of meeting market segmentation demands without incurring additional costs or time. If we can be profitable providing solutions in low volume, we would likely be very successful in those larger populations in the marketplace.

Parts off the Shelf

If the part is not a strategic part for the organization, we may elect to use a standardized part for a portion of the subassembly. We will consider this approach not only in the design for manufacturing aspects, but also in our make or buy analysis, which we discussed earlier in this book. Use of standardized parts in a subassembly means that we volume purchasing in our favor and the price of the part will reflect that.

If our organization builds a number of similar products, we may settle in on a set of components that we refer to as standard parts we use for products. For example, a SAE 485-bus transceiver can be used in a number of applications. There is probably no good reason for having multiple bus transceivers possible for the product line of the company. If there is a preferred transceiver for performance characteristics, we can use that part in all of our designs.

Design Parts to Fill Multiple Roles

When we find we have a design requirement that we can meet with discrete integrated circuit, we have an opportunity. For example we may need an AND gate function for our logic, but we do not have a microcontroller, nor a mixed-signal ASIC nor do we wish to purchase a 7400 series part when all we need is one of these gates. In those cases, we employ components that we use elsewhere in our designs. Diodes and resistors we use in other parts of our designs. We use parts we are already purchasing, consume less printed circuit board space, and only use the devices we need.

We meet this objective when we find ways to use a specific part in multiple ways. We use these parts to fulfill many roles or functions. For example, we may use diodes in our power supplies to keep the unwanted electrical signals or transients from parts of our circuitry. This is the typical application of diodes, but we can also use these same diodes to produce a logical OR gate.

We can use our NPN transistors as inverters—if we need a single inverter gate and do not want to purchase an integrated circuit that has more than we need. In each of these cases we have used parts in an atypical way to achieve the design objective and to improve the value.

Fabrication

We want to minimize the costs due to fabrication of the product. When we over-specify or unnecessarily harden the product, we alter the value proposition for our customer. This cost is passed on and the benefit may not be improved (that is the definition of overspecifying). Painting, refinishing during the final operation are not value added activities and do not improve your value proposition. These activities inflate the production cost, and that is not improving the situation.

Fasteners

Common parts and volume discounts are an area that is commonly considered. However, we are also saving money on the storage of the material. We save money on storage or maintaining inventory as we are consuming from the inventory across a number of products. We have a more even consumption. For example, if our sales volume for a particular product drops, we still have the sales volume of our other products in our product line to consume the inventory. When we use unique fasteners for each product, when the product consumption rate goes down, we may have inventory on the shelf that is just sitting there.

Another benefit of common fasteners is the tools used to install said fastener. We need not keep many of these installation tools such as an assortment of hex head or Phillips head screwdrivers. We do not have to train our people the proper installation technique for this multiplicity of tools and fasteners.

Another benefit of reducing the number of fasteners, we reduce the possibility of installing the wrong fasteners on the product. When we have a set of fasteners that look similar and we have to maintain access to this variety of fasteners in the assembly area, we run the risk of installing the wrong fastener on the product. Reducing the variety of fasteners does not eliminate this risk; however it does reduce this possibility.

Handling

Moving the product around unnecessarily consumes energy and time. Both of these erode value propositions. We want to reduce material handling. We should carefully consider our processes that may unwittingly contribute to excessive material handling and associated wastes. We use tools like design for manufacturing and assembly to help uncover this waste.

D. Rapid Prototyping

Rapid prototyping is a term most often used when we have the equipment to deliver a usable model within a short period of time, days or weeks. One of the biggest shifts in prototyping occurred when three-dimensional printers dropped to less than $100,000 in cost (for small ones), allowing the creation of SLA (stereo lithographic) models. The primary difficulty with these kinds of models is that they *really* are models and not prototypes. We show examples of rapid prototyping equipment in Figure 12.8, Figure 12.9, Figure 12.10, and Figure 12.5. Any waste or residual material we can recycle (see Figure 12.12).

In general, we will elevate a "model" to a "prototype" when we can actually perform tests on the object. Prototype is an appropriate designation when we have parts such as:

- Prototype printed circuit boards (which are sometimes better than the final product boards)

- Plastic mechanical parts injection molded from a soft tool (good for about 5,000 pieces)

- Metal mechanical parts injection molded from a soft tool (good for about 5,000 pieces)

- Actual connectors

- Actual wire harnesses (if we are in a business which uses them)

The great advantage to prototype parts is that we can test them very much as if we were working with production parts. The results from prototypes will have meaning for the rest of the development project. If we are building prototypes for a cost reduction, we need to include the cost of the prototyping into the business case for the cost reduction.

Figure 12.8 Any tool that helps us build models is a good tool.

Even if we pay for a soft tool, the cost of which can be upward of 80% of the hard tool, we can still use the soft tool to make production parts as long as we have appropriate controls in place and customer acquiescence. Controls might include tolerance measurements on the tool itself, control charts to analyze for measurement drift, designed experiments to keep us in the sweet spot, and a hard number at which we no longer will use the tool.

We have recommended several times that the engineers should consider the use of simulation. We can reduce wasted money with this step. One simple way to do this is to verify (if we sell electronics) that the components we place on the printed circuit board will fit within the enclosure. This approach is not always simple since we often do not have supplier drawings of the part to drop into our own drawings; however, when we have a misfit, it causes difficulties on the production line and probable future returns due to higher-than-expected wear out.

In the 21st century, we can use tools such as Autodesk Inventor or PTC Creo to model the form and fit in three dimensions. Once we verify our fit, we can move to prototype parts. We know this approach is powerful because we have seen a situation where we merged our drawings with our customer's drawings and discovered a multiple millimeter mismatch between our part and the attachment/supporting flange on the customer instrument panel—this situation resulted in torsion on the supplier's parts, causing cracking in the plastic lens for the part!

Although working models are at a "lower" level than prototype parts, they can still give us some idea about the limitations and abilities of the new product. Once again, we need to build the cost of these activities into our cost reduction proposal. However, experimentation is often at the heart of improvements and we may find through designed experimentation that we have other opportunities for improvement in the part. Working models can use such materials as:

- Wood

- Thermoplastic

- Thermoset

- Clay (often used in the automotive industry for nonworking models)

- Cardboard

- Stone

- Cement

- Papier-maché

- Plaster of Paris

- Paper and glue

- Food (sounds weird, but casting is easy!)

- Wire

- Cloth

- Hair-like materials

- Ceramics

- Ice

- Biomass

- Tar
- Duct tape
- Plastic tape
- Paper tape

Important tools in our modeling efforts can include a Dremel tool, drills, saws, and scissors; in fact, anything that can work with the materials we choose to use. We should not limit ourselves to technologically high and very expensive devices when we might be able to discover what we need at much less expense. For example, if we do not have software support for form and fit of a printed circuit board into an enclosure, we can put components on cardboard and build either an SLA enclosure or a cardboard enclosure and see if they fit.

Figure 12.9 Prototype PCP.

In fact, the materials we use for modeling are only limited by our imagination and the purposes for which we use them. Sometimes, the cheaper the material, the better. We do not invest that much, but we learn something about the product, perhaps changing direction on the cost reduction based on what we discover.

One of the concepts that should arise when building initial models is the idea of "play." If we have no play, we most likely are simply repeating what we have already done. Part of the play can include radical ideas, such as:

- Set the new cost at half of the current cost and design for cost

- Propose the elimination of entire processes by designing them away (for example, the use of screws in the assembly or elimination of expensive robots like selective solder machines).

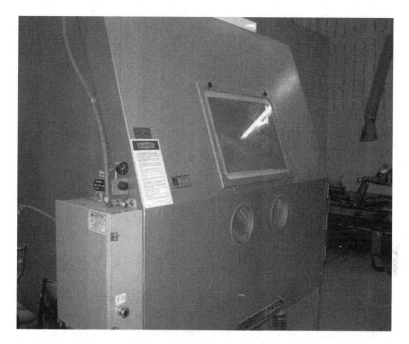

Figure 12.10 This air sander prototype allows us to study its properties.

- Make the cost reduction into a game!
- Put concepts on the World Wide Web for comment
- Make a cost reduction design contest with Internet submissions
- See what happens if we make all parts discrete
- See what happens if we integrate components to the maximum level
- Arbitrarily eliminate components and see what occurs
- Ask for combination of functions
- See if we can do the task with software
- Adapt a part to another use
- Work with somebody from the arts world for a new slant on the design
- Change the space available for the enclosure
- What happens if we locate the part somewhere else in the larger system (for example, the Toyota Yaris has most of the instrumentation in the middle of the dash, allowing for the steering wheel to be located on either side and making it a world car)
- Can we repurpose another product?
- Use the speed of qualitative analysis to tell us what we need to know during the

Figure 12.11 Laser cutters are a trifle exotic, but they are a great help when we need precision cuts.

beginning stage so we do not do something exceptionally stupid (use cardboard, glue, tape, etc.).

V. EXERCISES

- How can you justify prototype tooling and still have a cost reduction?

- Do some research online to ascertain how far you can go in the analysis of the cost reduction by using simulation. Will you have to buy the simulation software? Can you amortize the cost of simulation software over multiple products and/or multiple products?

- What methods have we missed in this book? Please send your answer to either one of the authors at www.valuetransform.com.

- If we are using a simulator, how do we perform validation? Are simulator results sufficient? Or do we need to use our standard process to check out the cost reduction? What are the risks?

- What is the difference between operational improvement and a process improvement? (Hint: Think about Shingo's definition.)

- If cost reductions potentially result in a reduction in head count, is the result justified? How are you going to sell this to other employees? Reductions result in head count reductions—how will we get employees to look for cost reductions?

- How do we test for cost reductions if they are relatively small; for example, if they only had up to a few hundred dollars?

Figure 12.12 We can even cut prototype panels.

- Does the Six Sigma style champion system make sense regardless of the kind of cost reduction we are involved with?

- How important is margin improvement through cost reduction? Is it more important than compound annual growth? Is it equal importance to compound annual growth?

- Is it ever reasonable to hide cost reductions from a customer? Under what conditions?

- How many cost reductions can we achieve by cooperating with the customer? And what is the likelihood that we will attain even more cost reductions when working with the customer?

- How would we optimize the cost reduction? What tools would we use to find "the sweet spot" in a cost reduction continue on? How do we account for the risk when we try to optimize cost reduction?

- What project management technique lends itself to prompt cost reductions while still minimizing risk?

- How do we track our cost reductions? If we are using myriad techniques, what is the best way to monitor our savings?

- Which part of the enterprise provides greatest likelihood of giving us the checks and balances—that is to say, validation—that we need in order to ensure that our savings are real?

- What is the best way to report cost reductions to upper management? Defend your point of view with at least three examples.

- How do we disseminate cost reductions across multiple parts of the organization, including manufacturing plants, design facilities, and laboratories?

ENDNOTES

1. http://www.smithsonianmag.com/history-archaeology/On-the-March-Terra-Cotta-Soldiers.html.

CHAPTER 13 – Finding Cost Reductions

I. Rubric for Finding Cost Reductions

Criteria	Level 1 (50–59%)	Level 2 (60–69%)	Level 3 (70–79%)	Level 4 (80–100%)
Apply different laws and regulations for waste disposal	Infrequently applies different laws and regulations for waste disposal	Sometimes applies different laws and regulations for waste disposal	Often applies different laws and regulations for waste disposal	Routinely applies different laws and regulations for waste disposal
Apply practices for recycling and waste management	Infrequently applies practices for recycling and waste management	Sometimes applies practices for recycling and waste management	Often applies practices for recycling and waste management	Routinely applies practices for recycling and waste management
Apply standards for health and safety	Rarely applies standards for health and safety	Sometime applies standards for health and safety	Often applies standards for health and safety	Always or almost always applies standards for health and safety
Apply treatments and procedures based on analysis	Uses treatment and procedures based on prior analysis safely and correctly only with supervision	Uses treatment and procedures based on prior analysis safely and correctly with some supervision	Uses treatment and procedures based on prior analysis safely and correctly	Demonstrates and promotes the safe use of treatment and procedures based on prior analysis
Create a list outlining 20 cost savings ideas available in the community	Is able to outline only 10 cost savings ideas available in the community	Is able to outline only 15 cost savings ideas available in the community	Is able to outline 20 cost savings ideas available in the community	Is able to outline more than 20 cost savings ideas available in the community
Demonstrate a problem-solving method	Demonstrates limited ability to use a problem-solving method	Demonstrates some ability to use a problem-solving method	Demonstrates good ability to use a problem-solving method	Demonstrates exceptional ability to use a problem-solving method
Demonstrate advanced interviewing techniques	Demonstrates limited ability to use advanced interviewing techniques	Demonstrates some ability to use advanced interviewing techniques	Demonstrates considerable ability to use advanced interviewing techniques	Demonstrates a high level of ability to use advanced interviewing techniques
Demonstrate record keeping skills	Rarely demonstrates record keeping skills	Sometimes demonstrates record keeping skills	Often demonstrates record keeping skills	Always or almost always demonstrates record keeping skills
Describe cost savings examples	Description of cost savings makes limited reference to examples	Description of cost savings makes some reference to examples	Description of cost savings makes considerable reference to examples	Description of cost savings makes thorough reference to examples
Describe different laws and regulations for waste disposal	Describes different laws and regulations for waste disposal providing limited information	Describes different laws and regulations for waste disposal providing some information	Describes different laws and regulations for waste disposal providing considerable information	Describes different laws and regulations for waste disposal providing thorough information
Describe disposal procedures for waste food products	Briefly describes disposal procedures for waste food products	Adequately describes disposal procedures for waste food products	Competently describes disposal procedures for waste food products	Thoroughly describes disposal procedures for waste food products

Criteria	Level 1 (50–59%)	Level 2 (60–69%)	Level 3 (70–79%)	Level 4 (80–100%)
Describe functions and responsibilities of front and back of the house personnel	Describes functions and responsibilities of front and back of the house personnel providing limited detail	Describes functions and responsibilities of front and back of the house personnel providing adequate detail	Describes functions and responsibilities of front and back of the house personnel providing good detail	Describes functions and responsibilities of front and back of the house personnel providing thorough detail
Describe "malpractice" and other liability issues	Description of malpractice and other liability issues demonstrates limited research	Description of malpractice and other liability issues demonstrates some research	Description of malpractice and other liability issues demonstrates considerable research	Description of malpractice and other liability issues demonstrates thorough research
Describe methods used both traditional and new	Communicates information about traditional and new methods and procedures with limited clarity	Communicates information about traditional and new methods and procedures with some clarity	Communicates information about traditional and new methods and procedures with considerable clarity	Communicates information about traditional and new methods and procedures with a high degree of clarity
Describe practices for recycling and waste management	Description of practices for recycling and waste management demonstrates limited knowledge	Description of practices for recycling and waste management demonstrates some knowledge	Description of practices for recycling and waste management demonstrates considerable knowledge	Description of practices for recycling and waste management demonstrates thorough knowledge
Describe the basic principles of customer service	Briefly describes the basic principles of customer service	Adequately describes the basic principles of customer service	Competently describes the basic principles of customer service	Thoroughly describes the basic principles of customer service
Describe the environmental impact of products	Communicates information about the environmental impact of products used in the industry with limited clarity	Communicates information about the environmental impact of products used in the industry with some clarity	Communicates information about the environmental impact of products used in the industry with considerable clarity	Communicates information about the environmental impact of products used in the industry with a high degree of clarity
Describe the importance of production schedules in planning events	Briefly describes the importance of production schedules in planning events	Adequately describes the importance of production schedules in planning events	Competently describes the importance of production schedules in planning events	Thoroughly describes the importance of production schedules in planning events
Describe various materials, process and equipment	Demonstrates limited knowledge of procedures, processes, and equipment	Demonstrates some knowledge of procedures, processes, and equipment	Demonstrates considerable knowledge of procedures, processes, and equipment	Demonstrates thorough knowledge of procedures, processes, and equipment
Develop an appropriate production schedule for selected events	Develops an appropriate production schedule for selected events with limited detail	Develops an appropriate production schedule for selected events with some detail	Develops an appropriate production schedule for selected events with considerable detail	Develops an appropriate production schedule for selected events with thorough detail
Employ techniques that meet industry standards	Employs techniques that rarely meet industry standards	Employs techniques that sometimes meet industry standards	Employs techniques that often meet industry standards	Employs techniques that always or almost always meet industry standards

Criteria	Level 1 (50–59%)	Level 2 (60–69%)	Level 3 (70–79%)	Level 4 (80–100%)
Explain how businesses increase market share	Explains how businesses increase market share with limited reference to the impact of that action	Explains how businesses increase market share with some reference to the impact of that action	Explains how businesses increase market share with considerable reference to the impact of that action	Explains how businesses increase market share with thorough reference to the impact of that action
Identify and apply procedures for inventory control	Identifies and applies procedures for inventory control with limited success	Identifies and applies procedures for inventory control with some success	Identifies and applies procedures for inventory control with good success	Identifies and applies procedures for inventory control with excellent success
Identify and apply procedures for ordering, shipping, and receiving products	Identifies and applies procedures for ordering, shipping, and receiving products with limited success	Identifies and applies procedures for ordering, shipping, and receiving products with some success	Identifies and applies procedures for ordering, shipping, and receiving products with considerable success	Identifies and applies procedures for ordering, shipping, and receiving products with excellent success
Identify common instrument equipment and materials	Demonstrates limited knowledge of common instrument equipment and materials used for client care in the health care industry	Demonstrates some knowledge of common instrument equipment and materials used for client care in the health care industry	Demonstrates considerable knowledge of common instrument equipment and materials used for client care in the health care industry	Demonstrates thorough knowledge of common instrument equipment and materials used for client care in the health care industry
Identify products that are environmentally friendly	Demonstrates limited knowledge of environmentally friendly products	Demonstrates some knowledge of environmentally friendly products	Demonstrates considerable knowledge of environmentally friendly products	Demonstrates thorough knowledge of environmentally friendly products
Identify resources needed to implement intervention plans	Identifies few resources needed to implement intervention plans	Identifies some resources needed to implement intervention plans	Identifies many resources needed to implement intervention plans	Identifies all or almost all resources needed to implement intervention plans
Safe use of tools and equipment	Uses procedures, equipment and applies industry safety standards safely and correctly only with supervision	Uses procedures, equipment and applies industry safety standards safely and correctly with some supervision	Uses procedures, equipment and applies industry safety standards safely and correctly	Demonstrates and promotes the safe use of procedures, equipment and applies industry safety standards
Use a variety of teamwork and interpersonal skills	Demonstrates limited knowledge of various teamwork and interpersonal skills	Demonstrates some knowledge of various teamwork and interpersonal skills	Demonstrates considerable knowledge of various teamwork and interpersonal skills	Demonstrates a high degree of knowledge of various teamwork and interpersonal skills

II. Questions to Ponder

• How can we create a hierarchical map that will help our employees look high and low for cost reductions?

• Will the organization chart help us in the sense that we can look for savings in discrete departments?

• How do we account for cost with a process enhancement?

- Why is accounting sometimes not the best department to use in the search for savings?
- Who should drive these initiatives?
- What is the "raindrop" method?
- Do small savings matter?
- Must we log small internal cost reductions with our customers?

III. Cost Improvement Scenario

A. Situation

A simple plastic-to-plastic metal screw held a production part together. The screw itself was expensive.

B. Objectives

We wanted to reduce the cost of a commodity part like a screw, but we did not want to reduce the quality of final assembly.

C. Actions

An operator noticed that we had an approved replacement part that we had used previously when the designated screw was unavailable. This other part was 1/27 of the cost of the designated screw.

We initiated an engineering configuration proposal to replace the designated screw with the backup screw.

D. Results

This change was surprisingly difficult to implement, given the magnitude of the savings and the nearly complete lack of risk.

E. Aftermath

After months of work by the cost reduction team, the part was finally approved for production. The cost of delay was the number of parts times the approximate $0.27 cost of the original screw. Four of these screws added up to a little over a dollar. If we had 16 screws per final assembly and we sold 20,000 assemblies over the intervening time, we would have lost *$80,000* in delay cost—a perfect example of opportunity cost!

IV. Finding Cost Reductions in the Plant

The "raindrop" method comes from an old saying that says, "many raindrops make an ocean." We are not always going to see huge cost reductions; however, a horde of small cost reductions can help reduce margins, instill a culture of savings, and make for much less risk. If we improve a process such as handoffs in the accounting department, we do not need to inform our customers, since this change does not directly affect their product or the processes that directly make the product. Cost reductions such as these are pleasant to approve for this reason.

A. Operations

Stockroom/Warehouse

Inventory control is somewhat of an art. Lean manufacturing gurus try to reduce inventory in the stockroom to an absolute minimum and handle the production needs through frequent delivery. The trick here is to assure ourselves that we are not paying more for delivery than we are for the reduction in stockroom material.

Release to the Floor

We primarily look to Lean approaches to find cost reduction opportunities when releasing material to the floor. We want to minimize on-the-floor inventory and waste. Additionally, we should be seeking to reduce movement of material. Let's look at the seven wastes:

- Transportation—we can reduce movement of material into the stockroom by locating the delivery ramp close to the location of the stock.

- Inventory—we want to control delivery inventory, since it can be harder to quantify material once it lands on the shelf.

- Motion—motion refers to operator motion with the actual material. We can reduce motion with clever design of material handling carts. Pallet handling should use motorized equipment if we have a large stockroom.

- Wait—at no point should the material handler be waiting to receive the material.

- Overprocessing—we should not be doing excessive package removal or other material processing activities. We want delivered material to be easily accounted for. Our procurement function should vet the supplier for accurate delivery.

- Overproduction—we should not ever produce more than we need.

- Defect—the materials handler can do a cursory check of the quality of the material before stowing it in the stockroom.

Assembly

Poka-Yoke
We save in the long term if we use true poka-yoke whenever possible on the floor. A true poka-yoke means we designed the component so it is difficult to assemble incorrectly. We see this approach on automobiles that have "keyed" connectors that fit one way. We save money with poka-yoke because we do not need product testing for every part and we certainly do not need automated optical inspection or human inspection because we already know the part has been assembled correctly.

Parallelism

We achieve parallelism when we can process more than one item at a time. One example is having a single operator control three or four devices instead of being dedicated to one machine. Another parallel approach occurs when we test multiple nodes simultaneously using, for example, an in-circuit tester.

Another approach to parallelism involves using latent features we may have in our products. For example, many of the larger microcontrollers have boundary scan capability; that is, they can scan the area of the circuit board around them to determine if the parts are there, if they measure correctly, and if they are the correct component.

Mechanical parallelism is often more difficult to achieve because of the rules of physics and the physical space occupied by the part. However, we have seen situations where the company hired a robot to do what is called "selective soldering" on printed circuit boards, which in actuality, is letting a machine do hand soldering. It would make more sense to try and achieve reflow soldering or wave soldering, which are both much quicker than the selective approach. If all three approaches are in use, we might consider redesigning the product to eliminate unnecessary processes.

Shipping

As with delivery, shipping should be located where part counting is easy and transfer to the shipping vehicle is also expedited by the location. If delivery comes in one side of the building, perhaps shipping should be at the other end of the building.

Production Testing

In the electronics industry, in-circuit testing allows for high-speed and relatively thorough testing of printed circuit boards, particularly those that have just received reflow soldering. In one facility, we eliminated open/shorts testers in favor of in-circuit testers to our benefit—the ICT can check much more than the simple continuity check performed by an opens/shorts tester.

Wire harness manufacturers may use continuity checking to verify their production parts; however, this test is really insufficient if it does not also verify that leads are in the proper locations on the connectors. In our experience, harness suppliers frequently do not perform sufficient checking.

So, where are the cost reductions in these two situations? We do production testing to eliminate type II failures ("consumer's risk"), which are likely to produce customer dissatisfaction. Additionally, one of us was part of the purchase of *used* in-circuit testers at about a quarter of their original cost. Continuity testers for harnesses are simple enough and the risk is even lower than using these devices to verify wire harnesses.

Lean

Conveyors

In general, conveyors are only necessary if we are moving heavy material; for example, engine blocks or heads. For lighter materials, we recommend that conveyors be removed and sold to less enlightened companies. We have seen surprising levels of resistance to the removal of conveyors, even with items that are predominantly made of plastic.

If our lines run synchronously, we would not expect to see more than one piece on a surface at a given moment. This approach may become difficult when we must use forced batching; for example, reflow soldering (surface mount) printed circuit boards are normally run in batches due to the amount of time it takes to change the machine setup. We know of no case with current machines where this situation is not the case, alas.

Even in the case where conveyors are necessary, we can attempt to simulate one-piece flow by correctly timing the movement of parts through the cell/line. Since we control the speed of the conveyors (if mechanized) or the operator controls the speed (if unmechanized), then we see no reason why the conveyor should not move at a speed that simulates one-piece flow.

Single-Operator Devices

Using a single-operator per machine is a waste of resources unless we are dealing with a critical safety issue. We designed our "C"-shaped cells so that a single operator can monitor and control multiple machines.

B. Engineering

Design

Hardware

Hardware testing during the design phase should be oriented toward finding flaws expeditiously. We have several options for doing this:

- We can run highly accelerated life testing (HALT) which significantly reduces test time by increasing the severity of the stress on the device under test (DUT)—the goal is to find the weak spots in the design

- We can run high-stress, multiple environments simultaneously for the same reasons as HALT, except that we are producing an even more severe environment

So long as we understand that we may see some specious failures, we can test in hours what would ordinarily take days or weeks. We then turn around our results to the design engineers as the anomalies begin to surface—even before the putative end of the test sequence. We are also allowed to perform minor repairs in order to continue *this* sequence.

We have abused products with this kind of testing, often against internal and external resistance—in spite of the fact that we were pushing for a stronger product. The design engineers must use a modicum of judgment in order to avoid over-engineering the product. Each failure must be assessed for reality.

Software

We can also stress-test software in several ways:

- Increase the rate of testing

- Change the external environment (yes, this change can affect embedded projects!) by varying temperature, voltage, current, and other factors
- Random button pushing
- High loads on the data bus

Product Testing

In all cases of testing, we see no reason to repeat tests if nothing in the parts has changed and we tested a representative sample to begin with. We have seen companies rerun tests because they believe they are somehow meeting the strictures of ISO/TS 16949 or the APQP process. A test that tells us nothing is not really a useful test.

Hardware Laboratory

In general, laboratories can acquire used equipment when these pieces come from a known facility or come with some kind of warranty or the laboratory has sufficient technical ability to be able to repair the device themselves.

One approach we have used is to observe when the laboratory of another facility is having financial troubles and buy their equipment when they are forced to sell their hardware. This approach may sound cold and uncaring, but it is a legitimate part of doing business and, at least, gives the seller the benefit of selling the equipment to another lab for continued use.

Good candidates for a new lease on usefulness are items such as amplifiers, Helmholtz coils, antennae, and other electronic hardware picked up at a fraction of the original cost.

Electronic Testing

Electronic testing must capture failures related to transient pulses, electromagnetic compatibility, electrostatic discharge, and variety of more exotic tests. It is possible to construct our own devices, although they will need to be calibrated according to the international standards. We suggest a cost/benefit analysis before undertaking development of new test equipment. In many cases, we can achieve the desired savings by purchasing used equipment or refurbishing our own equipment.

Mechanical Testing

Mechanical test equipment includes vibration tables, environmental chambers, salt chambers, pressure equipment, sprays, and other exotic devices and tools. Again, we should look for used equipment. One of us saved tens of thousands of dollars using preowned environmental chambers and refurbishing other company equipment. Our dust box was homemade and, while it was not standard, the tests conducted in that box were actually harsher than a more standard piece of equipment.

Environmental Testing

Environmental testing usually involves the use of thermal, humidity, salt, pressure and other chambers. For the automotive business, these chambers can be large enough to fill a room in a small house. When such equipment is acquired during clearance, often the most expensive part of the transaction is the shipping of the equipment to the new site. This added cost suggests it is to our best benefit to survey the region in which we work for laboratories that are struggling.

Calibration

Calibration of equipment is one area where we can save money by establishing meaningful calibration intervals. For example, antennae used for electromagnetic compatibility typically exhibit a high degree of stability; hence, the calibration interval can sometimes be upwards of three years, particularly if we have historical data indicating no drift in values.

Software

Any software testing should include at least the following components: Five-Way Approach

- Compliance
  - Test to specification
  - Interpretation issues handled with client
  - Regression testing can be derived from main test suite
- Combinatorial
  - Pairwise
  - Designed experiments and orthogonal arrays
  - Three-way
  - Issues with interactions
- Stochastic/Exploratory
  - Test engineer uses "gut"
  - Successful tests added as new tests to test suite
  - Must be documented
- Extreme Value
  - Temperature extremes
  - Voltage and current randomness
  - Slews
  - Noise
- Attack
  - Fuzzing the inputs
  - Genetic algorithms

We would like to see the fifth approach added to any software testing toolbox; namely, testing that more closely resembles the kinds of attack used by "hackers" trying to destroy or intrude on a system. These approaches may look like overflows, underflows, fuzzing, and other approaches documented online and in hacker books.

Regardless, we are looking at saving money by not allowing bad product to escape to the customer. A single product recall at $2 million can wipe out tens of painstakingly developed cost reduction projects.

Human Testing

Human-based testing has the most power when we are exploring the problem space presented by the product. An experienced tester can use his or her innate pattern recognition capability to push the product to extremes of usage. We must remain aware, however, that humans can typically concentrate on something—their attention span—for about 15–20 minutes before dis-attention commences. That duration means we need to give our testers frequent breaks to avoid this problem.

Automated Testing

Automated testing allows us to use cameras, frame grabbers, test equipment, actuators, and other devices to stimulate the device under test (DUT). Our experience suggested a "break point" at around 10,000 test cases on instrumentation would significantly reduce the escapes to the customer. Again, we are assuming the cost of an avoided recall or campaign more than pays for this testing. For most enterprises, we could examine their warranty and claims history to verify that we are accomplishing something with the intensity of our testing.

Reliability Testing

Reliability testing presents the same issues as basic hardware testing; furthermore, we may be asked to calculate some anticipated "life" expectancy for the product. These formulae will have a chemical/physical basis (Arrhenius equation) or an empirical basis (inverse power law) or a mixture of both (Eyring equation). As with design testing, we recommend HALT or multienvironmental testing as a means to reduce cost and accelerate the turnaround time.

C. Accounting/Finance

Facilities

Facility renegotiations are always a fecund opportunity for cost savings. In general, if we have been good customers, the lessor should have some motivation to keep us as a lessee.

Additionally, we can look at our utilities usage: gas, electric, and water to potential savings and conservation. We can recycle grease from our cafeteria grease traps. We can look at waterless urinals, low-flow flush toilets, quick-release water faucets and other sources of water loss. In some cases, we can reduce the cooling/heating by modifying our insulation practices.

We may be able to sublet space on the floor or on the property if our agreement with the lessor allows us to take this action. Another option is to consolidate the operations of more than one division under the same roof if we have the space.

D. Purchasing

Suppliers

Our suppliers can be an incredible source of cost reduction information, for who knows their product better than they do? We must provide some kind of incentive to motivate our suppliers to initiate and implement cost reductions. Since we have the right of approval of any changes to the supplied product, we can offer to share the value of any cost reduction achieved by the supplier, thus allowing a win-win scenario.

We can also help our suppliers with our own Six Sigma and Lean capabilities. We can train their staff and engineers and we can help to implement improvements in their processes and products. Obviously, we need to have a close relationship with these suppliers.

Sole Source

Sole source (single source) purchases can produce heartburn for procurement organization, particularly those in government entities, such as school districts. We need to ensure that this supplier is not leveraging us on price. If such is the case, we might consider designing out the part. In the automotive realm, this approach can be difficult because we are often using electrical connectors that are patented and made by only one source.

Low Bids

Low bids may represent a cost reduction—they may also represent a major fiasco. Our quality and reliability organizations need to be involved from the onset of a low bid purchase to ensure that we are not purchasing substandard material for our product.

E. Marketing

Travel

We belong to the school of thought that suggests more rather than less marketing travel is beneficial. We are not as convinced when it comes to sending out engineers on quick time. In some cases, considerations of customer satisfaction may require on-site intervention from an engineer. However, these should be approved only by a high placed manager to avoid "knee-jerk" responses to customer issues.

In down economies, we suspect it is wise to increase the amount of marketing/sales travel with metrics in place to validate that a real marketing effort is occurring and business is growing.

Meals

One of your authors has food sensitivities, making him the "cheapest date in town." We do not have to be eating lobster and steak every night with drinks from the on-site microbrewery—this behavior is not doing business, it is self-indulgence on someone else's dollars.

Lodging

We do not recommend stinting on quality lodging. Travel is tough enough without saving a few nickels on subpar lodging.

F. Project Management

Scheduling

We can generally save time and, hence, opportunity cost by running as many tasks in parallel as we possibly can. Of course, the project manager must keep an eye on dependencies, but parallel scheduling and even cascading scheduling will often accelerate the project. Even when dependencies are present, tight scheduling will still reduce the project time.

Cost savings calculations will usually be based on estimates determined from previous project histories. Clearly, failure to meet regulatory requirements on time, yielding fines, can be factored in.

Costing

Realize that the Empire State Building was erected in 1936—the middle of the Great Depression—ahead of schedule and under budget! Our costing models must account for realistic risks and avoid optimistic assessments, particularly those made by well-meaning software engineers. Furthermore, we need to factor in testing, production runs, and material shortages. Failure to calculate a realistic budget will lead to last minute costing that generally is more expensive than doing it correctly in the first place.

Quality

Never hold back on quality. The cost of returned material and customer dissatisfaction has no positive payoff—ever. Our rule of thumb is that a returned part runs roughly 10 times the selling price of the original part by the time it is dismounted (at a cost) from the customer product, shipped, analyzed, and tested.

G. Human Resources

Staffing

Staffing can be a political issue. If we have empire-building managers who derive their sense of importance from the size of their crew, we can have a major surfeit of employees. In general, we favor some level of excess capacity, especially if our enterprise is growing.

Figure 13.1 Vending is a good source of "raindrop" income.

Layers of Management versus Span of Control

Short-term memory holds about seven to nine items, which is approximately the size of a reasonable span of control for a manager or a supervisor. If we have a large company, this suggests we might have many layers of management. Let's look at the U.S. Army for a moment:

- A fire team = three to four troops
- A squad = two fire teams

- A platoon = four squads
- A battalion = four to five companies
- A brigade = four to five battalions

The military system mentioned is a little rough around the edges, but the point is that a manager (NCO or officer) can only responsibly control a relatively small number of individuals.

Figure 13.2 Our "raindrop" income can come from many sources.

Clerical Staff

Is the day of the secretary a position of the past? One of us was an executive and never had an executive assistant to help out—we did not need one and by the time we explained what we were trying to do, we could do it ourselves better. In general, we have seen executive assistants/secretaries often employed more to indicate the status of the executive than to actually do anything. Of course, we have seen executives who could not type and who were too good to take notes. We have also seen exceptions— we know of one case where the executive assistant held a degree in accounting!

The point here is that the clerical staff merits reviews. School districts are teeming with individuals at this level, sometimes performing work above their qualifications. Proceed with caution.

Figure 13.3 Vending choices are only limited by the imagination. We should always get a portion of the "take."

Cafeteria (Offshore)

In some offshore situations (e.g., Mexico), the government requires that companies provide line operators with breakfast and lunch using a cafeteria. We need to meet all environmental requirements. However, we may have opportunities for cost savings:

- Sales of grease
- Portion control
- Recycling of water
- Cater or not cater depending on cost
- Leverage from large food purchases (economic order quantities)

Offshore

For any noninternal staffing solutions, we must always consider the total cost of operation (TCO). That means we have to consider the cost in the long term, even when the short-term cost seems excessive and may temporarily affect the bottom line. These considerations apply with consultants and contractors also.

Offshore employment is no exception to this idea. In addition, we need to consider potential difficulties caused by time zones, languages, cultural differences, and technologies. Furthermore, we should also have a method for reliably ascertaining the capability of the offshore staff. In some cases, we will hire them because they clearly provide a capability we do not currently possess; however, in other cases, we may need to travel or conduct some kind of proficiency test.

Figure 13.4 Happy employees lower expensive turnover.

Consulting

As with contractors, consultants are "expendable." That sounds nasty, but what it means is that we can "fire" them for nonperformance much more readily than we can with our full-time employees. Consultants and contractors are by definition "casual employment."

Contracting

Contractors may be slightly more difficult to "fire" than are consultants because we generally have a contract for a predefined duration. Once the contract is completed, we can release the contractors. Some contracts will have performance clauses written into them, since contracting a poor performer to a customer is not good business for the contracting firm.

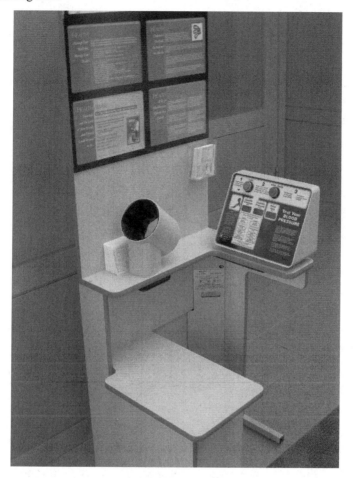

Figure 13.5 We can save money on benefits if our staff stays healthy.

Benefits

Benefits, especially insurance, are often a major source of cost. In Mexico, benefits may account for 50% of an employee's total cost to the company—although this seeming benefits black hole is often offset by the lower pay. U.S. employees generally cost 135% of their gross salary (according to multiple human resources managers with whom we spoke).

V. Finding Cost Reductions in the Office

A. Office Supplies

Total cost of operation is necessary information when we want to save on office supplies. These can range from the lowly stapler to massive group laser printers. Having multiple versions of printers causes a need for multiple sizes of printer cartridges,

Figure 13.6 We should be charging our banker for placing their business tool in our facility.

leading to complexity in ordering and stocking parts. The same thing applies to laptop and desktop computers as well as all other ancillary equipment. Standardization with an honest supplier should eliminate most of these difficulties.

B. Equipment

Computers

We favor laptop computers, especially stable systems like Apple Macintosh OS X, although Microsoft Windows has become significantly more stable since they bit the bullet, went to a 32-bit system, and introduced Windows 2000.

Sometimes, desktop systems are more capable and when that level of ability is required, then, by all means, we should go out and purchase it. The enterprise must define the *purpose* of these tools and procure accordingly.

Printers

In a word, we want *standardization*. Ink spraying printers have expensive replacement cartridges. Color lasers should only be used for finished work, not drafts. Plotters should not be used to print banners that employees proceed to ignore.

Trendy Electronics

iPad
While an Apple iPad (one of us has three!) is an interesting alternative to a laptop computer, it is barely useful for business-level typing. One might question whether the "end of typing" is on us, but in 2012 this hardly seems to be the case. An alternative would be voice recognition software, but a significant product for the Pad computers is only available from Nuance (http://www.nuance.com).

C. Copies/Printing

Paper can be expensive, but toner and maintenance are the heavy hitters with printers and copiers. We recommend that the enterprise have a key or password system to monitor usage.

D. Paper/Paperless

The paperless office is largely a joke, although Oticon Corporation has perhaps gotten closest to this chimerical issue. One of the problems is that we would generally benefit from a duplexing scanner, but these are expensive and somewhat hard to find.

Finding Cost Reductions in the Corporation
Beware of the illusion of control. Adjustments made at the local level may be more optimal than they first appear. The corporation will need an optimization model that can determine the global optimum.

VI. Finding Cost Reductions in Education

A. Operations

Stockroom/Warehouse

The cost-saving school district needs to find local suppliers who can hold some modicum of inventory in their distribution centers. That way, the district does not need to hold the inventory on-site. We have seen cases where districts have purchasedt high-tech hardware/software but do not have the time, the staff, or the skills to install the product, leading to waste.

Delivery

Delivery should be quick and we would hope that school districts design their facilities with high-speed in and out of delivery as well as take away.

Shipping

Shipping is not so much of an issue for school districts, although it becomes a bore when broken or nonfunctional material must be returned to the supplier. This situation is a case where a change in policy/procedure could accelerate the return.

B. Accounting/Finance

Facilities

The accounting function often has the opportunity to negotiate more favorable terms for the facilities (building, parking lot, etc.) that the enterprise uses. It is most common to lease the facilities. The downside to leasing occurs when the enterprise outgrows the existing facility or decides to combine their efforts in yet another facility.

Accounting can also look for other opportunities:

- Vending machines
- Day care services
- Banking rentals (the bank pays a fee to have their ATM collocated in the facility)
- Utilities
  - Gas
  - Air (pressurized)
  - Water
  - Electric
  - Sewage
- Rental of unused floor space if the lease allows for subletting

The accounting function can make agreements for a variety of vending services (see Figure 13.1 through Figure 13.6).

C. Purchasing

Suppliers

In lean manufacturing, we encourage organizations to develop long-term, trusting relationships with their suppliers. Such is not often the case in school districts, where procurement departments are encouraged to buy from a selection of three bidders (required minimum) and select the lowest bidder. In some cases, we will save money using this method. Unfortunately, we think the long-term prognosis is to ultimately receive little more than junk as we buy "cheap."

Clearly, we are suggesting the school organizations study their situation and not just pick the lowest bidder, who may not have the technical knowledge to produce a high-quality product at a fair price.

Sole Source

Many organizations have heartburn when dealing with sole source vendors. The term has overtones of monopoly and predatory capitalism. However, when we purchase *unique* equipment or products, we will have no choice. Really, we must take our metaphoric antacid and move on.

Low Bids

Low bids are not always the best deal, particularly when total cost of operation (TCO) is not very good. We might end up with poorly made products or deficiencies in features (often related to poor specifying procedures on our part). The Lean mavens often recommend establishing a long-term relationship with an honest supplier with actually lower TCO, even when the apparent cost is higher than that of other bidders.

D. Project Management

Scheduling

In the education business, we expect to see project management when dealing with grants and central office initiatives. We need to ensure we have the resource to accomplish our goals. If this is a building project derived from bond money, we should ensure that we have third-party oversight to make sure we know where the money is going.

Costing

Costing should be part of the proposal. In general, school districts try to avoid "in kind" monies, where the district provides some of the money to be used on the projects.

Quality

Quality may be an issue with hardware-oriented acquisitions and projects. We do not often see certified quality auditors, managers, and engineers in school districts. We are not trying to insult them, but this situation seems well-established.

E. Human Resources

Staffing

We have seen school districts where an army of clerks and former administrators, not one of whom possesses a human resources certification, runs the human resource function. We do not know if the lack of certification leads to process inadequacies or if these fiefdoms are largely the result of evolution and empire building by their hierarchies.

In one corporate case, we saw 4,000 being managed by a department of less than 15 people and this involved personnel law on both sides of the U.S./Mexican border!

Layers of Management versus Span of Control

One of us once tried managing 13 direct reports and found it to be extremely marginal in terms of the quality of the work. We found that we could fold departments into fewer departments and actually enhance communications and, thus, management.

Clerical Staff

In our experience, secretaries are often redundant in the age of word processing. Keep in mind that this primarily applies to the age group that can touch-type. Younger people who only know texting will need special software to convert their SMS to meaningful complete text.

We have seen high-level managers who cannot touch-type and we consider this to be a sign of technical ineptitude as well as forcing the need for a secretary or executive assistant that otherwise would be unnecessary. Please forget using these individuals as status symbols.

Cafeteria (Offshore)

Cafeteria service for operators is generally a requirement in Mexico as well as other south-of-the-border nations. The primary question here revolves around whether it is less costly to have in-house food services or, basically, to have the food catered to employees. In our experience, a large amount of the food goes to waste; hence, one method for saving cost in the cafeteria is to serve smaller portions.

Programs

School districts seem to have a rampant case of program-itis as they flail around trying to find canned solutions to existing problems. Instead of evolving solutions from within, they would rather burn money on the supposed quick fix. These kinds of quick fixes are much like the "Kaizen Blitz" events often used by naïve Lean manufacturing practitioners. Good cost reductions are sustainable.

Consulting

We have also seen districts hire consultants rather than use existing local talent.

Contracting

School enterprises will use contractors when they have a temporary need. This hiring practice only becomes problematic when the temporary individuals have become a permanent fixture. Contracts will often be negotiated on the same least-of-three approach used for hardware purchases, leading to the same problems.

Benefits

We think this area of savings is precarious, since the benefit is often protected by unions—organizations that are under attack in states such as Wisconsin. If the union is doing their job, then the agreements should be fair, without bringing the districts to their knees.

F. Sports and Extracurricular Activities

It would be nice if extra-curricular activities (sports, theater, etc.) were self-supporting through tickets, grants, and other support not from within the school district. Major universities work this way and we see no reason for not attempting to self-finance at the high school level.

VII. Finding Cost Reductions on the Personal Side

A. Used versus New Material

Does the new car make sense? Does the new house make sense? The same kind of thinking as with the enterprise applies at home, in the office, in the plant.

B. Quantity versus Quality

We are conditioned by the advertising industry to buy more of whatever we think we "need." Often, we will sacrifice quality simply to have a greater quantity of "stuff."

C. Food

We do not need restaurant food, fast food, or precooked junk for the dinner table. Is it that difficult to eat well? It is difficult to eat a healthy meal at many restaurants.

D. Clothing

Select a uniform. Who needs 40 outfits? Meet the requirements for presentability and leave it at that. Forget the dress-for-success movement.

E. Furniture

Again, we tend to purchase what we have been conditioned to purchase, rather than what we need. For example, do we really need a leather couch or will a Shaker-style bench do the job? Do we need the La-Z-Boy or are we just being lazy?

F. Housing

One author has lived in his house (as of this writing) for 18 years and the other author has been in his house for 12 years. Buy what you need and do not for a minute consider a house to be an investment. The most recent deep recession should be a caution against too much faith in a housing market that was a great investment only for professional investors (and sometimes, not even then!).

G. Vehicles

Buy a gas-sipping vehicle if you need one at all and drive it until pieces are falling off. Use mass transit when it makes sense.

VIII. EXERCISES

- Build a hierarchical chart of you enterprise, building as large as you think is feasible. How many discrete organizations do you have?

- For each discrete organization in the chart, add more detail. You may use a mind-mapping tool to do this exercise. We are going on a hunt for cost reductions!

- Using your chart, from the previous two activities, add

  - Man

  - Materials

  - Methods

  - Machines

  - Measurements

  - Policies

  - Procedures *to each node*

- For each item we attached to each node, we now want to find at least five potential cost reduction candidates. Do not overlook the more intangible items such as procedures and policies. Stupidity, habit, and ignorance in these areas can often provide us with huge reductions. We are looking for alternatives to "We always did it this way."

- For each of the five or more items you have listed that seem feasible, assess their current cost.

- For each of the five or more items you listed, speculate on the probability of being able to lower the current cost. In a small division with 12 departments, we should be able to take our (7 x 5) 35 ideas, now a total of 420 ideas and arrange them in a spreadsheet array.

- Sort the 420 ideas by probable savings (new cost—old cost—cost to implement).

- Sort the 420 ideas by time it takes to implement. We may want to execute some of the ideas immediately because it takes so little time to do them.

- If you work in a manufacturing facility, you can add product lines to your departments. Each product line can benefit from operational improvement (doing things more quickly) and process improvement (eliminating entire steps from the overall process). For each product line:

  - List every conveyor as a candidate for removal (unless we are dealing with truly heavy material).

  - List every production testing operation and review for redundancy and misplacement.

  - Look for any instances where we are using screws instead of snaps and assess for potential change.

  - Investigate soldering operations if you have them. For example, what kind of misbegotten design would need reflow soldering, wave soldering, selective soldering, and touch-up hand soldering?

  - Look for hidden factories: rework centers, rework tables, extra inspection sites, "special" testing, and forced packaging. Do any of these areas really add value to the operation?

  - Look for disorganization and filth. We may not see immediate savings from changing this situation, but things will improve in the long run because we will be able to see what is happening.

  - Investigate multifactor processes for potential optimization. We can use a designed experiment approach called "evolutionary operation" to optimize our subprocess while never stopping the line.

- We expect, say, 10 manufacturing lines to yield at 20 improvements per line for a total of 200 improvements.

- Investigate all supplier relationships! While MRP-oriented companies prefer fewer suppliers with long-term relationships to more suppliers with short-term relationships, this may simply be a by-product of the "illusion of control."

- We can generally find design flaw in our products.

  - Examine the product return history for potential reliability and/or quality issues.

- Interview people on the manufacturing line for areas where we have poor fit, misalignment on the production testers, and difficult to assemble products.

- Using the bill of materials, look for high-cost components and groups of components that collectively have high cost—these may be candidates for redesign and removal.

- Determine if the design is forcing the use of multiple types of solder operations.

- Look for opportunities for radical changes; for example, instead of using an arced lens on an instrument cluster, why not use a flat lens (much less expensive!)?

- Geometry modifications can yield improvements in form and fit.

- Try the paper (computer) experiment of reducing the number of components by favoring massive levels of integration. We may be able to move an entire chip set on a printed circuit board into one chip! Look at what happened to modems in the 1980s (remember modems?). The fewer the components, the more likely the reliability is to improve and the fewer the parts we have to manage.

- Examine the product for accessibility issues. Difficult to reach locations will slow down the activity on the manufacturing line.

- When looking at materials not only look at cost of material, look at cost to ship.

- Build a green savings spreadsheet.
    - List opportunities for recycling.
        - Look at water reusage.
        - Make a serious effort to reduce paper usage.
        - Sell the grease from the cafeteria. What else can we sell?
        - Sell materials like solder dross, wooden skids, surplus cardboard, unusable dunnage, and nonreusable metal components.
    - Examine the potential for cogeneration of power (most utilities must buy excess electricity by law).
    - Investigate the possibility of long-term savings by using solar and wind power as well as solar heating for hot water.
    - Explore the use of automatic shutoff of lights in little used rooms, auto-toilet flushing, auto-shutoff of faucets, and similar areas where we do not need to have the function on all the time.

- Investigate and report on potential for savings in shipping.

CHAPTER 14 – When Cost Improvement Goes Wrong

I. Rubric

We considered putting a moderately humorous, somewhat sarcastic rubric in this chapter. Unfortunately, we believe it would probably be misunderstood. Perhaps we will save that idea for a magazine article.

II. Questions to Ponder

- How can we tell when a cost improvement opportunity is a problem laying in wait?

- Should all cost improvement projects have the same level of diligence as typical product development projects—do we omit steps?

- Ponder a time when you were involved in a cost rationalization or improvement exercise. What do you think went awry?

- Consider what warning signs may be available to tell us that a given cost reduction is more liable to be a cost catastrophe.

- How would we account for risk when we make a cost reduction?

III. Cost Improvement Scenario 1

A. Situation

Recently, a project was concluded that delivered an electronic control unit (ECU) into the vehicle. At the start of this introduction we notice some failures of the product at the manufacturing facility. This was not deemed to be a catastrophic situation. By the time the levels of failures become really noticed, there are significant parts in the field. We eventually see the failures show up at our product return facility. There are so many failed parts being returned that it is nearly impossible to move around the facility. We are seeing failures of parts that have replaced the first parts in the system. The nature of the failure is the graphics display in the product.

B. Objective

Determine the reason for the failures and provide a corrective action.

C. Action

Explore the reasons for the failure and develop a corrective action. Given the severity of the problem, costing the company millions of dollars in warranty dollars, and find a quick solution. We are given considerable freedom in determining the appropriate corrective action.

Two immediate solutions were proposed. Those solutions are:

1. Find real root cause and correct

2. Find a way to substitute a later generation product

There are two teams, both led by one lead engineer. One team has the objective of determining how the substitution solution would work. This goal requires understanding the differences between the two iterations of the product from two different suppliers. The performance envelope for the two products is identical, as is the envelope for the connectors. However, the connector pin-out is significantly different. To make this solution work requires adding an interface harness and altering the software configuration for the component.

The other team has the goal of finding the root cause and real corrective action. The failing part is a subassembly to the larger component. In fact, as luck would have it, this subassembly is easily replaceable. The problem still remains: swapping the component out does not solve the problem. This action only extends some time for the next failure that will inevitably come, meaning customers are experiencing multiple failures for the same part of the product and are continuously required to swap the entire component or swap this subassembly. Neither one is a good solution.

Upon further exploration, the failure is in electrical connections between the subassembly and the upper level assembly printed circuit board. The LCD subassembly is mounted to the printed circuit board through interference fit tabs that compress when the LCD subassembly is pushed through the hole and then expand on the other side. These holes do not provide the electrical connections and control signals. The LCD connection to the main assembly is via "zebra strip" on the bottom of the assembly. The printed circuit board has flat pads that provide the electrical connections from the board to the subassembly. Under the subassembly are a number of via or through holes for the printed circuit board traces. On the other side of the printed circuit board is an area that has conformal coating (water resistant protective used on electrical and electronic parts) to protect the more sensitive components.

Our exploration indicates that under upper heat load of the product (but not atypical), the conformal coating loses viscosity and then migrates down the printed circuit board. The vias (printed circuit board through-holes) are large enough to allow the conformal coating to wick through and migrate between the printed circuit board and the "zebra strip" connection. The conformal coating between the electrical connections meant some level of inoperability. This issue gives the LCD the characteristic failure of lines through the display where parts of the LCD work while much does not.

D. Results

We now have two solutions. The immediate solution was to build interface harnesses for customers that had experienced the problem so many times they were irritated with the company. This solution was expensive because we required the interface harness and a new top-level assembly from the new supplier.

The other solution required a printed circuit board rework. Fortunately, the printed circuit board was a subassembly itself and relatively easy and quick to alter. The largest portion of the customers ended up with the solution that swapped out the LCD subassembly. Both solutions resolved the problem.

E. Aftermath

The corrective action solved the problem that was costing the company millions of dollars. While the customer wanted to blame the supplier, the design solution that caused the problem, specifically the "zebra strip." It is clear there was sufficient testing of the product and this specific attribute of the design solution.

IV. Cost Improvement Scenario 2

A. Situation

A procurement executive pushed a change in instrumentation backlighting (lamps) because it was significant cost reduction. The enterprise installed the new lamps with minimal testing (after all, the data book said they were drop-ins) and followed the proper documentation procedures.

Within a few weeks, the customer began to report failing lamps. It turns out, the new lamps did not seat as well as the old lamps and they were prone to vibrating out their socket.

B. Objective

Provide immediate containment followed by irreversible corrective action.

C. Action

The engineers stopped shipment of more instrumentation. Management decided to revert to the previous supplier and previously used lamps. Again, minimal testing occurred.

D. Results

In spite of the poor testing practice, the supplier was able to recover quickly. They pledged to replace all failing product also and any pretense of a cost reduction faded away!

E. Aftermath

The recommendation was that socketed items such as lamps always received vibration testing while lit (hot) for a substantial length of time using random spectrum frequencies.

V. Cost Improvement Scenario 3

A. Situation

An electrical engineer noticed that an operational amplifier ("op amp") on a small product could be replaced at less cost than the current component. The data book indicated that the op amps were equivalent. Little to no testing occurred as the design group bypassed the standard process in their enthusiasm to gain a significant cost reduction. The new op amp produced over 80% failures in the field within a week or two.

B. Objective

Provide immediate containment followed by irreversible corrective action.

C. Action

The supplier reverted to the previous op amp, again with minimal testing. All failing parts were shipped back to the supplier, who, in the meanwhile, had suspended shipment of parts until they could be reworked.

D. Results

We call this "death by data book." Once again, what appeared to be a cost reduction turned out to be an expense in terms of both money and reputation.

E. Aftermath

While we recommended proper testing of even apparent routine changes, the enterprise has continued to believe in the data books. After all, the supplier of the op amp fully tested their component against the other supplier's component, did they not? Why do companies so often assume the supplier has pursued appropriate vigilance with regard to their quality? We know of at least one case where a company used an LCD display from a supplier and all of the pin-in and pin-out information was incorrect, forcing the company to experiment in order to discover what the supplier should have written in their documentation! We should not be making assumptions about suppliers, customers, or ourselves.

VI. Material

A. Substitution Is a Poor Fit

As part of a cost improvement exercise, the overhead lamps on a vehicle were cost reduced. Another supplier offered a lower cost replacement part for the existing piece. The part was designed to be a drop in replacement; however, when the part was in the field when the operator went to turn the light on by pushing the face of the lamp, the entire lamp assembly went into the headliner. The spring load tabs on the part that held it in place into the headliner did not have the same spring force and were slightly narrower. This meant that the amount of force retaining the part, wedging as it were, was insufficient. The part was subsequently replaced with the original part.

B. Bulb Removal Tool

The instrument cluster for a class 8 vehicle manufacturer (class 8 is an 18-wheel semitruck tractor) had incandescent lamps providing backlighting. There were a number of these bulbs, and each bulb was removable from the back of the instrument cluster. This made replacement of burnt lamps quite easy, and that was a good thing, since the incandescent bulb life was less than the life of the vehicle.

The bulbs selected were mostly round at the base with two flat tabs. The bulb went into the back of the instrument housing and was then twisted, locking the bulb to the back of the housing and into the printed circuit board. Since the flat areas of the bulbs were exposed metal that conducted the current to the bulb, a bulb removal tool was placed on every key chain for every vehicle that went out. If a bulb burns out, the vehicle operator would gain access to the back of the cluster by using this plastic tool to remove the bulbs, insert a new bulb with the plastic tool, and then reinstall the instrument cluster. As a cost reduction idea, it was decided to delete the bulb removal tool.

The manufacturer started getting complaints from the field about dark spots on the instrument cluster. When the clusters were sent back to the supplier for a "postmortem," it was found that traces on the printed circuit board had burned up and become open circuits. Upon further investigation, it was learned that in absence of the plastic tool, the bulbs were being removed with needle nose pliers. Metal needle nose pliers that conduct more current than the printed circuit board could take—burning up the traces and making a section of the instrument cluster dark.

The subsequent corrective action was to thicken the printed circuit board traces and put the plastic bulb removal tool back on the key chain. Additionally, the bulbs were changed for bulbs that had the entire base enclosed in plastic, and these bulbs had a longer life as well.

C. Vehicle Diagnostics Connector

The diagnostic connector on an automobile is typically located under the dash on the driver side (see Figure 14.1). Using the data link connections on the vehicle uses this connector to gather diagnostics information from the vehicle after failures in the system. This connection to the vehicle on one end is attached through a cable to a personal computer or other diagnostics tool on the other end. The connecting end at the vehicle is a twist to connect—securing the interface between the diagnostics tool or personal computer and the vehicle. This connection point is used by the mechanics after production as well as through the manufacturing process of the vehicle.

One manufacturer found another solution—a less expensive connector (see Figure 14.2). The connector was, at least in part, less expensive because the mounting hardware had only two mechanical connection points instead of the previous four mechanical connection points.

This new connector configuration was introduced into production. A few months after the launch of this change, we found that when the cable from the personal computer to this changed vehicle connector was twisted onto the vehicle end, the connector fell back behind the dash. It was necessary for the mechanic to then reach behind this plastic dash part and push the connector back through the dash and then twist on the cable simultaneously. This condition was not catastrophic, but it did not make it easy to troubleshoot the vehicle with the diagnostics tool, either. Eventually, the new connector was cancelled and the company returned to the previous connector.

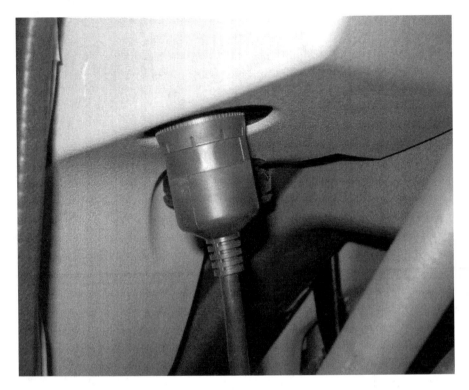

Figure 14.1 Diagnostic connector correctly plugged into the diagnostics tool.

D. Supplier Selection

It is not always material selection that goes awry. Sometimes we can find some overzealous purchasing people that want to make their cost reduction quota by improving on supplier pricing. Often the same purchasing people have to deliver cost improvements as a part of their major performance and employee evaluation. The procurement function has considerable clout in some organizations. This is especially true when these same purchasing people have found a supplier that will take on our project for much less than any of the other suppliers. That situation is not in itself a terrible act; however, it can become counterproductive when the procurement/ purchasing department favors the less-expensive supplier to the detriment of product quality and reliability as well as the long-term relationship with a now highly displeased customer.

We want our procurement function to work industriously on cost reductions, but not at the expense of quality. Hence, we need to have a balanced evaluation system for the staff that considers both cost reductions and cost increases.

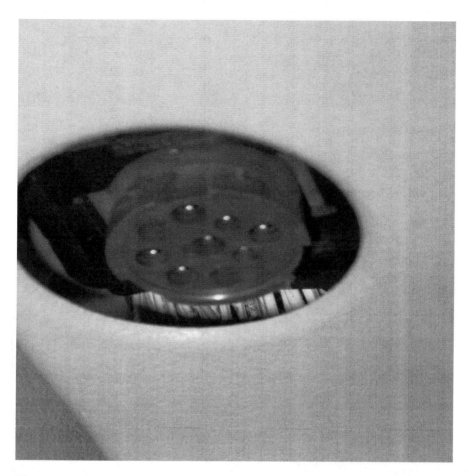

Figure 14.2 Diagnostic connector recessed too far back and attached only from one side. Attempting to connect the mating connector to this required a hand behind the dash to push the connector down.

E. Scope or Design Review

A small strand process control company receives a request from one of its customers and converts this request to a specification for the design staff. The product controls the fiber material (for example, wire, sutures, and fiberglass) from the source reel to the take up reel. This control includes tension as well as speed changes. A speed change in the source reel means a problem between source reel and the take up reel, specifically, a broken thread or fiber, or the problem could be an entanglement or a break in between the source and take up reels. The strand material can be costly and if a missing strand from the batch makes it into the end material means such material is now classified as a "second" or inferior in quality. Detection of a missing end requires a prompt termination of the process to ensure the missing material does not make it into the end product.

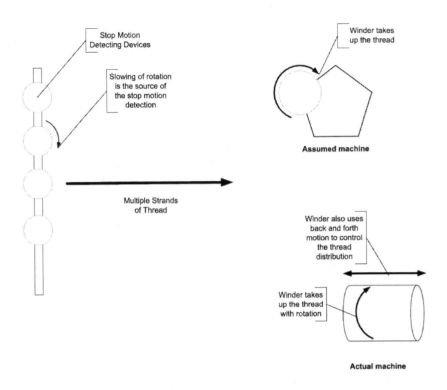

Figure 14.3 Specification and requirements have an effect on the end product quality. The design would work with one type of equipment, but we responded quickly to the change in speed of the other type of equipment.

The development group receives the specifications and develops the product to measure the speed and control the tension. The product is tested on in-house equipment and eventually delivered to the manufacturing personnel. The system is built and moved to the loading dock. It is at this time, with the material on the dock, that a key piece of information is discovered about the machine with which this system is to interface. The design documentation neglected to specify the type of machine that was to be the take up reel (see Figure 14.3). The assumption from the design group was that the machine was a continuous pull system. This meant the speed of the pull from the source reel to the take up reel was fairly continuous with the exception of the ramp up to the steady state. The design accounted for this ramp up and increases in speed that would be due to start of system operation.

As luck would have it, this assumption was invalid. As the product is on the shipping dock ready to go, an impromptu discussion with the salesperson leads to this clarification. The product was to integrate with a winder. A winder pulls the source fiber onto a spool in a back-and-forth motion. This back-and-forth motion guarantees the material is placed on the take up reel in a specific way, while being metered across the entire take up reel. To do this, the winder has to move from side to side across to take up reel area. This side-to-side motion comes with speed variations as the winder pulls from a top speed across the take up reel, but slows down as it changes direction and ramps back up to return the other direction. The design personnel immediately recognized the problem. The speed threshold was set using analog circuitry. To assure fast response time and a quick stop of the machine, the speed change to induce the stop motion and shut the system down was set to a fraction of the steady state operating speed. That would be acceptable for some equipment but not for a winder given this back-and-forth motion and changes to speed. The design staff made this known to the salesperson and the company decided to ship the product anyway. The design group responsible then ran tests on the product used for this other equipment and found the problem exactly as they had predicted. The system interpreted the speed changes due to the back-and-forth motion as a strand break and thereby stopped the entire machine. The customer now had material en route that certainly would not work as they expected —since the design group calculated and reworked some parts that remained at the facility. With the knowledge of the speed variation possible from this piece of equipment, the design staff went to the customer facility and altered all of the parts in the shipment to be able to work within this newly defined system context.

This correction required two people from the design staff to go to the customer facility and make the necessary modifications on every part of the system. Since considerable amount of material was involved, airline travel was not very practical. In the end, the design engineers were on the customer's site for a week of more than 12 hours per day of work to alter the entire system to function properly. For want of a scope review or design review, which in theory could have found this problem, we have incurred opportunity costs and disrupted our customer's plans.

Figure 14.4 Cluster printed circuit board and light guide attached.

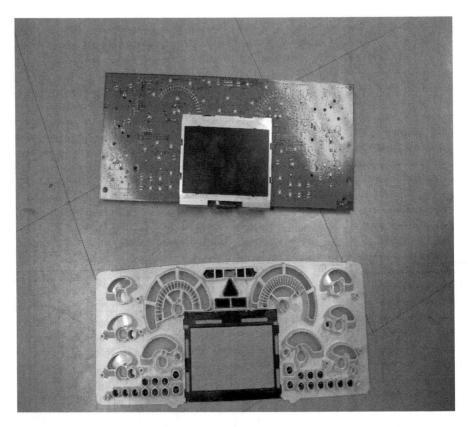

Figure 14.5 The known interference between the printed circuit board component and the light guide caused failures in the field.

F. Material Reuse

A supplier has two locations, one in Europe, and another in North America. Each of these two suppliers has a customer in each area. The European supplier is developing the product for both customers with the production occurring in each customer's region. The product is an instrument cluster that fits both the European and North American vehicles of the customer organization.

The European customer has a launch ahead of the North American launch. During the later part of the European launch, the supplier finds there is a product launch in Europe. The instrument cluster has a light guide that rides atop the printed circuit board (see Figure 14.4 and Figure 14.5). The light guide directs the surface mounted LED illumination to the overlay, making it possible to see things like the speedometer and other gauges at night in the dark. The light guide has direct contact with the printed circuit board, and has specially tooled recessed areas to accommodate the components whose wire leads extend through the printed circuit board, specifically the speedometer stepper motor. However, this recessed area did not exist in the early runs of the European product and the parts removed from production as the corrected parts created. This is not the end of the story. The North American portion of the company receives parts from the European company to build the North American customer's product. These errant parts are shipped to this supplier and the product is made from this failed part. The nonconformance is not found until the North American customer witnesses premature speedometer failures on the vehicles.

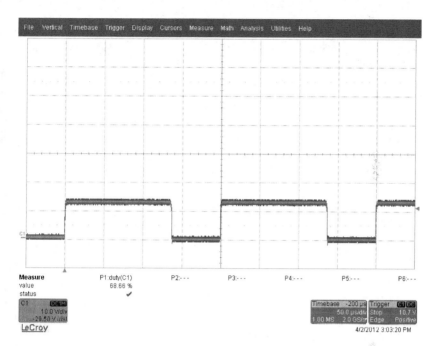

Figure 14.6 Previously designed transistor flasher for the turn signals.

G. Drop-In Replacement

The complexity of present day vehicles compared to the previous generation has grown. Electromechanical relays are not always used to turn on the lights, electric motors or turn signals as was typically done in the past. Solid-state switches such field effect transistors (FET) now perform some of these functions. These components have no moving parts to fail. In this instance, a particular vehicle manufacturer is already using a solid-state component that performs the function of activating and deactivating the turn signals causing them to turn lamps on when the turn signal switch has been engaged (see Figure 14.6). Early investigation finds that another supplier makes the same sort of solid-state switch at a lower price. The footprint of the newer product is the same as that of the older product. The cost difference between these two units is not a great amount of money. To make the business case valid means the engineers perform minimal exploration of that product's actual capability. With little time invested in the

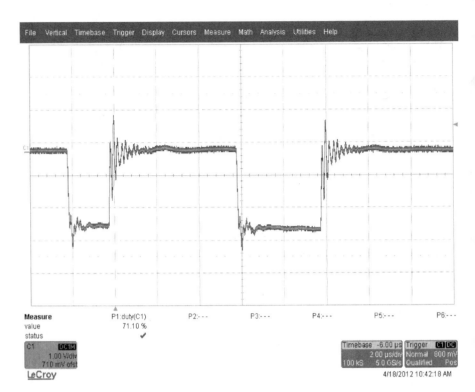

Figure 14.7 A drop-in replacement cost improvement for the turn signal flasher is not always a drop-in replacement. We see the performance of this switch affects the other components on the vehicle with conducted transients.

change, it is easier to justify the change since we spent practically nothing to make the change. The company updates internal drawings and makes sure the supplier is on the approved supplier list. The new flasher unit has a design change notification issued so the change becomes part of manufacturing the vehicle.

Six months pass and the vehicle manufacturer begins to witness issues with the antilocking brake system. The fault seems to be associated with activation of the turn signals of the vehicle during the startup of the electrical system. Upon further inspection we find that a transient from the solid-state turn signal device is coupled onto an input to the ABS unit. This transient affects the ABS diagnostics and causes the unit to make erroneous determination of the ABS level of functionality and a specific ABS fault is generated (see Figure 14.7).

The previous switch did not have this same malady. While the assumption was the parts were identical, in reality we see the performance is in fact not identical. The vehicle manufacturer abbreviated their process to make the business case for the change under the assumption that the change was a drop-in replacement; in other words, the vehicle manufacturer spent little to make the change to further make the business case more favorable. After the product was launched, the customers witnessed faults reported by the ABS unit, a key product for vehicle control.

Now the vehicle manufacturer has to address this issue in the present manufactured parts and may have to perform some retrofit of the vehicles that exhibit the symptom in the field. The business case did not account for the work to find the cause and address the field problems as a consequence of this simple drop-in replacement. A change in the product based upon the assumption of drop-in replacement is probably going to be a poor business case. We can provide an abundance of examples of the lack of success using this assumption-oriented approach. Usually, the cost to make things right after the fact is greater than any cost savings.

H. Reuse of Material

Under U.S. law, reused material must be marked. However, such is not always the case, since we know of plastic that contains a percentage of reground material without any kind of stamp on the product. "Regrind" is cheaper than "virgin" plastic.

In order to satisfy ourselves about using reground plastic, we must perform a substantial amount of mechanical and environmental testing, to include:

- Vibration testing with a random profile

- Vibration testing at an empirically determined point of resonance

- Salt chamber (salt fog)

- High temperature, high humidity

- High temperature, dry

- Exposure to ultraviolet light per standard

- Gravel bombardment if the part will see foreign particle impact

- High altitude if the product flies or we use it in high mountain scenarios

- Vibration testing, high temperature, and dry simultaneously

- Vibration testing, high temperature, and high humidity simultaneously

- Salt fog followed by vibration

- Immersion if unit is sealed

By now, it should be clear that proper validation of the product must be included in the cost reduction benefit calculations. The tests we list in this example could take weeks or months to execute, which also results in some level of opportunity cost, since we will not have the product with the cost reduction until testing completes.

We can anticipate the same kind of testing with metal parts as we do with plastic. The salt fog is still valid even with aluminum—we have seen aluminum parts exposed to magnesium chloride (a common road salt in the northern states and Canada) effloresce so badly they resembled a blossoming, metallic flower!

Metal parts must be stamped "used" if the part is reused with no melting and remolding. Even if the part is melted for reuse, we must ascertain the composition of the resulting material to verify that we have not allowed impurities into the alloy we desire. Although we can receive such results relatively quickly using x-ray diffraction and similar techniques, we will still see some cost associated with the extra labor and consumption of machine time.

We know that substantial motivation exists to recycle material in the age of green enterprises. We are not saying, "do not do it," we are saying, "move forward with substantial prudence and vigilance."

Consider this story. While this is not specifically a cost reduction problem, we believe this story illustrates how companies cause some of their own costing and therefore profit margin troubles. Consider a vehicle manufacturer (company A) that develops products globally. Company A is working on a project to alter the existing product to meet a new legal requirement to reduce the emission of pollutants. One of the suppliers (company B) to this company is part of the larger company. Company B is an internal supplier to the larger organization making the internal company to the larger organization. Company B provides large subsystem content for company A to integrate into the vehicle. Then company A tests company B's subsystem as it impacts the rest of the vehicle.

This company has work instructions for most everything they do. This work instruction defines that testing people evaluate the corrections for any of the fault reports they issue. The test people know exactly how the test case was performed. Additionally, the test staff has access to the exact test object that the failure was found. Both of these constraints present a rational and low approach to the closure of fault reports. Closing fault reports without objective evidence of the corrective action, or using different test cases or test specimens presents the risk of premature fault report closing.

Company B provides an iteration of the subsystem, and company A tests this iteration. The testing reveals considerable failures many of which are deemed catastrophic should these make it to the customer. These parts are prototype and therefore will not go to customers. A subsequent subsystem release and testing reveals even more fault reports. Both company A and company B have key performance indicators that track the number of fault reports in a project as well the amount of time required to close these fault of reports. After 1.5 rounds of testing, the number of faults reported is quite high and the corrective actions implemented are not sufficient to reduce the total open number of fault reports.

Company B proposes to reduce the fault reports, that work instruction be ignored and allow anybody from company B to close an open fault report—even on software that will never see the light of day. Company A resists knowing that closing fault reports on hope and some future planned activity is not a productive way in which to work. Company A cites the limitations of testing prototype software (unreleased) without the original test cases, and with inadequate test specimens. Company A also provides examples in this particular project where fault reports are closed and the failure persists. As additional proof, company A also points to the fact that many of the problems found would have been found by company B if they, in fact, had actually tested the subsystem before providing it to company A. Further investigation of company B's test capability found many flaws in their test scope, test process and execution of the testing. This only further strengthened the resolve of company A regarding the fault closing process.

Company B does not like being thwarted, and escalates the issue to the executive management. The key performance indicators are one of the items upon which the executive management measured. A senior vice president (let us call this person CL) is flown from Europe to the local site to talk with company A. A team from company A discusses the rationale behind the present process as well as the limitations of the proposed version. This team provides the same evidence of faults that persist after company B indicates corrective action has been exercised. The senior vice president does not care, and after throwing his pen on the table a number of times, company A is forced to accept the new process that is in violation of their work instructions.

Over time we see the fault reports that were previously closed, open once again, and a new corrective action developed—and opened again. The solving entity responsible need not investigate at a detailed level the correction to understand the real root cause. The solving entity only needs to present a plausible source of the problem and then produce actions to solve. We end up seeing the same faults over and over before we get to the real corrective action.

The "team" atmosphere evaporated between the two organizations as the customer, company A, were coerced into accepting a process they showed was inferior. The evidence was clear; the testing capabilities at company B were remedial at best. The team at company A believed there could only be one reason for adopting this deficient process, and that was political and to make things appear better than it was in fact. In the end there was little reduction of the failures reported. The faults continue to accumulate as faults closed once again rear their head.

VII. EXERCISES

- See if you can come up with at least three cost reduction fiascoes and describe them to your peers. You may hide the names to protect the guilty and/or innocent.

- At the beginning of this chapter, we ask you to consider what omens might suggest to us we are looking at a potential catastrophe. Make a list of signals that would enlighten us about the risk present and a cost reduction. Be prepared to defend your position.

- How would we categorize risk when doing cost reductions? Do we not also assume risk when we do not execute the cost reduction?

- Consider this idea: use a Pareto chart to identify areas of risk.

- Which parts of our enterprise have had the most or the largest failures?

- Which individuals produce the greatest catastrophes? (Uses one with great caution). What kind or type of cost reductions produce a greatest number of problems?

- Which customers lend themselves to fiascoes?

- If we are supplier, and we supply subsystems, which customer products seem inclined to be part of a catastrophe?

- Produce a risk management plan that, at a minimum, contains most or all of the risk when exercising cost reductions.

- How can we use our configuration management plan as part of our risk management practice?
- Validation of the cost reduction in the sense of product or process testing is often a hot button for management. How do we stop management from shortchanging the test process?
- Discuss the potential benefit of using a failure mode and effects analysis to reduce risk. What metrics can we use to prove that our risk is in fact reduced?
- Is there ever a reasonable justification for eliminating or reducing the test process?
- How many fiascoes have we seen that were supposed to be routine compound changes?
- Who in the enterprise should be responsible for monitoring the reality of the cost reduction?
- What can we do when we have a new fiasco?
- Do we need to test our product or service when we restore it to the previous condition after the aforementioned fiasco?
- Are we covered if the customer agrees to the cost reduction and chairs and the benefits? In this case, who owns the liability?
- How do we protect ourselves from influential executives who derive part of their bonus from how much they saved and cost reduction? For example, it is not unusual for procurement/purchasing departments to have written goals that include some annual dollar amount of cost reductions.
- Are purchase price variances ever a real cost reduction? How do we keep it from becoming unscrupulous?
- What is the best way to calculate standard cost? How do we eliminate game playing with purchase price variance (ppv)?

INDEX

Symbols

5S 199

A

Accounting/finance 33, 292
Agenda 173
Ant Path Optimization 250
Arbitrary cost down 58
Automated testing 292

B

Benchmarking 121
  performance 121
  process
    adapt 125
    analyze 125
    code of conduct 126
    plan 122
    recycle 126
Black belt 163
Brainstorming 41
Breakeven analysis 37
Budget
  account closed 181
  awaiting money 181
  below 181
  closed forever 181
  delayed 181
  no money 181
  on 181
  over 181
  unknown 181

C

Calibration 291
Capital expense
  reduce 80
Capital expenses 180
Computers 301
Continuous flow 200
Cost 106

Cost down process 59
Cost generators 68
  cost cutting 69
Cost of quality 165
  appraisal 165
  external failure 165
  internal failure 165
  prevention 165
Cost recovery 253
  benefits 258
  definition 257
  not use 257
  steps 258
  two-way 259
Cost reduction 6, 5
  case 8
Cost teardown 82
Critical to assembly 164
Critical to cost 164
Critical to customer 164
Critical to delivery 164
Critical to materials 164
Critical to process 164
Critical to quality 164
Critical to reliability 164
Critical to safety 164
Cycle-time reduction 200

D

Data convergence 98
Defect 287
Deployment
  enterprise-wide 159
Design for assembly 270
Design for manufacturing 272
Design for Six Sigma 158
DFA 270
DOD approach
  benefits 103
  function 105
Dynamic teardown 79

E

Education

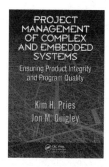 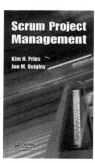 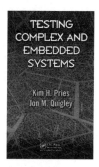